A New Basis for Moral Philosophy

International Library of Philosophy

Editor: Ted Honderich
Professor of Philosophy, University College London

A catalogue of books already published in the
International Library of Philosophy
will be found at the end of this volume.

A New Basis
for Moral
Philosophy

Keekok Lee

Lecturer in Philosophy,
University of Manchester

ROUTLEDGE & KEGAN PAUL

London, Boston, Melbourne and Henley

First published in 1985
by Routledge & Kegan Paul plc

14 Leicester Square, London WC2H 7PH, England

9 Park Street, Boston, Mass. 02108, USA

464 St Kilda Road, Melbourne,
Victoria 3004, Australia and

Broadway House, Newtown Road,
Henley on Thames, Oxon RG9 1EN, England

Set in 10/12 Times
by Input Typesetting Ltd, London SW19 8DR
and printed in Great Britain
by Billing and Sons Ltd,
Worcester and London

Library of Congress Cataloging in Publication Data

Lee, Keekok, 1938–

A new basis for moral philosophy.
(International library of philosophy)
Bibliography: p.
Includes index.
1. Ethics. I. Title. II. Series.
BJ1012.L44 1985   170   84–24937
ISBN 0–7102–0445–0

In memory of F
For Alice who is
unlikely to
want to read it

CONTENTS

Contents

Contents

PREFACE

This book sets out to challenge the existing philosophical orthodoxy about the fact/value distinction. Values are said to be subjective, arbitrary or irrational because there is no strict implication
(entailment) between the 'is' and the 'ought'. It follows that the
only 'justification' of 'oughts' is in terms of sincere commitment,
choice or decision. The author does not wish to dispute the thesis
that strict implication fails to hold between 'is' and 'ought' propositions; however, this book argues that the demand of strict
implication leads to an overkill. It cannot be satisfied not only in
moral discourse but also cognitive discourse in general. To be
consistent such cognitive (non-moral) discourse must also be
condemned as being subjective, arbitrary or irrational; and by the
same token, the only 'justification' available to it must be in terms
of sincere commitment, choice or decision. But these conclusions
are patently absurd. Those who support the Naturalistic Fallacy*
are, therefore, faced with the choice of embracing cognitive relativism or scepticism or cease to level the charge of irrationalism
at moral discourse if they wish to be consistent. What they can no
longer do is to insist on detaching moral discourse from cognitive

*In this book, the term 'supporter (upholder or subscriber) of the Natural-
istic Fallacy' is used in the following sense: one who argues that moral
discourse is irrational/non-rational because 'is' propositions do not
strictly imply or entail 'ought' propositions. It is *not* used in the sense
that it refers to someone who believes that 'is' propositions strictly imply
or entail 'ought' propositions. Those who do are described as having
committed the Naturalistic Fallacy.

discourse in general and by such a strategy render it peculiarly vulnerable. The postulated asymmetry between facts and values is not justified.

Moral discourse belongs to that part of cognitive discourse which may be said to constitute ordinary knowledge. This domain of knowledge may be characterised as follows:

(a) it is practice-oriented and not theoretically oriented;
(b) its goal is neither explanatory nor predictive but justificatory;
(c) it invokes and relies on extant scientific knowledge and pre-scientific knowledge, that is, on generalisations for which at the moment no explanatory scientific theory (or satisfactory theory) exists.

The author wishes to say that epistemology may be studied or approached with three domains in mind:

(a) science and the critical growth of knowledge where explanation is the goal;
(b) ordinary knowledge (as characterised above) where justification is the goal;
(c) perceptual knowledge where the fundamental problem is to account for how a grouping of words may be said to give an accurate description of what is the case.

The domain of ordinary knowledge has been overlooked in epistemology because: (a) Empiricists have been busy tackling perceptual knowledge but construing the problem to be one of getting hold of certain knowledge in the 'given' of sensory experience, while their counterparts, the Rationalists, attempt to find certain knowledge in self-evident truths; (b) the positivist tradition in the philosophy of science which seems to have dictated terms which are not only inappropriate to science (in the light of a realist critique of it), but also has the equally unfortunate effect of laying down the criteria of what counts as knowledge outside of science. One such powerful criterion shared by all forms of positivism is that of logical derivability – from a proposition which is to be tested (usually itself not directly observable), an observable proposition must be deduced from it (together with other propositions) if it is to satisfy scientificity – hence the Deductive-Nomological (D-N) method of explanation, prediction and theory-testing. But when this is borrowed by moral philosophers, D-N is transformed somewhat – the demand of observation drops out of the picture (as this clearly cannot be met) and the moral principle (analogous to the law(s) in the D-N model) is said to be justified if it can be derived from (or subsumed under) a higher principle, so that of the highest principle, 'justification', consists of making a sincere commitment to it. This may be called the Deducibility-Commitment model. It leads to the 'command theory of knowledge' under which the only type of legitimate justification consists of subsumption and not, where justification consists of giving reasons or evidence to support or defend the command, belief or judgment.

Justification in terms of reasons or evidence is ruled out of court because philosophers hold strict implication as the only legitimate logical relationship between propositions. But the logic of justification in the domain of ordinary knowledge is neither strict implication nor material implication. It is, however, the logic of verification/falsification, but suitably enriched. This may be called *epistemic implication*. The enrichment leans one to the side of those who argue for 'relevance' in logic. However, the systems of relevance logic devised by logicians such as Belnap and Anderson are not what is required as far as the logic of justification is concerned in the domain of ordinary knowledge. Moreover, epistemic implication is not intended to go beyond classical two-value logic. This author cannot hope to provide a *logica docens* for epistemic implication. All that this book can do is to provide a sketch of a philosophical semantics which will then show why relevance is required (and in what sense), and also why the Deducibility-Commitment model in moral philosophy is untenable. *Via* epistemic implication, the attempt to build an objective critical moral theory could become philosophically possible and respectable again by laying to rest the ghost of the Naturalistic Fallacy.

The book will also look at the ideological underpinning of the fact/value distinction as it is normally understood today under the influence of twentieth-century positivism. It will show that liberalism, far from requiring a meta-ethics of subjectivism/relativism/irrationalism, is compatible with and needs the presupposition that objectivity/rationality is possible. It will vindicate Mill, the father of classical liberalism in the English tradition. It will also indicate that Mill's arguments are not dissimilar to those advanced in this book – the two approaches are based on fallibilism as an epistemology. It is, therefore, ironical that the problems created by the straitjacket of logical derivability imposed by twentieth-century positivism may be solved by a return to a form of nineteenth-century positivism, namely, that held by Mill – a variety of positivism which has proved to be an embarrassment to contemporary philosophical sensibility and hence forgotten. It will also show why Popper, because of his mistaken ideological beliefs about liberalism, finds himself subverting his entire epistemology (and consequently his philosophy of science), in spite of his avowed adherence, too, to fallibilism as an epistemology, thereby rendering his philosophy incoherent and self-defeating.

ACKNOWLEDGMENTS

I wish to thank all those former students, particularly John Shand, who allowed themselves to be willing and helpful 'guinea pigs' in the ethics tutorials when the germ of the main thesis was tested on them. I am also indebted to members of Hillel Steiner's Thursday evening seminar group for allowing me to pursue my hobby horse on numerous occasions; but especially to Peter Halfpenny whose interest in and knowledge of positivism have greatly helped me to clarify my own thoughts on the subject, and moreover, whose clarity of mind enabled me to see my way through what at times appeared to be impenetrable fog. I am also extremely grateful to Professor Honderich and Dr Haack for their many suggestions for improvement, and particularly to the latter for saving me from several errors, great and small. I must, however, add that none of those I have acknowledged above are in any way responsible for whatever defects still remain in the book.

Finally, I wish to record my heartfelt thanks to those colleagues and ex-colleagues in the department, in the university, and friends in other universities and elsewhere who supported me morally during an extremely difficult period when the bulk of the book was being written – without their sympathy and kindness, this book could not have been written or finished.

University of Manchester
Autumn, 1983

I

THE SOURCES OF THE FACT/ VALUE DISTINCTION

The Naturalistic Fallacy is considered to be the biggest single obstacle to any attempt to argue for a rational basis to ethics or for the possibility of naturalism. Without going into the fine details of scholarship about its provenance, suffice it to say that meta-ethics today cites at least the following authorities, which roughly historically sequenced are: Hume, Moore, logical positivism, the first wave of language analysis, ethical relativism based on the 'form of life' argument (constituting the second wave of Wittgenstein's insights in the *Investigations*). The first six sections of this chapter briefly assess each of these influences, while section 7 will concentrate on the Naturalistic Fallacy as it is shaped and structured by the demand of formal logic in terms of logical derivability or strict implication which is shown as part of the positivist influence at work in moral discourse. Sections 8 and 9 will look at some recent attempts to combat this influence.

1 HUME

Naturalism (in ethics) seems to maintain that moral properties, although logically distinct from natural properties, are, nevertheless, entailed by them. In a naturalistic argument, Hume says that the premises contain 'is' propositions, while the conclusion contains an 'ought' proposition, which is a new term not already contained in the premises. It is analogous to his argument against induction – in an inductive argument, the premises refer to specific

1

events, events which have happened or are happening, yet the conclusion refers to all events of a certain kind, including future events. Such an argument is defective. There is a logical gap between the premises and the conclusion.

As a general argument, however, it seems to prove too much. If Hume's complaint is taken to mean that the 'ought' is illegitimate because it introduces a new relation, then as Swinburne[1] has pointed out, by the same token nearly all philosophical reasoning is defective since it is of the essence of philosophy to try to derive new relations from old. Philosophers deduce that God exists from the observation that the world is orderly (design argument); that mind exists because people think, say and do things in certain ways, etc. Now these deductions may not be convincing upon closer scrutiny for other reasons (such as, that the world is orderly, may already embody seeing the world through the eyes of a benevolent creator), but to rule out all such deductions would rule out all philosophising along that mode. This would be in keeping with Hume's out and out scepticism.

However, scepticism as a philosophical position may itself have to rely on that very mode of operation in order to formulate its own thesis and to make its point against those it is criticising. For instance, if part of Hume's evidence for saying that no attempt at deriving 'ought' from 'is' could be successful is his demolition of such attempts already made, then he too might be accused of introducing a new relation in his conclusion.

It is important to note that Hume's ethical scepticism is part of his general scepticism and of his empiricist epistemology and ontology. Other minds, material objects and values are problematic, since one is not confronted directly by them in sensory experience. One may know them *via* less problematic modes of existence like behaviour, sense data, feelings of pleasure or pain, etc. However, such a method of grappling with the problematic is basically flawed, since there is a logical gap between the conclusion (that 'X exists' or 'X is real') and the evidence proffered for its existence or reality. Hence the mind/body, the material object/ sense data, the inductive, the is/ought gaps.

To emphasise the unity of thought in Hume is significant for the following reasons: (1) this gap-problem arises within the empiricist/positivist tradition and is unlikely to be solved within it; (2) that a selective piecemeal attempt to meet Hume's sceptical

2

challenge may give rise to inconsistencies – some philosophers have tried to sidestep his problem of induction, or other minds, for example, but have not seen fit to object to his indictment of ethical values. On the contrary, they have welcomed it whilst fiercely resisting him in other areas of cognitive discourse. Those who invoke Hume nowadays in moral philosophy do not wish to have any truck with his general sceptical onslaught. They are happy to take it seriously only in the sphere of moral discourse. This is odd (the basis of this reaction will be examined in Chapter Six) as the different instantiations of the gap-problem all come from the same stable. As a result, one powerful strand of contemporary philosophical orthodoxy takes for granted that while scepticism with regard to facts is intellectually uncomfortable and suspect, scepticism with regard to values is *de rigueur*. This saves science but sacrifices values with no hint of unease. However, this book wishes to argue that the asymmetry created between facts and values is unjustified, that the correct way to meet Hume's challenge is a wholesale rejection of the terms with which he presents his general gap-problem, namely, the basic assumption that the relationship of logical derivability is the only wholesome, legitimate logical (and hence rational) relationship that may obtain between any two or more propositions. If p is not deducible from q, then p is problematic, uncertain or irrationally held. This presupposition will be examined in detail later on in the chapter.

2 MOORE

While Hume's sceptical spectre haunts contemporary Western philosophy, yet as far as meta-ethics is concerned within the broadly English-speaking tradition, it is G. E. Moore who has by far exercised a more profound influence upon its development in the last seventy-five years than may be said to be good for it. Moore's single most devastating argument is said to be the Open-Question Argument. He used it to show how Mill (utilitarianism), Social Darwinism as well as those who wish to anchor ethics in theology failed to pass the test he proposed, and thereby failed to provide an objective basis to their respective ethical systems. The argument consists of saying that it always makes sense to ask of the *definiens* which seeks to define the notion 'good' whether

3

it itself is good. Thus, if Mill is taken to be defining 'good' in terms of pleasure in the proposition 'pleasure is good', if the Social Darwinists are defining 'good' in terms of 'evolutionary success', and theologically inclined ethical theorists in terms of 'what God commands', then it is meaningful to ask the question 'Is pleasure good?', or 'Is what is evolutionarily successful good?' or 'Is what God commands good?'. Since the meaningfulness of these questions cannot be denied, Moore then concluded that all the three attempts cited failed to give what he called a correct definition of the term 'good'. For Moore a correct definition is such that there is an exact equivalence between the *definiens* and the *definiendum*, so that it would be nonsensical to ask of the *definiens*, for example, 'a figure of three sides', whether it is a 'triangle', which is the *definiendum* in the profferred definition – 'a triangle is a figure of three sides'.

Moore seemed to have been obsessed with definitions and, moreover, definitions of a peculiarly limited and special kind. Firstly, his paradigm of a correct definition is confined solely to what may be called 'closed' terms which may obtain in mathematical formal systems. The only test for such systems is that of internal consistency. The terms themselves need never be physically interpreted, and hence never face the problems which interpreted terms with applications to the world outside the formal framework of symbols have to face. In ethics, it is obvious that one's interest is not in formal systems with uninterpreted terms; hence an argument which gets its point by assuming closed terms as a paradigm of a correct definition seems to be less than relevant to an inquiry whose basic concepts are not closed in the way required. Secondly, his paradigm also indicates that he had in mind either lexicographical or stipulative definition. The former reports how in current usage a term is defined. The latter lays down how someone proposes to use a term even if it is not so used at present. 'A triangle is a figure of three sides' is both a stipulative and a lexical definition. Ethics, in so far as it is concerned with the provision of definitions, is not interested in either of these types, since in the end they deal purely with verbal linguistic matters. Instead it is concerned with 'real' definitions,[2] something which, to be very charitable to Moore, he could be said to be vaguely grasping at implicitly, but if so, he grasped it in such an unsatisfactory manner that in the end it led him to postulate the existence

4

of simple non-natural properties in terms of which 'good' is to be analysed. Moore wavered between being a 'modernist' in the sense of turning all philosophical matters into verbal linguistic matters (he is often acknowledged as one of the founding fathers of the analytical approach even though no one could be sure whether it was common language or common sense he was analysing) and being a 'traditionalist', of invoking the metaphysics of logical atomism which was fashionable at the time as the basis of analysis. The postulation of simple non-natural properties seems more properly to belong to the latter sphere of preoccupation.

Frankena[3] showed nearly forty years ago that the Naturalistic Fallacy is neither a fallacy nor is it naturalistic. From the examples Moore used, it is clear he believed not only that Mill and the Social Darwinists have committed it, since 'pleasure' and 'evolutionary success' refer to what may be 'natural' matters, but also those who give a transcendent underpinning to ethics. God (a theistic deity) can hardly be said to be a natural term, since by definition it is transcendent. So the attribute 'naturalistic' cannot be taken seriously. But if even transcendent terms are not admissible, then Moore must be referring to another fallacy, what Frankena called the definist fallacy – Butler's dictum 'Everything is as it is and not another thing' which he cited approvingly on the front page of the *Principia Ethica*. According to this fallacy, it is inadmissible to define one term in terms of another, unless the first can be completely reduced to the second so that they can be used interchangeably, and the *definiendum* becomes a shorthand for the *definiens*. It is, however, unwise to go along with this fallacy, since it would rule out all attempts to define terms outside such narrow confines.

Moore's limited conception of definition and his hankering for the metaphysics of logical simples, the distinction between simple and complex, that between natural and non-natural which focused on the unfortunate example of the differences between 'yellow' and 'good', set modern moral philosophy off on a course chasing numerous red herrings. From this point of view, one is not sure if the influence of Moore on moral philosophy in the long run can be said to be salutary, although the problem about the 'is/ought' distinction he raised is a genuine problem. However, the way he presented it, and the arguments he put forward, took their colour so much from his other presuppositions, that they could only be said to hold, if these presuppositions survived challenge, which they appear not to have done.

But once challenged, the Open-Question Argument is then no longer the lethal weapon it claims itself to be in demolishing all attempts to put ethics on a rational basis. His emphasis on his paradigm of a correct definition misconstrued what ethical theorists like Mill and others were attempting to do. They were trying to lay down what for them is the fundamental criterion or postulate for their system. They did not see themselves providing either a lexical or stipulative definition of the term 'good'. To the Social Darwinists, it is self-evident that what is evolutionarily successful is good. Mill did not fall back on self-evidence, and also admitted that such a principle is not susceptible to proof in the strict sense. (For details of Mill's position, see Chapter Six.) This might make the system unsatisfactory to one who might like to get at a more rational basis for an ethical system than self-evidence or something not susceptible to proof in the strict sense; and its unsatisfactory nature in this respect might be cited by others as yet another attempt to build a rational ethic coming to grief. But to criticise thus is to use a different argument from that of the Open-Question Argument.

Moreover, Moore himself in the end was doing no more than what Mill had done – namely, to lay down the fundamental postulate of his own ethical system. Moore too, like Mill, could not provide any strict proof that love, friendship and aesthetic experiences rather than pleasure constitute the good. Both theories are teleological and utilitarian. Moore may be said to be an ideal utilitarian; and so too, may Mill, as his conception of utility is clearly non-Benthamite and non-hedonistic and can easily encompass within his account of the good the Moorean states of mind. There is an overlap in their moral visions. Consequently the stricture against Mill that he has committed the Naturalistic Fallacy applies with equal force against Moore's own account. If there is something fishy about the leap from 'pleasure is desired' to 'pleasure is good', there is something equally fishy about the leap from 'certain states of mind are desired' to 'certain states of mind are good'. *Pace* Frankena, one may rescue both arguments from the attack by pointing out that they only appear deficient because they are enthymemes, and go on to supply the suppressed premise in each case, namely, 'what is desired is good'. At this point, Moore would fall back on intuition should the critic query the basis of that missing premise. But if Moore were to choose to regard it as a definition, then it would fail to pass his own Open-Question Argument test, as it clearly makes sense to ask whether what is desired is good.

The *Principia Ethica* may be assessed in the following ways: (1) in the context of Moore's own thought; and (2) in the context of the influence upon the development of moral philosophy.[4] With regard to the former, it appears to be consonant with Moore's general philosophical eagerness to defend commonsense beliefs and common language against sceptical attack. He tried to provide a proof that he had knowledge of the external world, by holding up both hands and uttering 'Here are two hands' – therefore there are at least two material objects, and therefore, an external world exists or is real. His ploy lies in maintaining that any proposition embodying the sceptic's reasons for doubting the truth of the proposition that he, G. E. Moore, had two hands, is less certainly true than the proposition itself. In other words he was merely re-affirming the claim that he had knowledge of the external world in the face of the sceptic's reasons for doubting such knowledge. In the same way, in the face of the sceptic's reasons for doubting moral knowledge, Moore equally affirmed the claim that he knew that certain mental states are ethically good. Analogous to the holding up of hands in the proof of an external world is the 'pointing to' or intuiting of certain desired mental states.

This unified attempt to meet the sceptic's challenge may provoke one of two unfavourable responses: (a) the sceptic may not be over-impressed by the nature of the 'proof' in both instances; or (b) neither might the non-sceptic who shares Moore's desire to surmount the sceptical hurdles, but who, nevertheless, believes that the mere re-affirmation of commonsense beliefs or the deliverances of intuition would not do, and who may wish to argue for the possibility of holding commonsense beliefs in a more critical manner.

The parallel efforts on Moore's part to defend both common-sense beliefs about the external world and moral beliefs is obscured by his attack on Mill, the Social Darwinists and others *via* the Naturalistic Fallacy. This might give the misleading impression that he was on the side of moral scepticism. But actually he thought that his analysis of 'good' as a simple non-natural term would enable him to avoid the Naturalistic Fallacy to which Mill and others fell prey, and to surmount scepticism at the same time. However, those who claim themselves to be influenced by the *Principia Ethica* simply regard it as setting the scene in the English-speaking world of moral philosophy this century, for the bifurcation of facts and values and for moral scepticism. Philosophers would tend to applaud Moore for his attempt to give a 'proof' of the external world, even though they might not think much of it as a proof (but they would agree that he was right to have tried), but at the same time equally applaud the Naturalistic Fallacy without perceiving any inconsistency whatsoever in so doing.[5] As a result it is taken for granted today that the *Principia Ethica* is the starting point of the growth of modern meta-ethics, a meta-ethics which legislates out of court any attempt to provide a critical basis for moral beliefs, apart from the constraint of consistency which it may permit.[6]

3 LOGICAL POSITIVISM AND ITS POLEMICAL HEYDAY

This meta-ethics was later explicitly reinforced by the arrival of logical positivism on English soil when A. J. Ayer brought the good news belatedly from Vienna. Although the actual form of the thesis might be hailed as new, the spirit of positivism itself was not.[7] As is commonly acknowledged, logical positivism may be regarded as a linguistic refinement of empiricism. Its explicit aim is to render science philosophically respectable, and anything which fails to conform to the scientific paradigm of meaningfulness is to be consigned to the bonfire of metaphysical nonsense. Values are, of course, one of the most obvious candidates for fuelling the conflagration. By postulating only two sorts of meaningfulness, the analytic *a priori* and the synthetic *a posteriori*, the logical positivist collapses two sets of distinctions into an expanded single set – the *a priori* is identified with the analytic and the *a posteriori* with the synthetic. The central tenet of empiricism-cum-positivism is that we cannot know anything about the world independent of experience, that is, in an *a priori* manner. Hence there is no necessity about anything that happens in the world. Everything is contingent and could have been other than what it is. In other words, propositions about the world are synthetic as well as known *a posteriori*. Analytic statements if true cannot be denied without contradiction, wherein lies their necessity. They are also *a priori* since anything known *a posteriori* is contingent. The logical positivist renders the class of the *analytic a priori* harmless by saying that the truths are linguistic, decreed by *fiat* and make no empirical assertions whatever.

Mathematics and logic are unproblematic because they fall into the analytic *a priori* category; physics (the doyen of the natural sciences) belongs to the synthetic *a posteriori* in so far as its factual components can be detached from its mathematical formalism. Physics (and other natural sciences), however, has the inconvenient habit of importing theoretical entities into its structure which are not directly observable. This feature led to much agonising, since what is not directly verifiable stands in danger of not qualifying to be meaningful. Indirect verification has to be introduced to save the situation. But loosening the criterion of meaningfulness in this way might well open the flood gates to all sorts of propositions already consigned to the bonfire under the more stringent interpretation to make a re-appearance through the back door. The proposition 'Where God lives is blue' may be meaningless because it is not directly verifiable; conjoin it with 'The sky is where God lives' and together they entail a directly verifiable proposition 'The sky is blue'. Indirect verification obtains and therefore, the proposition may be said to be meaningful.

At the other end of the spectrum of difficulties is the problem of what counts as the basic ('protocol') sentences where the process of verification may be said to rest without further justification. Critics also pointed out the problematic status of the thesis of meaningfulness when it is turned upon itself. As a descriptive factual thesis it may just be false, as it is commonly acknowledged, that there are more than two kinds of meaningful propositions. As a prescriptive thesis, it is only trivially true in virtue of the stipulative definition of 'meaningless/meaningful' it lays down. But no one needs be deterred by other people's stipulative definitions; they can simply be ignored and one's own substituted. If neither analytic *a priori* nor synthetic *a posteriori*, must it be doomed to be meaningless itself?

The technical defects and difficulties are too well known to be rehearsed. The foregoing outline is meant to serve as a reminder of the reasons behind the demise of logical positivism as a polemical philosophical movement. However, its formal demise does not mean that its spirit no longer lives on. It is more like a case of 'The King is dead. Long live the King.' Positivism has deeply penetrated modern European thought, and although professional philosophers today are not likely to call themselves positivists, nevertheless, this does not mean that the problems posed in philosophy by them have not been shaped and informed by the positivistic outlook. In nearly all areas of philosophy, the philosophy of science, of law, moral philosophy, to name a few, issues are raised and posed within the terms and framework dictated by it. Later on this chapter will take up this theme in greater detail.

For moral philosophy, the immediate effect of logical positivism upon it was dramatic and traumatic. However, out of the debris, theorists like Stevenson and later Hare have tried gallantly to restore the subject somewhat. Negatively, logical positivism dismissed moral propositions as strictly speaking meaningless and unintelligible. But more positively, it drew attention to the dynamic use of moral language by saying that moral propositions are not assertion but expression of emotions to influence conduct. Stevenson, in *Ethics and Language*, worked on this insight; he elaborates this theme and develops the thesis that moral language is a combination of descriptive and emotive meanings. The admission of a descriptive component does not succeed in altering the meta-ethics which remains a subjectivist one, though not the subjectivism of an earlier kind, which is based on the fact-stating paradigm of language by saying that moral propositions are empirical propositions since they assert the existence of subjective feelings of approval or disapproval in individuals or in a particular community. To distinguish it from this older form of subjectivism, it may be called sophisticated subjectivism. (In the rest of this book, the reference to subjectivism is to this variety.) In contemporary literature, it is commonly called non-cognitivism. He said that moral language is used really to alter people's attitudes. But it turns out that his arguments demonstrate something less than this. They prove instead that moral language can only cater for but not alter attitudes.[8]

In *The Language of Morals*, Hare takes up the theme that moral language, because it is action-guiding, must entail imperatives. These imperatives, if challenged, could be justified in terms of yet other imperatives. But ultimately justification comes to an end. The highest imperative.must, therefore, rest on a personal decision or choice to adopt a particular lifestyle or existence. In this way the agent creates her/his own values. This comes close to the existentialist view which regards choice as the essence of human being. Hare, who is one of the most influential (if not the most influential) moral philosophers in the English-speaking world in the last quarter century, transmits and entrenches the spirit of positivism in meta-ethics. The gulf between facts and values becomes firmly unchallengeable. Values are choices, or decisions, or the result of other deliberative or emotional processes of the individual. The general conclusion endorsed is the Protagorean view of human beings that they are the measure of all values, or the Romantic conception of the individual, that the assertion of the will confers not only dignity and autonomy but also automatically bestows validity on whatever is willed. (On the later writings of Hare, see section 9 of this chapter.)

From the point of view of moral philosophy, the influence of Wittgenstein's *Philosophical Investigations* comes in two waves – the *locus classicus* of the first is Nowell-Smith's *Ethics* (1954) and that of the second is Winch's *The Idea of a Social Science* (1958), a work not itself directly concerned with moral philosophy but which clearly has implications for it. (A decade later, Phillips and Mounce's *Moral Practices*, 1969, and Beardsmore's *Moral Reasoning*, 1969, reflect this approach.) The first wave is not now much discussed or invoked but the second is very much alive. The former in the end comes down on the side of subjectivism, and the latter on that of relativism. As a result, today, those who wish to argue for an objective rational and critical basis for ethics have to contend with both subjectivism and relativism. (There is even a third wave which will be looked at in section 8 of this chapter.)

4 NOWELL-SMITH'S *ETHICS* AND LANGUAGE ANALYSIS

Linguistic analysis reveals a feature about moral language which has already been anticipated by Stevenson (and even Ayer) and others working more directly within the logical positivist tradition. It is that moral language may have many uses – to make choices, express preferences and decisions, to offer advice and exhortation, and generally to guide human behaviour. In other words, it is the dynamic use of language and not the fact-stating role which is its characteristic feature. It is not surprising then that this style of philosophising concurs with contemporary positivism in endorsing a subjective meta-ethics, in spite of Nowell-Smith's explicit efforts to distance himself from subjectivism by giving what he calls a multi-track instead of a single-track analysis of the use of moral language. Such language may indeed be used to perform various roles depending on the context, and there may be a connection between them which is neither a purely factual nor a purely logical one. Nowell-Smith uses the term 'logical oddness' to characterise the denial of the link between 'X is best' and 'I choose X' in the absence of further forthcoming explanations. But the chain leads backwards from the executive decision through the choice to the preference. Preferences rest on logically impregnable reasons given in terms of what he calls 'pro' and 'con' words. If this is so, then it amounts to (sophisticated) subjectivism, no more and no less. Reasons come to an end with the rock bottom retort 'I like it' or 'I find it revolting', although further back in the chain reasons may be available. The 'pro' and 'con' words seem to be a variant of 'hurrah' and 'boo' in Stevenson's emotive theory of ethics. Pro and con words may justify any belief or course of action whatever. There is *ex hypothesi* no further yardstick to distinguish morally justified from unjustified preferences.

5 WINCH'S ETHICAL RELATIVISM

Ethical relativism as a philosophical thesis maintains too that there can be no objective critical yardstick by which one may determine the correctness or otherwise of the many, diverse and conflicting moral codes and practices and beliefs in different societies and at different times. It is based on the correct sociological observation that there indeed exists a rich profusion of moralities. However, from the sociological premise, it jumps to a philosophical conclusion and in so doing may be said to be introducing a new relation, the very thing which Hume might have declared to be suspect and objectionable.

Ethical relativism is not a new thesis – in modern times, it had its heyday during the period of European imperialism and colonisation of the non-European world. So its nineteenth- and early twentieth-century impetus seemed to have been less philosophical than liberal and humanistic. It could be explained in part as a re-action against the absolute values of Christianity which were being foisted upon conquered tribes and peoples. Moral-cum-religious imperialism in the wake of the gunboat and free trade systematically suppressed or denigrated native cultures in the name of superior white civilisation. The feeling grew up amongst the more intelligent and the more sensitive that, if an earnest and serious attempt were made to understand alien values and cultures (conquering) outsiders would begin to see the point behind such beliefs and practices. Understanding would bring appreciation and appreciation in turn would bring tolerance. (Westermaack's writings may be seen in this light as the product of the sensitive consciousness of nineteenth-/twentieth-century scholarship.) Tolerance is then considered to be possible if one presupposes the equal validity and worth of all diverse views and in so doing, confuses objectivity and its possibility with absolutism and dogmatism. This confusion is one of the most enduring and powerful intellectual sources sustaining the fact/value distinction and will be examined in Chapter Six of the book.

But of late ethical relativism has been given a new and apparently more satisfactory foundation – the thesis of conceptual relativism, which is a far-reaching and comprehensive theory about the relativisation of knowledge. Under it, ethical relativism is just a species of cognitive relativism. Its current source of inspiration is said to be derived from the insights of the later Wittgenstein, with Winch being its most articulate and influential exponent. His conceptual relativism is based on the 'form of life' argument. Implicit in a way or form of life are its own standards of 'truth', 'validity', 'objectivity' and 'rationality'. The participants use them to determine what is 'correct' belief or behaviour. Different competing ways of life may have different standards. There can, however, be no cross-cultural comparisons in terms of a culture-free standard of rationality, etc. which is universal and necessary for assessing and appraising belief systems. In the end all that is available is a particular standard of truth or rationality relative to the form of life to which the participant has committed her/himself or to which s/he habitually adheres. Ultimate commitment is itself incapable of further justification; it is what stops the infinite regress of justification within the system.

Applied to the field of morals, it yields the thesis that the different ethical modes displayed by different societies (or by different communities in a heterogenous one) are autonomous, and that the differences cannot be assessed and settled by reference to common critical yardsticks. One cannot criticise from an external observer's point of view using concepts which are not indigenous to that form of life. To understand from within is all that one can intelligibly do. If the norm of racial equality is alien to the apartheid form of life, one cannot criticise apartheid as immoral because it violates such a norm. Internal to the norms of the apartheid system, treating people with a certain skin colour in an inferior manner is correct behaviour and a proper application of the rules of the practice. The Afrikaaner is committed to the apartheid form of life and the white liberal in or outside South Africa is committed to another which upholds racial equality.

A substantial body of critical literature[9] has since grown up about 'form of life' type of relativism. Some of the main charges made against it are:

(1) it expresses a theory of rationality which at the same time lays down the limits of rationality.[10] Such a theory is unable to retain both its identity and its integrity;

(2) the very notion of disagreement on fundamental issues which is the given of this theory is not possible, as on the theory, there just simply follows mutual and total incomprehensibility and unintelligibility.[11] One can disagree with another only if one understands what the other is talking about. If *ex hypothesi* there is no possibility of communication, there can be no disagreement. People do of course, sometimes appear to experience such a yawning gap in communication with others which they express as follows: 'we seem to live in totally different worlds and never the twain will meet' or words to that effect. However, they do not literally mean that they have reached the limits of intelligibility. What they try to convey is the tremendous differences, and the shock attendant upon discovering them, between the sets of beliefs or ways of life, not that they literally find the other's beliefs

14

unintelligible, for to conclude that there are differences presupposes that one understands what is being said by the other. Suppose one comes across a tribe which buries alive the personal attendants of the king when he dies. An outsider, like oneself, is bound to find this practice bizarre and revolting. A member of the tribe might be able to justify it in terms which leaves the outsider totally unconvinced and shocked. All the same, one *understands* the other's attempt at justification but fails to be impressed. There is no literal breakdown in communication;

(3) that reality is not given by language, even though one cannot say what reality is like except *via* language. To maintain an identity between the two leads one to confuse X with the concept of X, to confuse questions about things with questions about the concepts of such things;[12]

(4) that it leads to the impossibility of criticism by its exclusive emphasis upon the 'inner' (which Collingwood and others in the hermeneutical tradition have also pointed out). This dimension, and the understanding of it, is, of course, a very important feature of human conduct and of one's assessment of it. But to understand is not to pardon all. Proper understanding yields correct description. But correct description is not the same as, although it is the basis for critical assessment, appraisal and evaluation, which are all intellectually respectable and legitimate tasks to perform if knowledge is to grow. Because this thesis is inclined to rule them out, Gellner has seen fit to label it a 'negative endorsement' theory.[13] As such it justifies the *status quo* – any existing set of beliefs is all right in virtue of the fact that people believe in them and are able to cite reasons and evidence within their structure of beliefs to justify them according to their criteria of truth and validity;

(5) that it rests on the mistaken assumption that different forms of life are autonomous and isolated, that there is and can be no overlap,[14] that societies are uniformly and absolutely closed societies;

(6) that there is a problem in identifying any so-called form of life in a complex and heterogenous society.[15] Does every fundamental difference entail new forms of life? There is danger that there will be as many forms of life as there are fundamental differences. A form of life conjures up something stable and enduring, not something fragile that is in constant danger of

15

disintegrating and splintering into new and different forms of life whenever a fundamental difference appears on the horizon. If a fundamental disagreement is used to identify a form of life, and then the form of life thus identified is used to explain why and how the fundamental disagreement exists and cannot be resolved, then the thesis runs the risk of saying that fundamental disagreements are incapable of resolution by definition. However, if every fundamental disagreement does not entail different forms of life, and if forms of life are not identified in terms of fundamental disagreements, then it is not obvious that fundamental disagreement is in principle incapable of resolution because of a conceptual yawning gap entailing unintelligibility between the disputing parties. For instance, one would admit that there is a fundamental disagreement between people in our society about the morality of abortion. It is a very important issue about potential life and death, it involves a conflict of rights between groups and potential groups in society, etc. Yet one would hesitate to say that the pro- and anti-abortionists belong to two different forms of life, each committing themselves to its own standards of truth, validity and rationality, so that there is conceptually and logically no possible common ground between them. For a start, they seem to understand one another perfectly. Is this a delusion? They seem even to share certain non-factual beliefs – for instance, that the post-natal life of a child is of great concern and significance – as well as factual ones – for instance, that medical knowledge about embryological developments and medical technology are not static matters. They also share certain critical standards in argument, such as consistency, not committing known fallacies of reasoning, not erecting generalisations upon insufficient and otherwise defective evidence, etc.;

(7) language is a form of life; it clearly is on the Wittgenstein/ Winch view. One important goal of language is communication. To communicate in human language, even at an elementary level, one must rely on the descriptive use of language. A description may be correct or mistaken. People may disagree whether a certain description is true or false. But the possibility of determining what is the case and what is not the case must be presupposed; otherwise, there cannot be communication. If truth is merely what is true for each individual (or groups of individuals in a community), language could be made to say anything and

16

therefore nothing.[16] Description and misdescription must refer to the one same public world; otherwise, there can be no possibility of objectivity and rationality. Without these there can be no language either. What is the case and what is not the case cannot both be true – any theory of rationality which violates such a fundamental principle of rationality by laying down the limits of rationality is, therefore, incoherent and wrong.

6 GALLIE'S 'ESSENTIALLY CONTESTED CONCEPTS'

In 1956 Gallie addressed the Aristotelian Society. The address, entitled 'Essentially Contested Concepts',[17] turns out to be influential not only in moral philosophy but also political philosophy and elsewhere. In spirit it has something in common with Winch's thesis, and Gallie's general approach to the philosophy of history *via* the notion of a story or narrative is not out of place within the Winchean outlook. However, Gallie's conception of philosophy in general (unlike the Wittgensteinian one which officially regards philosophy as a self-liquidating mode of activity) is what he calls the 'agonistic' style, and that it is of the essence of philosophy to produce intense competition amongst rival philosophers. The struggle is endemic – triumph on the part of one view is at best short-lived. Waiting by the wings of the stage are its competitors working furiously to topple it from its dominant position. In the process, old arguments would be trundled out, refurbished by adding to or subtracting from them, sometimes new ones would be co-opted (inspired by discoveries elsewhere and borrowed). Philosophers are doomed to such perpetual strife and contest. Philosophy is not alone in this struggle. He seems to say, although it is a point he does not emphasise much, that the essence of all intellectual activity (using the term to include science, art and religion) is *Sturm und Drang*. This account appears to him to be true and convincing from a study of the histories of such activities.

The *Sturm und Drang* conception of intellectual endeavour is not unique to Gallie. Another extremely influential philosopher, Popper, shares it. In Chapter Six, it will be argued that Popper, in spite of his avowed enthusiasm for rationality, in the end is driven to a position very near to that of Gallie, namely, that the

17

'essential contestedness' of science, art, religion, morality and politics (at least concepts like democracy and social justice) makes it intrinsically impossible to say of any of the competing uses of the central concepts in these fields of endeavour which is the better or the more correct of the lot. In other words, the nature of the contest is such that in principle there is no way of rationally determining who has the better case. It is not a contest motivated by the search for truth, or approximation to the truth (as Popper would have it), since there is no truth available by which to judge the competing claims. So like Sisyphus, philosophers are doomed by the Gods to argue amongst themselves; or are compelled, like the victim of an obsession, to defend their pet theories while viciously demolishing those of their rivals. It is a way of life to which they have become addicted.

To assess Gallie's thesis properly, one must distinguish between Gallie's own account of what is going on in the various intellectual enterprises (that is, second-order or meta-talk) from participant first-order talk, which is the account that the contestants themselves might give of their disputes. From the critical participant point of view where what Gallie calls an essentially contested concept is involved, the following happens: different groups of people disagree about what a certain notion like democracy amounts to. They address themselves to the question 'What is real democracy?'. The accounts given are many and even conflicting. Can they be all equally correct especially when they contradict one another? And even if they do not contradict outright, they do not say the same thing. So which one is mistaken, or more mistaken than another might be? Are they all internally consistent in what they are each maintaining? Out of this plethora, the participant backs a particular thesis because to her/him, for the variety of considerations just outlined, that is superior to its rivals. And until holes are successfully picked in the arguments s/he backs, s/he would support it as the correct account of the real X, and reject rival accounts as inadequate or defective in some way. The fundamental rule of the game operated by the critical participants is: unless you can show me where I have gone wrong, and provided your objections cannot be successfully met, you must grant that I have a better case than you. (The participants are assumed to be more or less consciously critical; the non-critical individual does not go in for intellectual contests.)

From the Gallie-observer's point of view, the following account obtains: the various contestants are using the concept X in different ways; the diverse competing uses are on all fours with one another – they are equally legitimate and correct; although correct, they are, nevertheless, contesting a single meaning that the concept is said to possess; there is no possibility of resolving the dispute by argument, even in the long run; but all the same, the dispute is genuine and is sustained by argument and evidence.

Under the Gallien representation, the contest is about different uses of a concept (this could be due to the Wittgensteinian influence) which is not necessarily how naive participants (naive in the sense of being ignorant of, and not, therefore corrupted by, Gallie's view) see what they are doing. They are likely to believe that they are in search of truth or reality, of (real) democracy or (real) social justice. Contemporary philosophers have a special abhorrence of such metaphysical mystification. Gallie is no exception. In the wake of Wittgenstein, he translates the dispute about the nature (dare one use the word 'essence'?) of X into a linguistic dispute about the uses of 'X'. Next he assumes no one use can be said to be more correct than another – every group of linguistic users can claim respectability by tracing lineage to what Gallie calls an exemplar.

So far one follows the broad outline of his thesis. The next stage is not so clear. According to the 'meaning = use' school (which Gallie seems to be implicitly following), it would follow that since there are diverse uses, then there must be diverse meanings (and as many concepts as there are meanings and uses). Yet Gallie maintains that there is a single meaning that is being contested which is possessed by the concept in question. However, the single meaning that is said to exist is a bit of a mystery as it seems to commit him to the equivalent of the representative theory of perception about meaning. All that Locke said we ever have are sense-impressions of an object, but never the object itself. Yet there must be an object which stands behind the sense-impressions and causes them. All that Gallie has are the uses which compete with one another. Yet there must be a single meaning about which they are contesting. But this meaning is never accessible. In which case there are proffered different and conflicting meanings, not a single one. Now it is true that each contestant maintains that her/his own account constitutes the

19

'true' or the 'real' meaning but that does not commit her/him to maintaining that there is a single meaning that could be contested. In the eyes of the contestant in any case, s/he is not so much contesting the meaning, as claiming that there is one and only one proper meaning and that her/his account embodies or approximates to it. So the postulation of 'a single meaning that could be contested' neither belongs to participant-talk nor even to Gallie-meta-talk, since it is not obvious what such a meaning could be, given the tacit acceptance of the equation 'meaning = use'.

There is difficulty too with the other parts of Gallie's thesis. In his opinion, the intrinsic impossibility of resolving disputes involving essentially contested concepts by argument, nevertheless, does not detract from their status of being genuine or rational disputes. It is sufficient, he says, that the contestants adduce arguments and evidence in support of their respective claims. For him the possibility of obtaining agreement in the long run by argument is not a necessary criterion of the genuineness of the dispute as a rational dispute. For him, however, universal agreement in principle in the long run by argument is possible only if logical justification obtains. He writes: 'if the notion of logical justification can be applied only to such theses and arguments as can be presumed capable of gaining universal agreement in the long run, the disputes to which the uses of any essentially contested concept give rise are not genuine or rational disputes.'[18]

But is logical justification the only type of justification which generates universal agreement? What is 'logical justification' anyway? Gallie does not elaborate. But presumably it refers to the logical relationship of derivability or deducibility (that is, strict implication) obtaining between premises and conclusion. Gallie is right in rejecting the notion of logical justification as a condition for saying that a dispute is genuine or rational as the price to be paid is too high (it will be shown later why it is too high). But he may not be correct in maintaining that the possibility of obtaining universal agreement in the long run by argument is too stringent a criterion to operate in granting the status of being a genuine or rational dispute. He mistakenly assumes that the possibility of obtaining universal agreement by argument is dependent solely upon logical justification obtaining. Since the latter is unobtainable, he concludes that the former too is unavailable. But it is the main burden of this book to show that even with the jettisoning of logical justification, it does not mean that there may not be other principles of logical relationship at work which will enable us to achieve the possibility of obtaining universal agreement by argument in the long run. Gallie is right in maintaining that logical justification is too severe a criterion, but wrong in maintaining that the possibility of universal agreement by argument is itself too stringent a test for the bestowal of rationality upon a dispute.

Critical but naive participants can only make sense of their own engagement in the dispute by presupposing just such a possibility, that there could be agreement in the long run by argument. This presupposition is necessary for critical debate to be an on-going concern; otherwise, debate and discussion becomes merely an obsessive indulgence. Indeed Gallie himself must adhere to this presupposition by entering the fray, as it were. He must believe that his own thesis about the essential contestedness of philo-sophical theories embodies the truth, and he hopes by using argu-ment to convince others (to procure universal agreement in the long run) that he is right. Or is he simply indulging in obsessive polemic for its own sake? If not, then with regard to his own thesis, he must be an engaged naive participant. As such he believes that he has put forward arguments, which unless a critic can successfully pick holes in them, he would stand by as the correct account. His critic, like the author of this book, advances a demolition of his thesis. Both act on the presupposition that agreement is possible *via* argument; indeed, the whole point of contesting each other's theses is precisely to eliminate error. In other words, the dispute between Gallie and his critics, which is a philosophical dispute about philosophy itself, is a replication of philosophical disputes in science, art, religion, morality, etc. If it is resolvable by rational argument, then there is no reason to believe that other disputes are not similarly amenable to rational resolution. Disputes to be genuine or rational must be capable of being settled by argument in the long run.

The notion of an examplar which he introduces is also not free from difficulties. It is one of the characteristics which a concept must possess to qualify as an essentially contested one in order: (i) to distinguish it from one which is merely radically confused; (ii) to meet the charge that people are not contesting a single meaning of the concept but are merely proffering competing but different concepts; (iii) to provide a rock bottom anchorage for an essentially contested notion; otherwise, critics could persist in saying that the concept is not unitary; and (iv) to prevent all concepts from being essentially contested ones by the mere existence of disputes about them. For Gallie, then, it is vital that the different uses of a concept could be shown to be derivable from 'an original exemplar whose authority is acknowledged by all the contestant users of the concept'.[19]

The problem that arises is to determine the status of this notion and where it belongs. Gallie implies that it belongs to both participant-talk as well as his own talk. It is because participants themselves acknowledge such an exemplar as authority that he, Gallie, can incorporate it in his meta-talk about essential contestedness. It follows that if it is not a *bona fide* notion operated by participants, its meta-status as an explanatory notion is no longer valid or justified. Two questions must then be raised: (a) as a matter of fact do participants always and necessarily acknowledge such an exemplar as authority?; (b) if they do, how do they set about identifying it?

Take religion or Christianity, which is the variant that Gallie chooses to discuss. He probably has Protestant Christianity in mind. He cited various elements or aspects of it which he claims are all essentially contested. He then asserts that it is obvious the various uses of the phrase 'the Christian life' are derived from a commonly acknowledged source. But what is this source? He does not actually say. The Bible, one presumes. But the status of the Bible is itself open to different interpretations amongst Protestant religious believers. Fundamentalists believe in the literal truth of what is written there. Others do not. Some very sophisticated Christians even do away with the text altogether, arguing that the book is irrelevant to the Christian way of life; in any case its historical status is questionable and there is no need to pin one's faith on such bits and pieces of dubious texts. If one were to widen Christianity to include Catholicism, here again, the Bible as the acknowledged source becomes problematic. The Church is the authority, not the Bible.

Would Gallie have to admit that the 'exemplar' turns out to be as much essentially contested as the various themes which may be said to be derived from it? There seems to be no exemplar acknowledged by all to be an authority. Yet if one is unable to trace back to such an exemplar how can the notion qualify to be

22

an essentially contested one? If it exists, it is not obvious where it is located and how it is to be identified. Participants themselves seem to get along nicely without it. This is because they each regard themselves to be the true guardian or possessor of the real truth and those who disagree are just wrong or mistaken in their understanding of the religion. Now, of course, in a spirit of ecumenism, they might sink all their differences and present a united view and claim that the Bible, or the Pope, is the exemplar. But when this happens, essential contestedness, which is the life-blood of the agonistic style, begins to wane or disappear altogether.

In other words, essential contestedness cannot get off the ground – either the exemplar cannot be easily identified and located which then makes it impossible to formulate the thesis, or it may be found, but participants cease to be contestants to become co-operative, peaceful, common believers or subscribers. The conclusion must then be, that an exemplar is not a *bona fide* notion operated by participants themselves when they engage in a contest about the real nature of X. Contestants in general either cannot agree about a common source or if they can, it is the mere form of words they are assenting to while hotly disputing about what the words really mean or amount to. Various political move-ments, for instance, may indeed claim that they derive inspiration from the French or American Revolution, but they would each understand such revolutions to stand for different things in legitim-ating their own political aspirations. They would each persist in saying that the true significance of the Paris Commune, say, is X and that rival understandings are just misunderstandings. Gallie could only locate his exemplar by adopting an extremely nomin-alist position which makes nonsense of the realities behind the mere form of words.

Gallie's thesis appeals because: (i) it seems to account for a very obvious aspect of intellectual life, its agonistic style; (ii) for the thrill of the journey without ever arriving at any destination – argument will go on endlessly without even temporary respite; (iii) it celebrates the possibility of competing diversities; and (iv) it seems to free one from the impossible demand of logical justific-ation without intellectual debate having to surrender its claim to the status of being genuine, critical and rational dispute. Unfortu-nately, he fails to deliver the goods. One cannot have a coherent theory of rationality which says that in principle even in the long run disagreements cannot be settled by argument, just as in Winch's case, one cannot have a coherent theory of rationality which lays down the limits of rationality.

The survey in the foregoing pages shows that there are now two major deep currents sustaining the fact/value distinction – one is the empiricist-cum-positivist tradition as understood today, and the other, officially the anti-positivist tradition (which in the social science literature is referred to as the hermeneutical tradition), culminates in the conceptual relativism of Winch in the English-speaking world. Both of these broad philosophical outlooks, however, have internal difficulties and tensions which moral philosophers, by concentrating single-mindedly on the preoccupations of their own area of study, tend to overlook when they rely on these traditions in the formulation of their problems. They concentrate on the obvious contention of contemporary positivism, that values are defective, failing to pass certain tests of objectivity or rationality (or meaninglessness) which facts can pass; or on the obvious implication for moral philosophy of the thesis of conceptual relativism, that the 'truth' of moral beliefs is relative to the standards of rationality, validity and objectivity of the people holding the beliefs. But they usually ignore the fact that these implications are teased from a theory which is meant to be a comprehensive theory of knowledge. Logical positivism, as we saw, as a comprehensive epistemology runs into severe difficulties. So does conceptual relativism. An unfortunate drawback results from this artificial isolation and parochialism – moral philosophy is regarded as autonomous, a subject matter with its own peculiarities and vulnerabilities which set it apart from other branches of philosophical studies.

The Naturalistic Fallacy is perceived as the most vulnerable characteristic of moral 'reasoning'. Yet this characteristic which has the effect of rendering moral 'knowledge' as pseudo-knowledge is hardly perceived as part of general scepticism. It is often not mentioned in moral philosophy in connection with that famous passage from Hume about the 'is/ought' gap that its author's general philosophy is one of carrying empiricism to its sceptical conclusions. The difficulties of such a position are hardly ever discussed, the assumptions and presuppositions behind Hume's scepticism are not alluded to. As a result, moral philosophers are caught within a narrow cage entirely of their own making, and so long as they do not break out of this cage to invade the wider philosophical territory, they will not be able to solve the difficulties which beset them. A ploy of this book is to try to re-integrate moral philosophy with the rest of philosophy, and to consider the problem posed by the Naturalistic Fallacy afresh by putting it within a broader epistemological perspective.

7 THE STRUCTURING OF THE NATURALISTIC FALLACY BY THE LOGICAL DEMANDS OF POSITIVISM

This section makes a start by getting back, further behind the scene, as it were, of the two main currents sustaining the fact/value distinction to see if any light could be thrown on the problem posed by the Naturalistic Fallacy in moral philosophy. First of all, one must remind oneself that a major impulse behind positivism is to put scientific knowledge on a firm philosophical footing. To this end, it develops a model of scientific reasoning. One such influential model is that of Hempel, the Deductive-Nomological model of explanation-cum-prediction (on this model, explanation and prediction are symmetrical). Very briefly, it consists of a law/theory (cast in the form of a universal proposition) and a statement about initial conditions, which together constitute the *explanans* and entail the *explanandum*, or the statement containing the prediction. If the context is one of explanation, the explanation holds if the statement containing it derived from the *explanans*, is shown to be true. If the context is one of predicting an event, the same logical structure obtains, except for the change in the tense of the conclusion, that is to say, the statement containing the prediction now reads 'X will Y'. The same process of logical derivation may be repeated in trying to explain a law or predict a law, in this way building a hierarchy of laws. This model is meant to be applicable to both the natural and the social sciences. Fundamental to the positivist outlook is the belief in the unity of method. Some positivists go further in maintaining that eventually all knowledge will be reduced to a single science, like physics.

This philosophy of science is itself under attack by conceptual relativism from two directions. First, Winch (and others belonging to the so-called hermeneutical tradition, although they use some-what different arguments[20]) resist this model of explanation as the appropriate one to use in the social sciences. The main objection lies in the fact that human conduct, which constitutes the subject matter of these sciences, unlike inert matter is capable not only of consciousness, but self-consciousness, of the very monitoring of such self-conscious reflections. This is done *via* language which construes and determines reality. Winch, as already described, develops the view that the method of the social sciences is concep-tual (philosophical), to get at the meaning of the central concepts which inform the conduct of the participants of a form of life in order to understand the rules, institutions and practices embodying them. On the other hand, the method of the natural sciences is empirical and its basic concern is not to get at the meaning for there is none, but to determine and obtain causal regularities in natural phenomena. Second, Kuhn (*The Structure of Scientific Revolutions*, 1962) who, although he does not regard himself as a conceptual relativist, is, nevertheless, regarded by many to be very much within the spirit of the form of life outlook. He argues that rationality criteria which operate in science are after all only criteria that the scientific community as a matter of fact endorses, implying that their bindingness and necessity are nothing more than the result of group loyalty and commitment, and that there is nothing 'rational' about such a commitment. Conceptual relativism in recent times is developed as a reaction to positivism in the philosophy of science and is its foil or anti-thesis.

The Deductive-Nomological model rests upon the primacy of the logical relationship of deducibility or derivability – a prop-osition is rationally established if it is a conclusion that is validly deduced from its premises. This is referred to as one of the 'logical conditions' which Hempel says an explanation must satisfy to be considered adequate, namely, that the *explanandum* must be a logical consequence of the *explanans*.[21] The others he cites are: that the *explanans* must contain general laws; these must actually be required in the derivation of the *explanandum*; and the *explanans* must have empirical content. Another criterion apart from the logical ones is that the *explanans* must be true.

However, satisfying these conditions has the peculiar consequence of rendering the following explanation scientific, as Harré[22] has pointed out:

All wooden things are good conductors of electricity
All metals are wooden things

All metals are good conductors of electricity

The conclusion follows logically from the premises; both premises are in the form of what passes for general laws and they are actually used in the derivation of the conclusion; the premises have empirical content. So the logical conditions are satisfied. Now it might be thought that the fourth non-logical condition is not met, since the *explanans* appears to be false. However, it can be said to be false if one is not operating the Hempelian positivist account of explanation and of truth. On his model, what is true is precisely what leads eventually to correct predictions. In the example cited, the *explanans* does lead to the correct prediction that all metals are good conductors of electricity and/or that this metal, A, is a good conductor of electricity. This philosophy of science, says Harré, suffers from the misfortune of being eventually engulfed by the dogma of the deductive relation:

the insight that it is sometimes a sufficient condition for a theory to be said to explain a fact, that the statements expressing the fact be deducible from the statements expressing the theory, together with statements of conditions, has been transformed into the dogma that explanation consists in nothing but the setting up of a deductive link from what is to be explained to what explains it.[23]

On the surface, the fascination for twentieth-century positivism of the deductive relationship is curious, given that it sustains the distinction between the analytic *a priori* and the synthetic *a posteriori*. The former category, on its understanding, consists of trivial truths linguistically guaranteed. Their certainty and necessity lie in their tautological character. As such they do not say anything about the world. To this category they say, mathematics and logic belong. The sciences, on the other hand, attempt to say something about the world; their propositions are meant to be informative. But any informative statement about the world is contingent. Yet why is it that twentieth-century positivism, in

27

giving an account of scientific knowledge which is synthetic *a posteriori*, leans on the exclusive primacy of the logical relationship of deducibility and ends up regarding mathematics as the paradigm of knowledge which science, to be respectable, must emulate and approximate?

This is because even twentieth-century positivism ultimately accepts certainty (logical) as the hallmark of true knowledge,[24] that very characteristic which positivism, in its earlier history, accused its seventeenth-century opponents of celebrating. The philosophers positivism was castigating were trying to find out what the world is like, why it necessarily is what it appears to be like. Causal connections for them were necessary connections which would account for the appearance of orderly sequences and regularities in nature. Hume, as we know, attacked this view with vigour, using the empirico-positivist weapon, that what is not phenomenally given is occult or metaphysical nonsense. But Hume demolished the distinction between essence and phenomenon and later positivists the category of the synthetic *a priori*. Yet positivism seems to hanker for certainty as the exclusive hallmark of true knowledge. Since logical certainty is the only permissible type of certainty within its framework, it has no option but to turn to mathematics and logic as the paradigm of true knowledge, even though on its own admission, the truths that obtain in these fields, in so far as they are certain and necessary, are truths of definitions. So really in the end, for twentieth-century positivism, physics is not the queen of the sciences, but mathematics, to which physics must approximate. Mathematics, as the most highly systematised and axiomatised structure of thought, is built on the logical relationship of deducibility. Logic, conceived as such a relationship, is then the basis of the twentieth-century positivist programme and its fundamental tenet.

Indeed one may go so far as to say that according to it: (a) a conclusion is not and cannot be said to be justified unless it is entailed by its premises; and (b) whatever is thus entailed or derived is not only valid but true. This means: (i) that no other logical relationship save that of logical derivability provides justification for knowledge claims; and (ii) that logical derivability exhausts the notion of truth so that to say that a statement is true is to say no more than that it is validly derived from another set of statements, whose truth in turn is guaranteed by its derivability from yet another set and so on. In other words, in spite of its empiricist origins and connections, the empiricist element with its insistence upon the primacy of the phenomenally given tends to be edged from the centre of the scene by the demand of logic as strict implication. The question of determining the truth of a statement, if not actually rendered redundant, is at least indefinitely postponed or sidestepped by the strategy of logical derivability.

The logical hardcore to twentieth-century positivism is all-pervasive in modern Western thought. It occurs not only in the philosophy of science, but also in moral philosophy and political philosophy, as well as in the philosophy of law, all underpinned by this fundamental logical tenet transformed into a theory of epistemology. As such it may be dubbed the logical theory of knowledge. It is all-pervasive not only in its positive form but also negatively by those who ostensibly challenge the positivist thesis itself, like Winch in the name of conceptual relativism. For Winch and others tacitly concur with the criterion that logical derivability alone confers unproblematic respectability. Winch is only able to shield the social sciences from such a demand by admitting that they are circumscribed by a theory of rationality which lays down the limits of rationality. Kuhn, on the other hand, seeing some of the distortions to which the criterion can lead, is quite eager often (though not consistently) to admit that the demand is not met even by the natural sciences, and to embrace a similar theory of rationality which in the end renders the whole domain of science shaky by resting it on an irrational commitment to rationality. Theorists like Hare in moral philosophy and Kelsen in jurisprudence combine the positivist criterion of logical derivability with the relativist/subjectivist requirement that the community or the individual commits itself to a certain moral, legal or political form of life. Deducibility is possible and criteria of validity are available within each system, but it is not possible to talk about the correctness of one system against the incorrectness of another; one can only commit oneself to any one such system and in so doing, one decides to abide by the rules of validity internal to it.

In science, it is no doubt true that the more mature a science, the more it tends to assume a deductive structure. However, from this it does not follow that the mere possibility of systematisation by itself is sufficient to render it scientific. Nor is it correct to assume that just because a theory employs mathematical formulae, it consists of nothing more than its mathematical formalism. Few practising scientists fall for this. Instead they assume that the theory has a factual content beyond the formalism and that a mathematical formula embedded in a particular theory is not a pure abstract equation but one which has been given a factual (either tacitly or explicitly) interpretation.[25] (They tend to interpret it in operationist terms, which may, of course, be criticised for being inadequate,[26] but this is another matter.)

However, the good sense of practising scientists does not always filter through to those who write about the philosophy of science, an activity which is conducted from a particular philosophical standpoint. So they tend to interpret and understand science in terms of their philosophy and then to reinforce the latter by an appeal to science (as interpreted through it) itself. And by the time this reinforced philosophical viewpoint is in turn filtered down to areas of philosophy outside the philosophy of science, an even more simplified and distorted account of the whole matter is put across and in turn taken for granted. Philosophers of science imbued with the spirit of positivism look at the more mature sciences, are impressed by the magnificent deductive structures embedded in them, then proceed to reinforce their philosophical requirement of logical deducibility by casting science within such a mould. The message is then put out to philosophers elsewhere that scientific explanation consists of satisfying the requirements of the deducibility relationship. Such philosophers then proceed to assess their own subject matter in the light of this relationship and its demands. They then conclude, either that their own discipline satisfies the requirements, in which case it is respectable and may carry the honorific title of being scientific, or that, unfortunately, it does not measure up to the demands, in which case in order to remedy the situation, the subject matter would have to be manipulated so that eventually it might fit the mould, or at least fit it as near enough as possible, or, finally, simply accept the inevitable, that the discipline is irredeemably unscientific or irrational because it can in no way be made to match the requirements of strict implication or deducibility.

Moral philosophers, for instance, all agree that moral 'reasoning' simply does not fulfil the demand. Some accept the inevitable and conclude that morals are hopelessly irrational, arbitrary, subjective or whatever. Others try to salvage the situation (like Hare in *The Language of Morals*) by combining, as we saw, deducibility as an internal feature of the system with commitment to the system. Still others, like Gallie, correctly reject the criterion of 'logical justification' as the criterion for conferring rational status upon a dispute, but nevertheless maintain that even the impossibility in the long run of procuring agreement through argument bestows rationality status. Gallie, unlike the others, tries to meet the positivist thesis by rejecting and not accommodating it, by developing an anti-thesis to it. But unfortunately the anti-thesis is not a viable one.

So moral philosophers on the whole tend to shackle themselves within a framework of demands which has been filtered down from the philosophy of science interpreted through twentieth-century positivist lenses. Within this inherited but self-imposed framework, certain problems arise which cannot be solved without deserting it for another. There is no need to stick to it, especially when it is being challenged in the philosophy of science and philosophy in general, both of which are showing increasing signs of moving out from the positivist stranglehold as well as from the anti-thesis which seeks to challenge it but still within its own terms. The broad stages of development in philosophy this century may be said to be: first the rise of twentieth-century positivism with the rise of the Vienna Circle; later the rejection of the *Tractatus* by Wittgenstein himself in favour of the *Investigations* which signals the formulation of its anti-thesis in philosophy in general (by Winch in the social sciences in particular and by Kuhn, who amongst others was influenced by Quine and his attack of the empiricist-cum-positivist tradition, in the natural sciences); and of late the slow but growing impetus of going beyond both the thesis and the anti-thesis for an outlook which may be characterised very loosely as critical and realist, arguing for the possibility of objectivity and rationality not only in the natural sciences but also in the social sciences, and in philosophy in general, arguing for a critical or scientific realism with regard to theoretical terms as opposed to the reductionist account which underpins contemporary positivist epistemology.[27] Given this new mood and outlook, the time seems ripe to re-examine the contemporary positivist implication for moral philosophy, and to try to find a way out of the impasse created by its requirement of strict implication or deducibility, that does not suffer from the defects of previous rescue attempts which do not really succeed in restoring the possibility of objectivity and rationality to moral inquiry. The thesis to be developed in this book is a contribution made in this spirit of going beyond the positivism and conceptual relativism of our time.

However, a word of clarification is essential before closing this section. Positivism is by no means a simple single doctrine or even a homogeneous set of doctrines. Upon investigation, it turns out to be a nest of theses, not all of which are subscribed to by philosophers who care to call themselves by that label.[28] Moreover, it has a very long and complex history, going well beyond its official beginning with Comte, whose philosophy is regarded as a mature form of positivism of the nineteenth century.[29] Twentieth-century positivism, largely but not solely based on logical positivism, is in fact a reaction to nineteenth-century Comteanism. It differs from the latter mainly by its application of the logicistic method of analysis pioneered by Russell, Whitehead and others, culminating in the *Principia Mathematica*.[30]

The philosophy of science that then emerged is shaped by logical positivism based on the logic of the *Principia Mathematica*. That version of the positivist philosophy of science associated with Hempel and called the Deductive-Nomological model may be seen as a product of that influence. But there are other versions of the positivist philosophy of science in this century, such as Popper's which differs in some respects from the Hempelian D-N model, and has even eclipsed it in the English-speaking world with the publication of Popper's *The Logic of Scientific Discovery* in 1959.[31] However, for the purpose of this book, which is to combat the contemporary positivist influence on moral philosophy through its conception of rationality as logical justification, logical derivability/deducibility, strict proof or strict implication, it may not be unjustified to simplify matters and use the D-N model as a focus for discussion. For all forms of positivism, in spite of their differences, agree that the relationship of deducibility is crucial to the scientificity of a discipline.[32] The D-N model is invoked in this spirit to display the centrality of that relationship.

But there is another strain of positivism which must be singled out for special mention, and that is the variety represented by J. S. Mill, another version of nineteenth-century positivism, based on the inductivist wing of the positivist spectrum. To anticipate a little, it turns out that the thesis of epistemic implication, developed in Chapter Three of this book, is a form of fallibilism. Fallibilism, it appears, is the mode favoured by Mill in his attempt to give a rational basis to his defence of liberty and his utilitarianism (see Chapter Six). Contemporary positivism, so wedded to its fact/value distinction, seems to have suffered either from embarrassment or amnesia about the fact that in the history of positivism, there is a variety which argues for the possibility of rationality/objectivity in the domain of values.[33] This book did not set out wittingly to apply and develop Mill's fallibilism or to defend Mill's inductivist brand of positivism. But as there turn out to be overlapping similarities between the Millean outlook and the thesis of epistemic implication, this leads to the ironical conclusion that in a sense, the beginning of a cure for the defects of twentieth-century positivism as far as norms/values are concerned lies within the history of positivism itself.

The relevance of that history has been obscured for two reasons. Firstly, Moore misunderstood Mill, accusing him of committing the Naturalistic Fallacy. That misunderstanding was taken over by other moral philosophers. Secondly, in the philosophy of science itself, Mill's enthusiasm for inductivism also led to a decline in his fortunes as inductive logic is dismissed as both unobtainable and irrelevant by Popper's variety of twentieth-century positivism (though not by logical positivism). As a result, philosophers who have imbibed the spirit of contemporary positivism would tend to overlook Mill's solution to the problem of norms/values.

8 THE REJECTION OF NON-COGNITIVISM AND THE RISE OF MORAL REALISM

The meta-ethical view associated with C. L. Stevenson's *Ethics and Language* and Hare's *Language of Morals*, commonly called non-cognitivism, has come to dominate the post-Second World War discussion in moral philosophy, at least in the English-speaking world. It maintains: (a) that moral language is a combination of two sorts of meanings, descriptive and emotive for Stevenson, but prescriptive for Hare; (b) the emotive/prescriptive component is the dominant partner, which accounts for why moral propositions are not logically derivable from non-moral (factual) propositions; (c) its dominance also implies that moral disagreement is possible even if there is no disagreement of facts between two people; (d) what renders the disagreement intelligible is that morality is primarily an expression of emotion or attitudes; (e) emotions/attitudes or more generally speaking, values are free-floating and may attach themselves to any set of facts or situation; (f) what makes something morally right is simply the case that the agent has a favourable attitude towards it, and that this favourable attitude is manifested through the agent's carrying out the prescription which embodies it.

The dominance of this view was first challenged by Philippa Foot who calls it the 'private enterprise theory' of morals.[34] This was later taken up by Iris Murdoch in *The Sovereignty of the Good* (1970). The self portrayed by non-cognitivism is one of restless activity through choice and commitment. To this, Murdoch opposes the image of the contemplative self. Moral knowledge is gained by contemplation of the good (a kind of neo-Platonism), and not by the self arbitrarily bestowing approval through commitment to willy-nilly any course of action.

In 1976, David Wiggins in his address to the British Academy – 'Truth, Invention and the Meaning of Life' – also criticised non-cognitivism, primarily for its failure to 'explore the possibility that the questions of truth and the meaning of life are the central questions of moral philosophy'.[35] On the non-cognitivist view, any activity could render life meaningful provided the agent is whole-heartedly committed to it. In Wiggins's opinion, to find meaning in life presupposes that certain activities are intrinsically worth-while, and this is a truth which itself is not dependent on a free-floating commitment. However, in spite of his strictures against non-cognitivism, Wiggins appears to endorse a limited form of non-cognitivism which regards the individual as the final authority of what it is to 'live most fully'.

Of late, a new outlook in moral philosophy has appeared on the scene, also opposed to non-cognitivism, which its practitioners call 'moral realism'. It is the conscious extension of the Davidsonian approach in the philosophy of language to moral philosophy. Its most obvious advocate is Mark Platts, who has devoted a whole chapter of his book *Ways of Meaning* (1979) to developing the new meta-ethics. This is not the place to discuss Davidson's contribution to the theory of meaning within an overall philosophy of language.[36] But, in brief, it is a truth-conditional account of meaning based on Tarski's theory of truth. Basically it says that the meaning of a sentence is to be given by stating its truth-conditions. As such, the concept of truth is fundamental to the theory of meaning and renders it testable by appealing to the notions of assent and dissent, that is to say, it is assumed that a speaker on the whole assents to true and dissents from false sentences. This enables us to recognise when what are said to be the truth-conditions for a sentence are really so.

It is held that truth-conditional semantics entails a particular type of metaphysics, namely, realism.[37] Realism is said to be the thesis that

the world is determinately constituted, that is, has its character independently of any knowledge or experience of it, so that sentences about the world are either determinately true or false in virtue of the way things are in the world, whether or not we can come to know how things are in the world and thus whether or not we can come to know those sentences to be true or false. On a realist thesis, the truth-conditions of sentences in a given class of sentences may transcend our capacity to recognise whether or not they obtain.[38]

When such a truth-conditional/realist view of language is extended to include moral discourse, as it is by Platts, moral judgments are

viewed as *factually cognitive*, as presenting claims about the world which can be assessed (like any other factual belief) as true or false, and whose truth or falsity are as much possible objects of human knowledge as any other factual claims about the world. This amounts in part to a denial of anything in the literal meaning of a moral judgment which compels us to assess those judgments on some dimension other than (or in addition to) that of the true and the false. It thus amounts also to the claim that if a moral judgment is true, it is true in virtue of the (independently existing) real world, and is true in virtue of that alone.[39]

This of course directly conflicts with the non-cognitivist view that moral judgments belong to the realm of values, not facts, that values are either totally emotive (as most logical positivists claim) or predominantly conative (as Hare claims). It clearly then repudiates the fact/value distinction as it is today commonly understood.

However, the moral realism that Platts is led to defend is a type of intuitionism.[40] This results, it appears, from an attempt to broaden the category of the kind of sentence which are 'barely true'.[41] These are sentences 'whose truth (where they are true) is not dependent upon the availability of a non-trivial answer to the question, "What *makes* it true?" A sentence which can be "barely true", in this sense, is a sentence of whose truth we can be *noninferentially* aware.'[42] Platts maintains that moral truths are non-inferential truths; hence his intuitionism.

Platts's intuitionism differs from classical intuitionism in several ways, of which the following two are particularly important:

> First, it is no part of this intuitionism to suggest that we detect the moral aspects of a situation by means of some *special faculty* of the mind, the intuition. We detect moral aspects in the same way we detect (nearly all) other aspects: by looking and seeing. Any further claim, like that positing a distinctive faculty of ethical intuition, is a contribution to the unintelligible pseudo-psychology of the faculties of the mind. Secondly, contrary to a persistent strand in classical intuitionist thought, certainty plays no role in this form of intuitionism. This is a consequence of taking realism seriously. By the process of careful attention to the world, we can improve our practical understanding, our sensitivity to the presence of instances of the moral concepts that figure in these beliefs. But this process of attention to improve beliefs and understanding will go on without end; there is no reason to believe that we shall ever be justified in being certain that we have now completely understood any of the moral concepts occurring in these beliefs. Our moral language, like all the realistic part of that language, transcends our present practical comprehensions in trying to grapple with an independent, indefinitely complex reality; only ignorance of that realism could prompt the hope of certainty.[43]

Such intuiting is a process of looking and seeing, akin to Murdoch's contemplating, and equally at odds with the non-cognitivist view of moral agency in terms of activity like choosing or committing oneself to something.

While this book is extremely sympathetic to Platts's efforts to combat non-cognitivism (it is not possible here to examine the merits or otherwise of the truth-conditional semantics of which his moral realism is an off-shoot), his intuitionism does not appear at first sight to be a fruitful method to adopt to work towards establishing the possibility of rationality/objectivity in moral discourse, in spite of the fact that his emphasis on the lack of certainty, and the open-ended nature of moral investigation, has much in common with the fallibilism argued for by this book. Chapter Five attempts to show that it is not helpful to assimilate moral sentences to sentences of the sort 'there is a tree in front of this house' or 'this grass is green', where it seems to make no sense to ask for evidence why grass is green other than by saying that one has looked, etc. In these cases, looking and seeing is the appropriate and the only thing one can do. But with moral sentences (A1), it makes sense to ask for evidence which is inferential (provided inference is not understood as strict implication), and they belong more appropriately with other sorts of sentences (like (A3) and (A2) – see Chapters Two and Three), where inferential evidence is also required. Sentences like (A1), (A2) and (A3) belong to the domain of ordinary knowledge whose task is justificatory (unlike scientific knowledge whose task primarily is explanatory though it may also be predictive). It is argued that if the sentences containing the evidence satisfy certain criteria, then the evidence serves to justify (rationally and objectively) the beliefs contained in sentences (A1), (A2) and (A3).

The latest and the most developed of these post-Davidsonian attempts to reject non-cognitivism in ethics is that by Sabina Lovibond in her book *Realism and Imagination in Ethics* (1983). She differs from Platts by relying in the main on the insights of Wittgenstein's later writings, and especially on the form of life argument, to generate an account of moral realism.[44]

Like Platts's book, this one has much in common with Lovibond's. It agrees with hers in diagnosing the inadequacies of non-cognitivism, especially in the following three respects: (i) that the sovereignty of the individual will as the final arbiter of what is right and wrong has unacceptable consequences; (ii) that the contemporary positivist fact/value distinction (what she calls 'empiricist') must be rejected if meta-ethics is to be re-integrated into the domain of the rational and the objective, that is, of critical discourse; (iii) the belief that irrational (but sincere) commitment to values is alone compatible with the notions of liberalism and tolerance is false.

However, her approach and that taken by this book in over-coming these deficiencies and in providing for an alternative meta-ethics are radically different. In the opinion of the latter, the form of life argument (what Lovibond calls 'expressivism') cannot generate, as we have seen earlier, an alternative epistemology to non-cognitivism which is genuinely rational and objective.[45] What expressivism does offer is the substitution of collectivity for indi-viduality – it is not so much the individual will as the collective will which is sovereign.

In this, she draws attention to the similar insights of Marx and Engels in their comments about language, and thus recalls the Hegelian source from which not only Marx but also, she claims, Wittgenstein may be said to descend.[46] She also echoes the efforts of Marx in his rejection of the thesis of abstract individualism.[47] For liberalism cohering with capitalism, the individual is auton-omous, against which is pitted the collectivity or society. However, the latter is construed to be logically posterior to the former – individuals are real and exist (in the crucial sense acceptable to the empiricist), whereas society is but a logical construction out of autonomous individuals. Statements about society can be reduced without remainder to statements about individuals. For Marx, the terms 'individual' and 'society' are dialectically related – the one concept cannot be understood without reference to the other. The one is not logically posterior or reducible to the other. Individuals and their identities are given or evolved within the collectivity of which they are a part. Similarly, Lovibond wishes to argue that the values held by individuals which constitute their identities are not created *in vacuo* by their autonomous wills. Rather they come to hold the values which are constitutive of their identities because they are participants of a form of life which embodies these values. They have learnt to absorb them so that they come to inform their lives. What individuals hold as valuable are learnt from society. Yet the values of society are but the values affirmed by individuals – they are not transcendently given.

On Lovibond's view, the process of learning is conceptually

linked with the notion of objectivity. Learning itself presupposes consensus or agreement. The consensus is upheld by what she calls 'intellectual authorities', which include teachers at every level of the educational ladder, researchers, parents and others who are acknowledged to know true from false, right from wrong. They are the people who know how to apply the rules which determine what is correct and what is incorrect.[48]

Lovibond cites with approval Wittgenstein's account of logical compulsion.[49] When we criticise someone for deviating from the rules of logic, this is but the product of a process of training which ends with the internalisation of the goal set before us by our trainers or educators. But that process begins with coercion – we are beaten (physically), frowned upon, chided, rejected emotionally by our parents and teachers, not given sweets or other treats whenever we make mistakes as beginners. Through reward and punishment, subtle or unsubtle, suitably meted out, successful conditioning results in an ability to apply the rules correctly (be they the rules of logic, of morals, or whatever). On achieving this, the process of initiation as full members of the form of life is completed, and we become an authority, certified to initiate others in turn. She says:

> what is both historically and logically prior to this sort of co-
> operative learning process is an operation in which coercion
> has the central place. It is in virtue of our having been
> subjected to this original, coercive type of training that we
> can be said to belong to a community which is bound together
> by a common education. . . . Wittgenstein reiterates his view
> that the uniformity of practice which makes objective discourse
> possible is sustained, ultimately, by material coercion. . . .
> The implication is that sanctions will be brought to bear upon
> anyone who seeks to think, act or talk in a deviant way.
> These sanctions may consist in acts of physical violence, as
> when a child is smacked for doing something 'naughty'; but
> of course there are other, less direct approaches which are
> used in cases of greater social complexity. Thus if someone
> takes himself to be pursuing a particular artistic or scientific
> discipline, but produces results which fail to meet our
> standard of good results for that discipline, we say he is no
> good at what he is doing and we give a material expression

to our adverse judgement – for example, by not buying the objects he produces, or by not appointing him to a university lecturing post.[50]

If Lovibond intends to use this account of learning based on authoritarianism to build a so-called theory of moral realism, as she clearly does – 'Our proposed theory of ethics, in short, is a realist theory in that it asserts the existence of *intellectual authority-relations* in the realm of morals,'[51] – then this book must part company with her. If her thesis is merely the application of the insight, namely, the 'discovery of the logical link between *objectivity* and *intellectual authority*, and of the embodiment of such authority in institutions which exert a coercive force upon individual participants in the language-game';[52] if for her 'Objectivity . . . is a function of what Quine calls a "pull" toward habits of judgement which are consistent with the adoption of a publicly accessible perspective on the world. Objective discourse is discourse in which, as a matter of logic, we cannot participate unless we are prepared to acknowledge certain intellectual authorities',[53] then her account of objectivity amounts to what in Chapter Two of this book is called the 'command theory of knowledge' (see Chapter Two).

Such a theory of knowledge presupposes a sense of authority which is based on a power relationship. Those who are acknowledged to know true from false, right from wrong, those competent to apply rules are teachers, employers, judges, agents and agencies which penalise those who deviate from or fail to conform to the rules and reward those who perform according to the rules. In Chapter Two, a distinction is made between 'political authorities' based on power and an 'epistemological authority' which has nothing to do with power relationships.[54] It is argued that the possibility of objectivity and rationality is logically linked to the latter and not the former. Political authorities impose, maintain and sustain consensus, but they have nothing to do with the possibility of objectivity in the epistemological sense that one is interested in when criticising non-cognitivism and providing an alternative to it (see Chapter Three). That sense of objectivity is both independent of the will of the individual as well as the stick and carrot used by the collectivity or the community or society in asserting its collective will by maintaining a consensus. From the point of view of this book, the theory of learning put forward by Lovibond/Wittgenstein fails to be a proper epistemological theory of learning, although it may be a fruitful sociological theory.

In Chapter Two, the point is also made that the command theory of knowledge based on 'political' (what Lovibond misleadingly calls 'intellectual') authorities is deeply entrenched in the positivist account of law. While such a theory may have some merits in the philosophy of law, it has none in moral philosophy or in plain epistemology. On Lovibond's account of Wittgenstein, the latter may be construed as applying the thesis of legal positivism to the philosophy of language. Legal positivism distinguishes legal rules from other rules (like moral rules) by saying that physical coercion is constitutive of legal rules – the violation of a valid legal rule entails the physical sanction. It is held that the rules of a municipal legal system clearly are rules of such a type. As such they entail the existence of policemen, judges, probation officers, prison officers and even hangmen whose business it is to apply and use coercion. This criterion of what constitutes a legal rule, therefore, has the effect of ruling out, for instance, international law as law in 'its proper understanding of law', as there is no body which exists to enforce sanctions and to use coercion in the events of its rules being violated. Some legal positivists, as a result, argue that international law is really a body of moral rules. When these are violated, indignation and disapproval are elicited but not physical sanction. It is held that expression of condemnation is constitutive of moral rules when these are violated.

Similarly, Lovibond says,

> Wittgenstein's account implies that where there is no material agency to coerce, there is no rule to compel; and there is, *ex hypothesi*, no one outside the *total* speech community who could exercise the necessary coercion. No one, that is to say, penalizes the total community if it adopts a different social practice in place of its current one.[55]

For Lovibond/Wittgenstein,

> In relation to the community itself, then, as distinct from its constituent members, linguistic rules are not prescriptive but descriptive. They are abstract representations of what is

41

actually done by speakers: representations, in other words, of particular aspects of the use of language. As such, they are *read off* from the various collective practices which constitute linguistic behaviour; they do not *govern* those practices *qua* collective.[56]

Linguistic rules *vis-à-vis* the community are reclassified as descriptive rules in the spirit that the legal positivist reclassifies international law as moral rules. *Vis-à-vis* individuals, expressivism allows one to say that 'what is right' is 'what the political authorities regard as right through the use of coercion'. *Vis-à-vis* the linguistic community, 'what is right' is simply 'what political authorities do'. In this context, the normative is reduced to the factual. However, one does not need to be a non-cognitivist to protest at this reduction – 'what is right' simply does not mean 'what the linguistic community as a matter of fact does'.[57]

It looks as if, then, Lovibond's account of moral realism is based on a confusion between epistemological objectivity/rationality and consensus. A consensus account of objectivity/rationality (what Putnam calls 'institutionalized criterial rationality'[58]), logically linked as it is with the notion of political authority, naturally conjures up a conservative rather than a liberal view of society. Lovibond sets out vigorously to combat such an image. She argues that conservatism is not a necessary accompaniment of the notions of consensus and political ('intellectual') authority. She is well aware that the idealist tradition, of which Wittgenstein's expressivism may be seen as a continuation, is regarded as a natural ally of those who wish to preserve the *status quo* and to outlaw dissent. She tries to break this natural affinity by reminding us that there is no need to accept the extreme position of one like Bradley, who maintains that dissent is logically impossible. In this, she does not seem to be successful. The failure can be traced directly to the very notion of objectivity/rationality as consensus and political authority. Again, at best these latter concepts can accommodate the idea of change and dissent in sociological terms, but not in epistemological terms.

For Lovibond dissent can be accommodated for two reasons: firstly, because political authorities are as a matter of fact not as well-entrenched, all-powerful, far-reaching and successful as they might be. If they 'do a thorough job', so to speak, and achieve near-total efficiency, then dissenters would not emerge or survive. She says:

> Adherence to an expressive conception of language does not mean that we have to represent ourselves as citizens of one of those 'devout, authoritarian, semi-primitive societies' . . . which appear to have inspired the development of that conception; we can retain the idea of language as expression – of linguistic institutions as embodying the objective spirit of a community – without making fanciful claims about the degree of internal cohesion or harmony which can be attributed to our own form of life. The importance of reserving philosophical space for a moderate, or pluralistic, interpretation of organicist view about language lies precisely in the power of such an interpretation to make sense, within the given theoretical context, of the phenomenon of rational dissent. For in a community where intellectual cohesion exists only in a low degree, there will be nothing to prevent individual members from rationalizing their distaste for a particular sub-set of the prevailing values (or institutions) in terms of an alternative or divergent scheme of values, through which they can sustain their identity as rational persons while renouncing the dominant mode of rationality. In this way, their criticism of the *sittlich* commitments of their fellow-citizens (which are also their own commitments, prior to reflection) will not necessarily prejudice their status as exponents of a way of life regulated by universal laws or principles.[59]

Secondly, as a matter of fact, these authorities and institutions are themselves diverse and conflicting, and do not constitute a single authority embodying a unified world view that has achieved hegemonic control of society.

> Any imperfectly coherent form of life necessarily encompasses institutions which are dedicated to incompatible (or dubiously compatible) ends, and that is why there can arise within it competing habits of judging and reasoning – the habits grounded respectively in these competing institutions – whose exponents can engage in mutual rational criticism. The dissenting values, too, are grounded in the form of life whose

partially alienated members draw upon them to articulate
and justify their own alienated condition.[60]

As for the first reason, she could be right as a matter of fact.
The success enjoyed by such authorities in any one society may
be a matter of degree. The second reason appears to reflect the
conditions of a pluralistic society. In such a society where the
various authorities compete and jostle for the allegiance of the
individuals, there is room for dissent naturally. Dissent is easily
explicable and intelligible when both assumptions obtain. But
what if a society is non-pluralistic (suppose such a one could be
found) and is successful in establishing hegemony, what then?
Under such conditions, dissent cannot be philosophically accommodated. In other words, her account works because she is
presupposing a form of life which may be said to be pluralistic
and liberal, where dissent and tolerance of dissent are already
values embodied in that form of life.

But the crucial test for an epistemology which argues for the
possibility of objectivity and rationality lies in the choice between
competing forms of life, for instance, the liberal or the illiberal
form of life. If the choice itself is not susceptible to rational/
objective (in the non-expressivist understanding which this book
argues for) critical scrutiny, then non-cognitivism can re-assert
itself. A non-cognitivist is not concerned to deny that someone
already within a liberal form of life can make space for dissent.
The point is precisely to show that liberalism makes sense if it is
already assumed that individuals have sincerely committed themselves to the basic value in question, just as illiberalism, as a form
of life, makes sense if it is assumed that individuals have sincerely
committed themselves to the basic value of that system or form
of life. But on the non-cognitivist thesis it makes no sense for the
liberal to accuse the non-liberal for being mistaken in accepting
illiberalism or *vice versa*.

But it turns out that on Lovibond/Wittgenstein's view of
expressivism, one cannot say: (i) of the linguistic rules *vis-à-vis*
one's community that they are prescriptive; (ii) of the linguistic
rules *vis-à-vis* another community that they are prescriptive; (iii)
that the linguistic rules of one community are more adequate,
rational or in any way better than those of another community.
Criteria of rationality are internal to any one form of life; no

trans-communal or trans-cultural criterion or criteria of rationality
exist or are intelligible. If this is so, then the actual differences
between non-cognitivism and Lovibond/Wittgenstein's expressivism amount to the replacement of: (a) the non-cognitivist individual by the Wittgensteinian collectivity acting coercively through
its various agencies or political authorities; (b) the non-cognitivist
process of conscious deliberate commitment by the individual to
certain norms and values by the Wittgensteinian process of
prolonged initiation through coercion leading finally to the internalisation of the values enforced.

The existence of coercive institutions and practices does not by
itself guarantee rationality and objectivity, any more than does
free-floating commitment on the part of the individual will. On
the contrary, it is at best irrelevant and at worst incompatible
with the conception of rationality and objectivity in the proper
epistemological sense of these terms argued for in Chapter Three.
Coercion is required in the absence of such a conception. If it
obtains, argumentation is possible. The philosopher who rejects
non-cognitivism because non-cognitivism elevates the individual
will to be the supreme and final arbiter of right and wrong is no
better off by embracing a conception of objectivity/rationality
which elevates the collective will through coercion to be the
supreme and final arbiter. The philosophical escape from arbitrariness lies in an epistemology which argues that it makes sense for
the will (individual or collective) to be rationally persuaded to
adopt certain values and to reject others.

This means that a further difference exists between Lovibond's
approach and that adopted by this book. Lovibond rejects the
fact/value distinction primarily from the metaphysical standpoint
– values are immanent in the world through the consensual behaviour of the community in following rules, just as facts are in the
world. What counts as a fact is dependent on the consensual
application of one set of linguistic rules; what counts as a moral
fact is dependent on the consensual application of a sub-set of
linguistic rules. Their shared ontological status leads to their
shared epistemological status, namely, that so-called objectivity
obtains, but it is a conception of objectivity logically linked with
consensus and the existence of political authorities.

The thesis pursued by this book, on the other hand, accepts the
positivist (though not exclusively positivist) fact/value distinction

on its ontological level. It has no quarrel as such with the onto-logical status of values as products of the will, that is, that they are conative. But it wishes to challenge the assumption presupposed by the contemporary understanding of the fact/value distinction, that the ontological status of being products of the will entails the epistemological status that such products are irrational/ non-rational. It rejects the dogma that the will is necessarily irrational/non-rational, and that the products of the will are essentially irrational/non-rational.[61]

To conclude, while there is much where this author can agree with Lovibond in her negative critique of non-cognitivism, there are radical differences in our respective accounts of an alternative meta-ethics which render them mutually incompatible – if expressivism applied to the domain of moral discourse is correct, then the thesis of epistemic implication is wrong-headed or irrelevant and *vice versa*.

9 HARE'S LATER WRITINGS

Hare's first book *The Language of Morals* (1952) may be regarded as the *locus classicus* of that position in moral philosophy which has come to be called non-cognitivism. In the foregoing sections, we have seen that in trying to avoid committing the Naturalistic Fallacy, Hare was then forced to combine the thesis of deducibility with its anti-thesis of irrational commitment to the first principle of a moral system (the Deducibility-Commitment model) in constructing a positivist science of ethics. To say this, however, is not to say that Hare at that time (or even subsequently) consciously saw himself doing just that. Although it is true that Hare himself has moved away from that position, the thesis of non-cognitivism has remained firmly entrenched in contemporary moral philosophy. This book, like Lovibond's and others, seeks to attack the thesis, to the formulation of which *The Language of Morals* historically is an outstanding contribution. But it would be fair and relevant to examine Hare's later writings as he himself was quick to recognise the limitations of non-cognitivism as the basis of a moral philosophy once these were pointed out by his critics.

The central limitation facing non-cognitivism is the by now

familiar one that it renders morality irrational or non-rational. But to non-cognitivists, this is the price that one must pay in order to avoid committing the Naturalistic Fallacy. Hare's writings since *The Language of Morals* may be seen as an attempt to avoid the Scylla of committing the Naturalistic Fallacy and the Charybdis of moral irrationality which seems to be entailed by the former. His enterprise may then be said to be similar in its central goal to that undertaken by this book, for it, too, seeks to argue that moral discourse is critical and rational discourse, but without maintaining that it is possible or necessary to logically derive 'ought' from 'is'. The difference, however, lies in their respective accounts of what constitutes critical/rational thinking. Although both accounts agree that it means bringing facts and logic to bear upon a case, they differ as to the characterisation of the facts and logic involved. This book argues (see Chapters Three and Five) that the facts must be referentially and causally relevant facts and the logic is that of verification and falsification (though not of 'conclusive' verification or falsification in two of the three senses of 'conclusive' identified). The term 'epistemic implication' is introduced to try to do justice to the 'if . . . then' relationship that is involved when one says, for example, 'if abortion in advanced pregnancy is wrong (right), then certain (causally relevant) facts obtain'. Hare argues that the facts refer to the preferences of the agent both in the actual role s/he occupies and in role reversal envisaged. The logic pertains to the logical property of universalisability of the moral 'ought' – to say that I ought (morally) to do X to Y entails that anyone like myself in the relevant respects (including Y) ought to do X to anyone who is like Y in the relevant aspects (including myself).

The first major attempt to establish the rationality of morals without committing the Naturalistic Fallacy on Hare's part was *Freedom and Reason* (1963) in which he distanced himself from both non-cognitivism and naturalism by putting forward the triple theses of weak descriptivism, universalisability and prescriptivism. The first two are meant to enable him to avoid the irrationality implicit in non-cognitivism while the last is meant to enable him to avoid committing the Naturalistic Fallacy that naturalism as strong descriptivism involves.

However, the arguments there led him into difficulties in at least four areas: (1) the charge that the rationality he hopes to show exists in moral discourse is really no more than a fortunate consensus amongst individuals making judgments – a charge he himself admits. As a matter of fact it turns out that most people would agree not to assent to a prescription in question once that prescription has been universalised; (2) that the application of the theses might involve logical difficulties about personal identity; (3) that the 'fanatic' is the paradigm of morality as it is the product of applying these theses; (4) that utilitarianism appears to be implicit in these theses.

Again Hare, in the light of these problems, carried out another phase of re-thinking in the decade and a half or more after the publication of *Freedom and Reason*. His most recent book, *Moral Thinking* (1981), is the product of that re-thinking.[62] It looks as if in Hare's opinion, the way forward is to 'come out' as a utilitarian instead of being the 'closet' utilitarian that he seemed to have been in *Freedom and Reason*. By doing so, taking the bull by the horns, so to speak, he hopes to overcome the problems mentioned under (1), (3) and (4) above, without having to compromise the twin goals, negatively, of avoiding the Naturalistic Fallacy and positively, of establishing that rationality obtains in moral discourse. (*Moral Thinking* retains the basic method advocated in *Freedom and Reason*, the triple theses, but this time, they are made to work in such a way which hopefully would overcome the difficulties isolated, with the addition, as we shall see, of some new elements.) Indeed, he now goes so far as to say that the method of critical thinking would lead to conclusions which are no different from utilitarianism. He says,

> The thesis of universalizability requires that if we make any moral judgement about this situation, we must be prepared to make it about any of the other precisely similar situations. . . . What critical thinking has to do is to find a moral judgement which the thinker is prepared to make about this conflict-situation and is also prepared to make about all the other similar situations. Since these will include situations in which he occupies, respectively, the positions of all the other parties in the actual situation, no judgement will be acceptable to him which does not do the best, all in all, for all the parties. Thus the logical apparatus of universal prescriptivism, if we understand what we are saying when we make moral

judgements, will lead us in critical thinking (without relying on any substantial moral intuitions) to make judgements which are the same as a careful act-utilitarian would make.[63]

Hence in *Moral Thinking* one finds Hare not only trying to defend his method against possible objections but also trying to defend act-utilitarianism from the many criticisms which are traditionally made against it.

One new strand he has introduced and to which he attaches a lot of significance is the distinction between (morally) intuitive thinking and critical thinking. (He points out that eschewing moral intuitive thinking is essential in order to establish that rationality obtains in moral judgments but relying on linguistic intuitions is quite acceptable – that the moral 'ought' has universalisability as a logical property is one such linguistic intuition.) Having identified the outcome of applying his method with that of applying act-utilitarianism, it is vital that he distinguishes between the two levels of moral thinking. Intuitive moral thinking is by and large unreflective, inculcated moral reflexes, the product of moral education which should see us through the routine of normal life. This is not to imply, however, he says, that such thinking cannot be given critical backing should one care to reflect upon such a matter. Critical thinking would indeed endorse and coincide with intuitive thinking within the context of unextraordinary, unmelodramatic human existence. However, critical thinking when conducted in the context of extraordinary circumstances facing the agent could lead to conclusions which run counter to those yielded by relying on intuitive thinking. But Hare quickly adds that as the extraordinary circumstances referred to are unrealistic ones and do not obtain in real life, one need pay no serious attention to them. This, as we shall see, is the central strategy used by Hare to deflect criticisms of his method which try to establish that it has unacceptable outcomes.

Traditionally act-utilitarianism has been accused of endorsing outrageous conclusions in precisely this extraordinary sort of context. The stock example immediately comes to mind of hanging the framed innocent victim when the real offender proved elusive, feelings against the crime in the community were running dangerously high and the higher authorities were pressing hard for results in solving crimes. Hare, now that he has assumed the mantle of defender of act-utilitarianism, comes to the rescue by arguing in two related ways: (a) that such cases are straw ones put up entirely with the motive of discrediting act-utilitarianism by its critics; in real life, the good or utility that is said to flow from a violation of the rule 'one ought not to punish the innocent' never outweighs the disutility when all things are considered; (b) that such cases though logically possible are highly improbable, so improbable that it makes no difference to real life moral judgments.

The first move runs into the following difficulty. In bringing facts and logic to bear upon a particular case by applying his method or act-utilitarianism, Hare has to bear in mind that the human agent is neither omniscient nor totally ignorant about how the world works and how it will continue to work in the future. If the human agent were totally ignorant, no moral judgment would be possible. If s/he were omniscient, the judgment arrived at would be different from those that are made under conditions of neither total ignorance nor omniscience. Hare says we occupy a position with regard to foreseeability of consequences somewhere in the middle between what he calls the prole and the archangel. If this were so, the notion 'all things considered' cannot be construed to mean all the consequences which the archangel could ascertain and foresee. The consequences must be those which a normal agent could ascertain and foresee given partial information and knowledge and without the benefit of hindsight. Under such 'realistic' circumstances, it is not so obvious that a particular violation of a rule is always disutilitarian. Perhaps one could conclude that it would always be disutilitarian if the agent were the archangel. But it is already conceded that the human agent is not.

Act-utilitarianism enjoins us to choose that course of action which produces greater utility over other possible alternatives in the calculation of the human agent who is neither the prole nor the archangel. Such an agent might be able to ascertain that on a particular occasion, violation of the rule would go undetected, that no character deterioration would set in and good would ensue, so that 'all things considered' in the real world, one would be justified to violate the rule. If so, even the framing of an innocent person would be justified. In the real world where things are stranger than fiction or the examples dreamt up by moral philosophers, the act-utilitarian judge might indeed have reasons to suspect that the defendant in the dock is not the real offender, that even indeed the defendant has been handsomely paid to stand in for the real offender. In a country where poverty is rife and corruption endemic, it could be arranged for a poor sick man to agree to admit that he is the real offender even if the penalty is death, provided the man in question has confidence that he would be paid a suitable price for this sacrifice. His family could then have a decent chance of survival after his death which it would not have without his self-sacrifice. It would be difficult to provide evidence which would satisfy the methodological rigours of a social scientist or a moral philosopher like Hare that such cases in real life exist, but they have certainly been reported by those who have first-hand knowledge of societies which are somewhat different from contemporary British life.

Let us take examples of a slightly different kind which would however illustrate the same point. Individuals imbued with a sense of justice are outraged when they encounter instances of corrupt practice which appear to be condoned by the institution of which they are members. A recruit to the police force might discover soon after arrival that some of the superior officers violate certain fundamental rules of just behaviour, such as that if a colleague were to use undue and unnecessary force in arresting someone and the person died as a result, one would always support the colleague's version of the events even if it were false and never the victim's account or that of the family. Should such an individual be asked to lie to cover up for a colleague in this way, justice appears to demand that s/he refuses to co-operate and to expose the corrupt practice in question. However, an act-utilitarian adviser would give the person different advice, namely, to co-operate or to resign but without publicising the matter. The former option is based on the following sorts of consideration – that making an issue of it does not necessarily mean that one would be successful in reforming the institution, or ensuring that the injustice to the victim would be redressed. In practice all that it means is that the higher officials would close rank, your version would be discredited, and at the first available opportunity a trumped-up charge of incompetence or insubordination would be laid at your door, and you would be dismissed from the force with ignominy. The latter option leaves the individual the luxury of not being actively engaged in condoning corrupt practices but s/he would still have to compromise about exposing the scandal, for exposure again does not remotely guarantee the redress of injustice or of reform. As a symbolic gesture of protest, it is fine but it would not have the outcome desired. All things considered, either stay or quit but with the mouth shut.

The utilitarian adviser does not need to be an archangel but only an observant student of the workings of bureaucracies, institutions and the hierarchies of power in general. Nine times out of ten, the act-utilitarian adviser would be right. On act-utilitarian grounds, it is difficult to see how one can justify the exposure of corrupt practices. On non-utilitarian grounds, one could simply justify it by claiming that it satisfies one's conscience, that even an ineffectual act is appropriate as an expression of moral disapproval and indignation, or simply that one ought as a matter of principle to do so. A well-documented case[64] of how on act-utilitarian grounds one ought not to spill beans concerns a senior employee of Hoffman La Roche. In his attempt to do what he clearly considered to be the right thing in exposing certain corrupt and illegal practices of his company, he ended up being arrested, his wife committing suicide, and himself and the rest of his family being harassed financially and in other ways. Eventually after having been hounded from one country in Europe to another, the British government granted him permission to settle in this country taking into account the fact that in the past he had acted as a consular official for the UK. Hoffman La Roche does not appear to have altered in any recognisable way in its operations although it was fined a relatively insignificant sum for its illegal practices. Good consequences nil; bad consequences innumerable. Therefore on act-utilitarian grounds, it is best to violate or ignore the rule which says injustices must be redressed and corrupt practices exposed.

Here is another example which has of late been sufficiently well-documented to make it realistic enough, one hopes, even for Hare. The US government, and its military and intelligence agencies after the Second World War, agreed not to prosecute those Japanese scientists and officials who were involved in research in biological warfare in Manchuria using Chinese, Russian and other prisoners of war as human guinea pigs in atrociously cruel experiments.[65] Washington offered immunity provided the Japanese agreed to hand over the results and their expertise to American researchers who acknowledged that the Japanese not only had an indisputable lead over them in this particular research programme but that their results obtained through the use of human guinea pigs could not be duplicated in the West. Unlike post-Nazi Germany where the Allies mounted an attempt to bring some if not all war criminals to justice, in Japan, apart from some very token effort, the transition to post-war existence was not troubled by such matters. Consequently those scientists and officials (some claim including the Emperor) engaged in those heinous experiments simply returned to civilian life occupying positions of power and status in universities, industries and the government services.

The American justification for this muting of justice is the act-utilitarian one that more good would come from hushing up and making use of the expertise in the post-war fight against the evils of Soviet communism. For those who are already convinced about the evils of communism (Soviet-style or not)[66] and the virtues of capitalism and its defence of freedom, an act-utilitarian justification is highly plausible and acceptable. After all, they could argue that the prisoners were already dead, that no amount of denunciation of the culprits would bring them back to life, that the evils of fascism were in 1945 historical evils whereas those of communism were the real threat facing the Western free world. As somebody less than an archangel, they claimed to be able to assess that the intentions of the Soviet Union were not benign, that if undeterred by superior military might, the Soviet Union would most certainly be tempted to act aggressively. At that time, there might have been a small handful of Kremlinologists who argued to the contrary, that the intentions of the Soviet Union were not any the less or the more benign than any other major world power, that it would not be tempted to imperialise given its own internal problems although it would be firmly committed to protecting its own borders by the establishment of friendly satellite states (a technique of self-protection which all major powers also adopt). Hindsight would confirm the diagnosis of the minority view[67] but the cold war hawks could reasonably argue that hindsight was neither here nor there. As predictions about the future behaviour of the Soviet Union, it could be argued that the hawkish prediction would be a plausible one to make at the end of the war.

Furthermore, the act-utilitarian supporter could add that US officials at that time could not have foreseen the passing of the Freedom of Information Act some thirty or so years later which enabled investigative journalists and historians to bring the deal to light. They had good grounds to believe that the secret would not be uncovered, at least within the lifetimes of all the participants.

In this real world, the American government and officials came to the act-utilitarian conclusion that it was right all things considered to arrange the *quid pro quo*. The anti-utilitarian viewpoint would argue that the heinous nature of the offence could not be traded off against other utilitarian considerations, no matter how great, even including the containment of communist evils. The right thing to do was to prosecute.

In arguing against Hare that such cases are not straw cases or Aunt Sallies, one has in a sense also argued against his second move, namely, that such cases, though logically possible, are highly improbable. Being logically possible commits one, he says, to agreeing that theoretically speaking the act-utilitarian answer is the correct one; being highly improbable means that in practice one would need never to violate any moral rules.

> If . . . he claims the right to introduce any *logically possible* example, then he is exposed to the other prong of your attack. For then he has put himself beyond the range of intuition and cannot appeal to it. Critical thinking can certainly deal with such cases, and will give a utilitarian answer. If he tailors the case so that the utilitarian answer is that murder is the right solution, then that is the answer he will get. What you have to say to the audience is that this does not in the least matter, because such cases are not going to occur. This has two important consequences for the argument. The first is that allowing that in such a case murder would be justified commits us to no prescription to murder in the actual world, in which we have to live our moral lives. The second is a generalization of the first: the prima facie principles which the critical thinker will select for use in this world can also, and will, include a ban on murder, because for the selection of these principles this peculiar case, since it will not occur, is irrelevant.[68]

But contrary to what Hare maintains, in real life, the utilitarian solution might have to be put into practice. Extraordinary circumstances are not as improbable as Hare seems to think that they are.

There is at least one other aspect of his alternative escape route which needs further investigation. This brings out the limitations of a moral philosophy which ignores highly improbable cases, and in turn to confirm a criticism of his earlier book *Freedom and Reason*, namely, that his method, even if it were to introduce rationality into moral thinking, is not applicable to certain areas of human conduct as these fall into the category of logically possible but highly improbable cases.

As Hare is well aware, two of the most lively moral concerns of contemporary times are the fight against racism and sexism. The fight against the former is directed at those people who possess a light skin pigmentation and who also possess power and high status over people who possess a dark skin pigmentation and who also by and large possess little or no power and low status. The fight against the latter is directed at human beings who possess male reproductive organs and who also possess power and high status over those human beings who possess female reproductive organs and who by and large also possess little or no power and low status. Using Hare's method, the dominated class appeals to the dominating class to use logic and facts, to universalise the 'ought' in the prescription 'I (a member of the dominating class) ought to discriminate against the dominated class', thereby through a role reversal acquiring the other person's preferences. (Let us assume that Hare has successfully overcome the difficulties about personal identity involved in such role reversals.) This exercise should lead the members of the dominating class to realise that the original prescription is morally unacceptable as in the reversed role, such members are unwilling to accept the universalised prescription.

However, upon a moment's reflection, the members of the dominating class would realise that Hare's alternative escape route is available to them. This consists of acknowledging that while it is logically possible for them to be in the reversed role and to acquire the preferences of their victims, as a matter of fact, it is highly improbable that they would ever occupy such a role and acquire the preferences of their victims. Theoretically speaking, they would have to admit that discrimination is wrong, but role reversal of the kind envisaged (to be black when you are in fact white, to be a woman when you are in fact a man, sex change operations apart) is so highly improbable that one needs pay no further notice in practice to the universalised prescription. In practice one would never be called upon to desist from practising discrimination. Speaking about the Marquis de Sade complex, Hare says

> nothing in the real world is going to be affected by having a
> method of *critical* moral thinking which allows one to say
> that *if* it occurred, the torturing should be done; at least, no
> harm would come of it unless the existence of this logical
> possibility were allowed to weaken our hold upon the prima
> facie principle which condemns cruelty. But if this did
> happen, it would be in contravention of the method, which
> forbids us, when selecting prima facie principles, to attend
> to cases which are not going to occur.[69]

Analogously, the racial/sexual discriminator would argue: nothing in the real world is going to be affected by having a method of *critical* moral thinking which allows one to say that *if* it occurred (role reversal), the discrimination ought to stop; at least no significant change would come of it unless the existence of this logical possibility were allowed to weaken our hold upon the *prima facie* principle which condones discrimination. But if this did happen, it would be a contravention of the method which forbids us, when selecting *prima facie* principles, to attend to cases which are not going to occur.

The strength of Hare's method lies precisely in those areas of its application where the role reversal envisaged is not merely logically possible but either probable or highly probable. There you would indeed get a high degree of consensus about rejecting a particular prescription once you get the author of the prescription to engage in role reversal and in universalising the 'ought' of the prescription. Most (rational) people would reject the original prescription, 'I ought not to help the needy through taxation', after critical thinking, given the uncertainties of human fortune, the practical certainty involved in the biological processes of growing old (this type of certainty is not acceptable to a philosophical sceptic of course, but that is another matter); given that

it is probable and in some cases highly probable that they would
fall ill some time (even if they are now healthy), that they might
become handicapped through disease or accident (even if they are
now whole). With such cases, Hare's method takes on the function
of an insurance policy. In this sense, the 'rationality' embedded
in his method becomes indistinguishable from that of pursuing
enlightened self-interest.

The pursuit of enlightened self-interest, of course, has a respectable place in utilitarian thought. It is argued that the maximisation
of one's longer-term self-interest coincides with the maximisation
of overall utility for everybody else in the community. Enlightened
and long-term self-interest would dictate that we who are not ill,
not handicapped, not senile, not infantile pay taxes to support
and care for those who are, as paying taxes is the most comprehensive form of insurance one could buy to cover all probable future
eventualities. The day might/will come when we become chron-
ically ill (no private insurance company is prepared to take on
such cases as they are not profitable or if it does, it has to charge
excessively high premiums), when we lose an arm or a leg, when
we become unable to earn a living through illness or old age, etc.

However, enlightened and long term self-interest would get you
so far and no further, say, in the matter of taxation in support of
a welfare state. For there are circumstances which do exist under
which enlightened self-interested persons might work out that it
is not worth their while paying such taxes. A few years ago a
newspaper in this country (unfortunately, the date and the precise
references have been lost) reported a case in California where a
particular region became very popular as a place for the retired
to live. By becoming a 'costa geriatrica', its demographic pattern
also became distorted. The affluent leisured retired class soon
proceeded to stand for election to local government offices. It
formed a majority in the town hall. When it came to voting for
funds for schools in the area, it voted against them on the grounds:
(a) that they themselves were highly unlikely to have children (or
even grandchildren as these lived on the East coast, the Mid-West
or other parts of the country) who would be making use of the
educational services; (b) that they were not particularly bothered
by the long-term consequences of an illiterate or inadequately
educated younger generation as most of them did not reckon that
they would live long enough to suffer the bad effects themselves;

(c) that of those who would live that long, they, with the money at their command, would be able to pay higher wages (but less than the taxes they were asked to pay) to attract better educated people from outside to work in the area so that they themselves would not have to suffer the bad effects of being served by illiterate milkmen, postmen, by inarticulate hairdressers, etc. Such people, of course, had worked out that, although it is logically possible for them to have children, to live another thirty years (when they were already seventy), it was highly improbable that they would do so.

Such utilitarian calculation differs little, if at all, from that of applying Hare's method. Hare is, therefore, correct in maintaining that the outcome of both approaches are identical or near-identical. Anything that is logically possible but highly improbable may be ignored in practice. If this were so, there has been no progress made since *Freedom and Reason* where Hare was a closet utilitarian. Admitting openly that he is a utilitarian in *Moral Thinking* does not appear to enable him to meet the charge that his method at best yields a consensus when applied to those areas of life where the chances of the agent occupying the reversed role are probable or highly probable. It also fails to meet the charge that the rationality embedded in his method may be no more and no less than the conception of rationality as enlightened and long-term self-interest.

Nor does Hare appear to be successful in trying to overcome the difficulties surrounding the fanatic. In *Freedom and Reason*, the fanatic is someone who, after applying the critical method, nevertheless is prepared to accept and endorse the original prescription by accepting and endorsing the universalised prescription when the latter would clearly run against her/his own interests. The example of the sincere Nazi was cited. He now argues that if his critical method or the utilitarian method were properly applied, no one could possibly arrive at a fanatical conclusion. The fanatic simply does not exist.

He distinguishes between two types of the 'pure fanatic' – call them pure fanatic (1) and pure fanatic (2).

> The first, which would indeed present a difficulty, would be if a case could be found in which the pure fanatic went on holding his opinions, and could not be budged from them by

critical arguments, and in which these opinions proved to be indeed different from those which a utilitarian would reach. The second, which would not present a difficulty of the same (or perhaps in the end of any) kind, would be if the pure fanatic went on holding his opinions, but it turned out that these were not, after all, inconsistent with utilitarianism. It is this latter case whose possibility I had not envisaged when I wrote FR. The tactic of the present chapter will be, after first discussing the impure fanatic (to which all real-life human fanatics, as I think, belong), to show that the second kind of pure fanatic logically can exist, though we shall not in practice meet him, and that this possibility raises no difficulty for our theory; but that the first kind of pure fanatic cannot exist, if the argument of ch. 5 is correct.[70]

Presumably the sincere Nazi in *Freedom and Reason* would qualify to be a pure fanatic (1), as it is clearly disutilitarian to endorse the prescription 'I ought to exterminate Jews' by endorsing its universalisation which entails that the proposer be exterminated should s/he acquire the characteristics of a Jew. In *Moral Thinking* he gives the example of the doctor who is determined to save life and postpone death regardless of the cost to the patient. Such individuals, he now argues, can be dissuaded from endorsing such a prescription by the realisation that their preferences, including those springing from their own moral convictions (that Nazism is correct/saving life is sacrosant) are insufficient to outweigh the preferences of those who would be harmed by the implementation of their preferences. But if they could not be so dissuaded, critical thinking would have to agree that their universalised prescription be accepted as correct.

The first possibility, if it were to happen, would simply mean that the proposer of the original prescription had not thought through the process of critical thinking, of the full extent of the suffering involved. The moment s/he realises the full extent of the suffering involved, the proposer would drop the prescription and thus cease to be a fanatic. The more interesting case is the second possibility where Hare is driven to admit that critical thinking has to endorse the universalised prescription as correct.

(If he claims that) his own preferences (together with those of people who think like him) are so strong and unalterable that they will continue to prevail, over those of the others whom his actions will cause or allow to suffer. If this claim be granted, then critical thinking will endorse the universal prescription that in such cases the fanatic's preferences should be implemented.[71]

However, having admitted this, Hare immediately tries to undo any possible damage to his thesis that no pure fanatic (1) could exist by (a) relying on his central strategy that such cases are mere logical possibilities; as such they do not matter –

> If these fantastic cases really have to be considered, critical thinking will give those answers. But since they are not going to occur, the counter-intuitiveness of the answers provides no argument against the method. For our intuitions were not made for use in such cases; they are, perhaps, good intuitions, and critical thinking would endorse them for use in the world as it is, as having the highest acceptance-utility; but if we address our critical thinking to queer cases, we shall get queer answers. This does not in the least matter; if the answers are counterintuitive, that just shows that our intuitions were, rightly, not chosen for such unreal cases.[72]

(b) implicitly and surreptitiously redefining his conception of utilitarianism. He claims that this logically possible though fantastic conclusion is still a utilitarian one. Therefore no case of pure fanaticism (1) has been established by admitting this logical possibility.

A pure fanatic (1) cannot exist only because Hare has altered his account of utilitarianism which he says is, by and large, a Benthamite one endorsed by classical economics, to a conception which is endorsed by neo-classical economics. The former presupposes: (i) the principle of marginal or diminishing utility; and (ii) the so-called principle of equality – each to count for one and none for more than one. The latter rejects both of these assumptions.[73] Neo-classical economics, for instance, regards the first as false psychology. (Abandonment of the first opens the way to abandonment of the second.) At best it applies to only very limited cases and circumstances. The example of food and certain other carnal desires come to mind. There appears to be a point of satiation over a short period of time beyond which yet another sumptuous meal would produce disutilitarian rather than utilitarian results. So if one has a hundred meals a day to dispose of (in the absence of deep freezers), it is correct to say that greater utility would be produced if a hundred hungry people were given a meal each than if the hundred meals were given all to one hungry individual. Given the principle of marginal utility, utility is maximised by adhering to the principle of equality, or at least to a more equal rather than a less equal distribution.

But if it is not perishable food, but some other good, like money (which Locke says does not rot) or status (psychic good) that is being distributed, neo-classical economists argue that it is not so obvious that utility would be maximised by adhering to the principle of equality. The so-called Brahmin argument is put forward. A Brahmin, being much more sensitive, cultured and educated than an untouchable, would derive greater utility from a bundle of resources allocated to him than that derived by an untouchable from a similar bundle. Utilitarianism would then be maximised through an unequal rather than an equal distribution of resources. A Brahmin would count for more than one and an untouchable for less than one or not at all. On this view, a Brahmin, using Hare's critical method, could endorse the universalised prescription 'All untouchables (including myself should I become one) ought to be discriminated against'. The preferences of the Brahmin caste, of the sincere Nazi; of the doctor who is convinced that prolonging life even at great cost to the patient, are so intense that greater utility could still be produced by the implementation of these preferences. That is how Hare could claim that prescriptions based on such preferences would still be utilitarian, and that no case of pure fanaticism (1) could be produced which though passing the test of critical thinking would be against utilitarianism.

But to make this point, he must abandon the Benthamite type of utilitarianism for that of neo-classical economics (as indeed, Bentham himself was tempted to do). However, if he were to opt for the neo-classical variety, he would no longer be able to rule out people who maintain that the preferences of a certain elite group carry more weight than the preferences of another group. Hare then must accept that it is all right for racists, sexists, Brahmins and others to prescribe courses of action which ignore or ride roughshod over the preferences of the lesser orders, simply on the grounds that the latter, being less sensitive, less educated, less cultured, less intelligent, etc. would generate less utility from any given bundle of resources, or suffer less disutility when subjected to discriminatory forms of treatment than the elite groups in society.

We have already seen that Hare has in any case provided a comforting escape route for such people. They could accept the universalised prescription that were they to become untouchables, women or blacks, they too could be discriminated against. As this merely involves a logical possibility, Hare assures us, nothing would change in the real world, that is to say, in these cases, discrimination could/would justifiably carry on.

He disposes of the pure fanatic (2) – someone who endorses a universalised prescription whose outcome is not inconsistent with utilitarianism – also with the same ploy.

> Because his existence is only a logical, not a practical
> possibility, critical thinking, although it can handle his case,
> will pay no attention to it when selecting prima facie principles
> for use in intuitive thinking in the real world. Therefore the
> intuitions of the well brought up man will not be adapted to
> deal with such a case, and even its existence will seem
> counterintuitive. This, so far from being an objection to our
> theory, is exactly what it leads us to expect.[74]

On the contrary, one wishes to say that pure fanatics (2) do exist and are not all that rare. They are those individuals who, as a matter of fact, are already occupying positions of power, prestige and privilege, but who morally disapprove of such power and privilege, and argue for their divestment in favour of the unprivileged, thereby generating greater utility, welfare or justice. They arrive at this view either as Hare envisages, using Benthamite utilitarian thinking, or his method of universalising the 'ought' or some other method of moral argument. Socialists amongst the rich and the privileged do exist (Robert Owens, Friedrich Engels, William Morris, to name a few famous ones); some white people in South Africa do genuinely approve of and work towards a non-racist society; some males do genuinely approve of and work towards a sexually more equal society. All these people are convinced that greater good, utility or welfare would come from a more equal rather than a less equal society, and that working towards such a goal would involve personal/class sacrifice. To say that pure fanaticism (2) is logically possible but in practice does not exist, is to lend substance to the suspicion that Hare might after all be simply working within that tradition of rationality which understands it, not even as advancing enlightened long-term self-interests, but advancing immediate narrow self-interests.

Hare explicitly maintains that his critical method yields conclusions which are indistinguishable from those yielded by what he calls Benthamite act-utilitarianism. Therefore the two methods for generating rationality in moral judgments are identical. But in the light of the discussion above, it appears plausible to maintain that, contrary to what he says, his utilitarianism is that of neo-classical economics, and the rationality is but the rationality of either enlightened long-term or narrow short-term self-interests. This conclusion is made more plausible by the realisation that the function performed by the role reversal strategy in Hare's thinking is an ambiguous one.

In one sense, it is a heuristic device and not a method independent of the logical thesis of universalisability of the moral 'ought'. That thesis on its own is sufficient to do the job of making the proposer of the particular prescription either to accept or reject the universalised prescription. 'I ought to torture Jews' entails 'Anyone who is an Aryan ought to torture anyone who is a Jew' by virtue of the logical property of universalisability of the moral 'ought'. This in turn entails that the victim, should he acquire the characteristics of being an Aryan, ought to torture anyone who possesses the characteristics of being Jewish, including the proposer of the prescription should s/he come to acquire the characteristics of being a Jew. Similarly 'I ought not to condone injustices' entails 'Anyone who has knowledge of unjust practices ought not to condone injustices' by virtue of the logical property of universalisability of the moral 'ought'. This in turn entails that the person who asks the proposer to condone injustices ought not to condone injustices. 'I ought to pay more taxes to support the social services' entails that 'Anyone who enjoys a level of income above £x ought to pay more taxes to support the social services'. This in turn entails that those who are below a certain level of income (lower than £x), should they acquire the characteristic of being rich, ought to pay more taxes. It also entails that should I lose the characteristic of being rich (earning more than £x), I ought no longer to pay more taxes. The reversal of role is simply an implication of the logical thesis of universalisability. It is not an independent device; it may be used as a teaching aid to make more vivid to someone what the thesis of universalisability really entails.

But in Hare's hand, it often assumes an independent existence. It plays the vital role of concentrating the mind on the implications and consequences of the prescription when universalised as far as one's self-interests are concerned, either enlightened long-term or narrow short-term self-interests. That is why an implication which is a mere logical possibility can be discounted as far as calculation of self-interest is concerned. The agent could safely ignore it and yet be seen as morally correct by accepting the universalised prescription. But this method of Hare for generating 'morally correct' judgments which nevertheless permits such a convenient escape route is surely deficient. At best it would only generate consensus over areas of conduct where the agents calculate that certain implications and consequences are not only logically possible but also probable or highly probable, and these consequences are seen by them to be damaging to their self interests. This exemplifies a conception of rationality, as we have mentioned earlier, endemic in utilitarianism, which understands rationality in terms of the advancement of self-interest, enlightened or unenlightened.

The rationality embedded in the logical thesis of universalisability of the moral 'ought' on the other hand is that of consistency. In *Freedom and Reason* where Hare was a closet utilitarian, this conception of rationality was predominant. The sincere Nazi is the typical product of understanding rationality as consistency. Consistency simply demands that if it is proposed to do X to Y, then X ought to be done to anyone who is like Y in the relevant respects. X could be exterminating Jews, giving treats to children or an adequate pension to old age pensioners. In other words X could be malevolent or benevolent in intention and outcome. Adhering to consistency is a purely formal demand of rationality.

We have seen that in *Moral Thinking*, the formal demand of rationality as consistency is married to the conception of rationality as advancing self-interest, which is a substantive motion. They could lead to very different conclusions in certain areas. Hare's central strategy of admitting certain cases as mere logical possibilities is an attempt to reconcile the divergences. By saying that logical possibilities are to be acknowledged as legitimate (as they are the outcome of applying the logical thesis of universalisability and of rationality as consistency) and at the same time to maintain that such logical possibilities do not exist in practice, he permits the agent to avoid doing what could damage his/her own self-interests. In this way he hopes to have the best of both worlds. However, such a morality has the effect of leaving large areas of conduct in which the status remains comfortably *quo*, that is, cases which involve racial, sexual and caste discrimination.

To labour this important point, let us look at an example, one which has already been mentioned. The Japanese justified their use of prisoners of war as guinea pigs by discounting them as human. All non-Japanese are non-human; they are *maruta*, meaning log of wood. One ought not to use human beings as guinea pigs in cruel experiments but one may use non-Japanese as they are non-human. Logically speaking, a Japanese could become *maruta* and *maruta* could become Japanese. So a Japanese could accept the universalised prescription 'All non-Japanese ought to be used as guinea pigs, including myself should I become non-Japanese', and be seen to be applying Hare's critical method. At the same time, s/he could carry on with the experimentation, having been assured by Hare that logical possibilities of this kind are improbable, so highly improbable that it would make no difference in practice to one's conduct. In the world as we know it, Japanese are human and would not become non-human. So the Japanese need not alter their moral principle 'One ought not to use Japanese as guinea pigs in cruel scientific experiments'. As a result, suffering and discrimination would continue in spite of thinking critically in moral matters à la Hare.

The term 'Japanese' is not a proper name like 'Tom Jones' or 'Yoko Ono' which are the names of individuals. It is a common name which refers to a class of individuals, just as 'stone' or 'the elderly' refers to a particular class of individuals. As such it can enter into a universal principle; so can the term 'non-Japanese'. The term 'Japanese' refers to a class of individuals who speak Japanese, participate in Japanese culture and life, whose ancestors are Japanese, etc. (This last characteristic is important, for the Japanese do not regard the descendants of Koreans, Chinese, Ainus and other ethnic minorities living in Japan as Japanese, even though these individuals speak Japanese, participate in

65

Japanese culture and life – indeed many of them speak no Korean or Chinese – and look like Japanese in every way. Before a Japanese family agrees to a marriage proposal, an investigation into the ancestry of the future groom or bride would be carried out. If it turns out that the prospective in-law is descended from non-Japanese genes, the proposal is almost certainly immediately rejected.) It is logically possible, as Hare might maintain, for them to become Japanese but it is highly unlikely that they could alter their ancestry.

Hare, of course, could retort by saying that the Japanese are simply wrong about a matter of fact. They falsely assume that only Japanese are human. Non-Japanese are human too. They have the same sort of nervous system, they feel pain and suffer when they are exposed to Arctic temperatures or when typhoid germs are injected into their bodies. This mistake of fact leads to a mistake in moral reasoning. However, it seems unlikely that the Japanese really hold such a false empirical belief about the physiological/neurological make-up of non-Japanese peoples. What they are really saying is this – although all would suffer pain if certain unpleasant things are done to them, the Japanese ought to be exempted from exposure to such unpleasant things because they are superior to non-Japanese. It is conceivable that some Japanese racialists, like the Brahmin, might argue that although all would feel pain, the Japanese, being more sensitive, might feel more. However, the main point that they would emphasise, if pressed, is the cultural/genetic superiority of being Japanese. Although it is logically possible for others to acquire this complex of characteristics, it is, nevertheless, highly improbable that they would acquire it. And by Hare's own admission, that is sufficient for them to retain their existing moral principles as morally correct ones.

II

THE CONSEQUENCES OF STRICT IMPLICATION

1 SYMMETRY BETWEEN MORAL 'OUGHT' (A1), NON-MORAL 'OUGHT' (A2) AND ORDINARY FACTUAL 'IS' (A3) STATEMENTS

The Naturalistic Fallacy may be briefly formulated as the thesis that moral 'ought' propositions are strictly implied by or logically derivable from factual 'is' propositions. In accordance with the positivist criterion of strict deducibility of what passes for knowledge and what does not, it follows that moral beliefs are irrational or pseudo-knowledge for those who wish to avoid committing the Naturalistic Fallacy. Strict implication may be spelt out as follows: to say that S_1 strictly implies (entails) S_2 is to say, on one formulation, that it is not possible that S_1 is true and S_2 false; on another formulation, S_1 strictly implies (entails) S_2 if the truth of S_1 is a sufficient condition of the truth of S_2 and the truth of S_2 is a necessary condition of the truth of S_1.

This criterion of what is a correct or justifiable conclusion leads to an overkill. It would condemn too much even in areas which the supporter of the Naturalistic Fallacy would not normally regard as non-cognitive or lacking in rationality. Take two such instances: (a) conclusions or statements containing non-moral 'oughts'; and (b) conclusions or statements which are plainly factual containing no 'oughts', whether moral or non-moral, which may be made in ordinary daily intercourse. There is symmetry between all these cases.

To demonstrate the symmetry, let us grant first of all that a proposition containing a moral 'ought' may be used to make an assertion which can be said to be correct or incorrect, justified or unjustified (the epithets 'true', 'false' need not be used if it is felt to be objectionable.) By saying that it may be used to make an assertion, one is not denying that it may also be used to perform other linguistic functions. All that one is maintaining is that these other functions are not the only ones, and that they do not necessarily exclude the assertion-making function. Maintaining this, however, does rule out the accounts given by either the very crude logical positivist or the very crude emotivist, since the former regards moral propositions to be strictly speaking nonsensical, and the latter regards them not as assertions but expressions of mere emotions.[1] But since subscribers of the Naturalistic Fallacy nowadays are hardly either the one or the other, the thesis that moral 'ought' propositions may be used to make assertions cannot be considered to be contentious. Let us grant that any proposition containing a non-moral 'ought' may be used to make an assertion. Similarly any straightforward ordinary low-grade factual proposition containing no 'ought' may also be used to make an assertion.

Second, any assertion in the three sorts of discourse referred to above seems to require the production of evidence to back it up. Let us call an assertion (A) for short and evidence (E); a moral assertion (A1) and its required evidence (E1); a non-moral assertion (A2) and its required evidence (E2); an ordinary factual assertion (A3) and its required evidence (E3). The term 'seems to require' is used to convey what appears to be an intuitive plausibility. This is to put it at its most cautious because one can only argue for something stronger in the next chapter. If someone wishes to quibble about the word 'evidence' in connection with (A1) and (A2) and say that it is not appropriate to use it in those two types of assertion and insist on 'reason', the substitute is acceptable, because the choice of word is not germane to the point that is being made. 'One ought not to kill' (A1) seems to require (E1) – if you are a utilitarian (E1) will take the form 'killing causes pain'; 'I ought to tidy up my room' (A2) seems to require (E2), such as 'I won't be given my week's pocket money if I don't'; 'the cat has given birth to four kittens' (A3) seems to require (E3) such as, 'I, or someone who is not hallucinating, has just witnessed the birth, etc.,' or the presence of four kittens plus a gynaecological inspection could be cited.

Third, the question then arises, what is the relationship between (E) and (A)? Is it one of strict implication, such that (E) may be said to entail (A)?

Fourth, clearly it is possible for (E1) to be true and (A1) to be false, for (E2) to be true and (A2) to be false, for (E3) to be true and (A3) to be false. As the Naturalistic Fallacy subscriber would point out, 'killing causes pain' is compatible with 'it is not the case that one ought not to kill'. Similarly, 'I won't be given the week's pocket money' is compatible with 'it is not the case that I ought to tidy up the room' (since I regard the allowance as too meagre in the first place to induce me to tidy up). So too, the eye-witness account of the birth is compatible with 'it is not the case that the cat has given birth to four kittens' (since unbeknown to me what I witnessed was not a real event, but a very skilful way of creating a three-dimensional picture of such an 'event'). Likewise (E1), (E2) or (E3) is not a sufficient condition of the truth respectively of (A1), (A2) or (A3); nor is the truth of (A1), (A2) or (A3) a necessary condition respectively of the truth of (E1), (E2) or (E3).

Fifth, it follows from the above that 'is' of (E1) does not entail (A1). Neither does the 'is' of (E2) entail (A2); nor does the 'is' of (E3) entail (A3).

Sixth, therefore, the inability to logically derive a moral 'ought' from a set of 'is' propositions is not peculiar to moral assertions. The inability arises in virtue of the absence of strict implication between evidence and assertion; the evidence just does not entail the assertion.

Seventh, the complaint against the upholders of the Naturalistic Fallacy is then this – why single out moral discourse, isolating it from other forms of discourse, as a result of observing that the relationship is not one of strict implication? (Of course, one is not disputing that they would be right to point out the impossibility to someone who actually tries to derive 'ought' from 'is'.) As we know, the effect of isolating it is to create a problem seemingly peculiar to moral discourse, the impossibility of breaking out from the circle of 'oughts' in justifying them, and the far-reaching conclusion, that moral discourse is irrational. But this policy of isolation is unjustified. If it is the case that strict implication fails to obtain between (E) and (A), and for this reason (A) is said to be incapable of rational justification, then not only is moral discourse irrational, but also non-moral as well as ordinary factual discourse in general. They are all tarred by the same brush.

Eighth, to be consistent, not only have the Naturalistic Fallacy subscribers to generalise their conclusion to these other types of assertion, but they must also generalise the 'solution' they have worked out for the 'justification' of (A1), since if it is appropriate for moral discourse, *ipso facto* it should do for (A2) and (A3). Their solution, as is well-known, is that the 'justification' of moral 'oughts' is ultimately in terms of sincere choice or commitment to the 'oughts' in question. The merit of this solution, it is claimed, lies in the fact that propositions about choice and commitment are not 'is' propositions or fact-stating. They do not refer to fact-stating properties of the kind 'sticking a needle in the flesh causes pain and damage to the body tissues'. Their role is one of decision-making. 'I ought not to kill' is now justified in terms of 'I have sincerely chosen, committed myself to, bestowed approval on, the non-violence norm'. This new reason or evidence will be called (E1.1). The extension of this solution to the 'justification' of (A2) and (A3) means that (E2) and (E3) will be replaced respectively by (E2.1) – 'I have sincerely chosen, committed myself to, bestowed approval on, the tidying-up course of action' – and (E3.1) – 'I have sincerely chosen, committed myself to, bestowed approval on, the belief that the cat has given birth to four kittens'. This procedure, adopted uniformly, would indeed render (A1), (A2) and (A3) all equally irrational.

Ninth, are the Naturalistic Fallacy supporters prepared to accept the logic of their solution? If they are not, what other reason have they got to differentiate between (A1) on the one hand and (A2) and (A3) on the other in virtue of which (E1.1) is an appropriate solution but not (E2.1) and (E3.1)?

2 THE OPTIONS OPEN TO THE SUPPORTER OF THE NATURALISTIC FALLACY IN THE FACE OF THE OVERKILL

Forced to face the overkill and its consequences, Naturalistic Fallacy subscribers might adopt one of three strategies: (a) they could join forces with the 'form of life' thesis to try to anaesthetise the arguments brought forward; (b) they could fight a rearguard action to try to surmount the adverse verdict of non-cognitive and irrational by combining, like Hare, the thesis of positivism with the anti-thesis of relativism, to argue (as in *The Language of Morals*) that within a moral system, strict implication obtains *via* subsumption while commitment to the first principle of the system is a matter not amenable to rational discussion and assessment; (c) they could tacitly drop the positivist criterion of strict implication, which really amounts to changing their identity, and argue that nevertheless (A1) is not 'irrational' because (E1.1) constitutes justification for (A1). 'Irrational' is not used in such a way as to exclude only absolute arbitrariness. An agent who ponders and deliberates before s/he sincerely commits her/himself to a moral 'ought' is not like someone who chooses moral 'oughts' out of a conflicting variety by writing them down on bits of paper, putting them in a tin and then pulling out the first. To say that the first 'ought' pulled out is the 'right' 'ought' is to misunderstand the problem of justifying 'oughts', whereas sincere commitment to an 'ought' constitutes justifying it. However, all three strategies run into difficulties.

Take the last. Even conceding as drastic a change as one in identity would not do the job of salvaging the wreckage wrought by the positivist criterion of rationality, since it is not obvious why sincere commitment, choice or decision should be said to constitute a 'rational justification' of a belief. It is obvious that such commitment to a purely factual belief does not constitute a rational justification of it. Moreover, it is typically when no rational justification is forthcoming that resort is made to sincere commitment as a *faut de mieux*. It is *ersatz* 'justification' and therefore no justification at all. If symmetry obtains between (A1), (A2) and (A3), then if (E3.1) constitutes no rational justification of (A3), *ipso facto* neither is (E2.1) nor (E1.1) a rational justification of (A2) or (A1) respectively. Suppose someone asserts that a neighbour is a wife-beater. Asked to cite evidence to back it (or to give reasons why s/he believes it to be true), s/he fails to provide any, such as that s/he and others have witnessed the man assaulting his wife, or that the woman has been seen sporting black eyes and broken legs following a violent session which could be heard through the adjoining walls, or that the victim has confided in the assertor of the spouse's violence (assuming that she is telling the truth and not suffering from paranoic persecution), etc. In the absence of any such evidence, or if such evidence turns out to be faulty and have no basis, then it would be rational to withdraw the assertion. To maintain that the assertion is correct and justified under such circumstances would be highly irrational, in the normal understanding of the term 'irrational'. Furthermore to insist that one can provide a 'justification' simply by declaring that the assertion is true because one has sincerely committed oneself to it is absurd. 'I sincerely commit myself to the belief that my neighbour is a wife-beater' no more justifies the belief that my neighbour is a wife-beater than one's sincere commitment to the belief that there are centaurs provides a rational warrant for the belief that there are centaurs. Similarly 'one ought not to mug people' is not justified by the speaker's sincere commitment to the norm of no-mugging. Likewise 'one ought to eat more roughage' is not rationally supported by one's sincere commitment to the norm of eating more roughage.

3 DISTINCTION BETWEEN (sE) AND (fE), THAT IS, SERIOUS AND FLIPPANT EVIDENCE

To make clear one's objections to (E1.1) as a solution to the problem of justifying (A1) or of (E2.1), (E3.1) to the respective problems of justifying (A2) and (A3), two terms will be introduced to characterise (E), namely, 'flippant' and 'serious'. When asked to cite evidence in support of (A), one may cite either flippant or serious evidence. Flippancy is typified by responses of the kinds: (i) 'I commit myself to it'; (ii) 'I decide or choose to do or believe it'; (iii) 'I happen to approve of it'; (iv) 'it turns me on'; (v) 'it happens to appeal'; etc. (Some people may wish to divide these responses into two sub-groups – (i) and (ii) belonging to the first and (iii) to (v) to the second. Supporters of the Naturalistic Fallacy may wish to emphasise the difference and to maintain that their (E1.1) belongs to the first and not the second. There may be a difference in the psychology behind the attitude of these two groups but this is of no significance as logically they are both 'flippant' in the technical meaning of this term which is being introduced.) Flippant responses may be sincere or insincere –

(E1.1) is clearly both flippant and sincere whereas it is conceivable that someone may be insincere about her/his commitment or choice, about what s/he likes or finds appealing. Sincerity is about the truthfulness of the speaker and not about the truth of the assertion. It is about the frame of mind and the intention, whether it is *bona fide*, of the person who utters the assertion. As such, it is appropriate that flippant responses be considered in this light, to see if they are sincere or insincere, as flippant responses are about the decisions and resolutions and preferences of the agent who makes them.

While a flippant response (call it (fE)) makes no attempt to discern any features in the situation referred to in (A), that can be assessed in a critical manner (what is 'critical' will be made clear in the next chapter), by contrast, a serious response makes such an effort. (Call it (sE)). For example, (sE3) involves someone examining the cat in question (before the birth, at the time of the birth and shortly after the birth if one wants to be as careful as one can be about the evidence one is citing), counting the number of kittens in the litter, etc. But (fE3.1) does nothing of the kind – it simply refers to the sincere commitment of the speaker to the belief that the cat has given birth to four kittens. Since (sE) is about certain features of the situation referred to in (A) which may be true or false and relevant or irrelevant to the truth of (A), and has nothing to do with decisions or resolutions of the speaker, it would be inappropriate to appraise it in terms of sincerity or insincerity. So while (fE) may be sincere or insincere, it makes no sense to talk of its truth or falsity being relevant to the truth or falsity of (A); while it makes no sense to talk of (sE) being sincere or insincere, it makes sense to determine its truth or falsity, its relevance or irrelevance to (A), and in the light of this to determine in turn the truth or falsity of (A) itself.

Logically speaking, (fE) and (sE) are not mutually exclusive. The former may be true or false independently of the latter being true or false. So (fE) may be true and (sE) false and *vice versa*. They in fact answer two very different questions. (sE) addresses itself to the question 'Have you got a case in maintaining (A)?'. This question presupposes that the commitment or decision of the individual *apropos* (A) is none of its concern. The speaker who cites (fE) in reply to it is, therefore, not answering it at all. S/he side-steps the question and instead poses and answers a different one altogether, such as 'How is it that you are doing X?', to which the following answers may be appropriate: 'The sergeant major ordered me to', or a flippant response like 'I just feel like doing it', or 'I have sincerely committed myself to doing it'. The question is usually asked out of a sense of puzzlement especially when the questioner is aware that no serious case can be made or is likely to be successfully made for the activity. Suppose you find someone painting coal white. In terms of (sE), there seems to be none available for maintaining that one ought to paint coal white. So you inquire of the agent why s/he is doing it, not to ascertain the point of the activity *per se*, since *ex hypothesi* none can be found, but why s/he persists in doing it in the absence of any (sE). The puzzlement is removed if s/he reveals that s/he is carrying out the command of someone who would make one suffer if one were not to comply, or if s/he tells you that s/he is doing it out of a whim or merely to pass the time.

An 'ought' question, whether moral or non-moral, however, calls for a different answer. For example, when you ask a potholer the question 'why ought one to go down holes?', you are not asking for a flippant reply no matter how sincere. Indeed, it calls for an answer independent and irrespective of whether s/he and others like-minded enjoy groping or crawling along dark subterranean passages. If no (sE) is forthcoming, then perhaps one should stop saying that people ought to go potholing and simply say that people may go potholing if they so wish and/or find it enjoyable. Similarly, when you pose the question 'Why ought one not to kill?', you do not expect a flippant answer, such as that it is all right to kill provided people enjoy (sincerely) doing it. A murderer who tries to 'justify' killing by saying he finds it exhilarating has not answered the question appropriately. As a person with moral concern, I am not interested in wondering why he spends all his spare time poisoning his office mates as opposed to potholing. In asking for justification of his activity, one demands (sE) which specifically rules out the consideration that he finds killing fascinating or indeed revolting for that matter.

An 'ought' question implies that there is a justification of the activity which is independent of one's inclination and feelings about it. The force of such a question is precisely to bring into the open its *raison d'être* which can then be critically assessed. To cite (fE) is to admit that one has no case or cannot make out a case for maintaining (A). To be consistent, those who cite (fE) for moral 'oughts' should really go on to say that since such 'oughts' are not justified, one should no longer ask any more 'ought' questions. 'Ought' questions are only meaningful if (sE1) or (sE2) is available. But since (sE) is not available, one should replace 'ought' questions with a question such as 'How is it that people do X rather than Y?'. The Naturalistic Fallacy subscriber is not right in believing that it is still intelligible to pose 'ought' questions even though (sE1) does not obtain, that somehow (fE1.1) could be construed as an appropriate answer provided it is sincere. But sincerity is not a suitable substitute for (sE1) and cannot provide a rational justification for 'oughts'.

4 HARE'S STRATEGY AND THE POSITIVIST DEDUCTIVE/NOMOLOGICAL MODEL OF EXPLANATION

Hare's strategy fares no better. Indeed it combines both the limitations of the positivist criterion with the undermining of rationality by the anti-thetical criterion of sincere commitment to first moral principles. It gets the worst of both worlds. The demand of logical derivability in science, as we saw in the last chapter, leads to the possibility of legitimising absurd and bizarre explanations. The criterion applied in moral philosophy would legitimate equally absurd and bizarre justifications. For instance, one could then justify the judgment 'On Tuesdays one ought to short-change one's customers' by deriving it from the major premise 'On even days of the week one ought to short-change one's customers' (which is equivalent to the universal law-like statement of the D-N model in science) and a minor premise 'Tuesday is an even day of the week' (which is equivalent to the statement of initial conditions). This practical syllogism is, of course, valid, but it would be ridiculous on that ground alone to regard the conclusion justified as a moral judgment. On this criterion, one could legitimate any judgment by simply creating or inventing a *justificans* (analogous to *explanans*) which would satisfy the condition of enabling one to derive the *justificandum* (analogous to *explanandum*) in question. This procedure is, however, no more acceptable as an account of scientific reasoning than it is of moral reasoning.

In characterising a positivist philosophy of science, it will be recalled that Hempel gives four conditions for an adequate explanation. To re-cap, these are: (1) that the *explanandum* is a logical consequence of the *explanans*; (2) that the *explanans* must contain general laws and these must actually be required in the derivation of the *explanandum*; (3) that the *explanans* must have empirical content; that (4) the *explanans* be true, that is, in the sense that it leads eventually to correct predictions. In appropriating this model from the philosophy of science (for explanation/prediction) and applying it to a justificatory context in moral philosophy, some modifications have to be made.

Condition (1) may be taken over intact; while the second part of condition (2) is uncontroversial and required, the first part must not be understood in the sense that moral laws are descriptions of regularities in human behaviour analogous to descriptions of regularities in the behaviour of matter in physical laws of nature – to do otherwise would be to confuse the normative order with the physical order. They are similar in that as laws, they are general in scope. 'Rain makes one wet' amounts to 'All occasions of being exposed to the rain are cases of getting wet' just as 'One ought not to lie' amounts to 'All occasions of lying are wrong and ought to be avoided'. Even condition (3) may be satisfied – to avoid committing the Naturalistic Fallacy, Hare needs only to ensure that the *justificans* does not have only empirical content. The major premise containing an 'ought' ensures that the normative element is intact whatever empirical content the proposition might also possess. Condition (4) is more difficult to satisfy since justification is not in the business of making predictions which can be empirically checked. So at this point it looks as if Hare changes tack. Instead of determining the 'truth' of the *justificans via* a downward thrust towards predictions, the moral philosopher establishes the 'truth' of the major premise *via* an upward thrust towards subsumption of it under a yet wider major premise from which (together with another minor premise), it in turn can be logically derived. 'Truth' becomes redundant by being assimilated to validity (or formal truth). In the original explanation/prediction model, some element of factual truth is retained by the requirement that the *explanans* eventually leads to a correct prediction.

5 THE DEDUCTIVE-NOMOLOGICAL MODEL MODIFIED TO BECOME THE DEDUCIBILITY-COMMITMENT MODEL AND APPLIED TO THE LAW

Such modifications allow the model to be applied not only to moral philosophy but also to the philosophy of law. On the positivist account of law, what renders a rule legally valid is that it satisfies the rules of validity created and sustained by the legal system in question. A particular bye-law at the level of the parish council is ascertained to be valid if it is made in accordance with the procedures laid down by the parish council and if the powers of jurisdiction exercised by the latter are themselves validly derived from a higher body, the power of which in turn is derived from yet another higher body until you come to the highest body or Kelsen's *Grundnorm*[2] or Hart's rule of recognition,[3] such as, that what the Queen says in Parliament is law. For Austin, the sovereign is that body which owes no obedience to anyone but which is habitually obeyed by everyone else. For Hart, the mass of the citizenry simply accepts the rule of recognition while the officials (like judges and policemen) apply and uphold it in their decisions and actions. But whether passive citizens or active officials, it may be said that one and all make a commitment to it either tacitly (analogous to Locke's tacit consent) or explicitly. The *Grundnorm* or the rule of recognition, *ex hypothesi*, cannot be validated in terms of derivability from yet another norm; therefore, it can only be 'justified' in terms of sincere commitment.

Commitment to it renders the legal system autonomous – the rules generated may be judged solely by the criteria of validity internal to it. As a result, a legal rule is valid so long as it satisfies such criteria and may not be rejected as law no matter how unacceptable its content might be on moral or other grounds. A legal system might actually incorporate certain desirable moral norms, like the upholding of human rights, or the norm of sexual equality, but if it does not, and enacts legislation which contravenes these moral norms, legislation remains valid provided it satisfies the criteria of validity. Critics who say that laws which violate moral norms are not laws are said to confuse legal with moral validity. Law is law and morals is morals. Moderate legal positivists like Hart may say that in cases of clear conflict one should condemn it (and perhaps even refuse to obey it) on moral grounds and not because they are not laws on account of their gross immorality. Extreme positivists go so far as to say, that what is just is what the law says is just; that there is no concept of justice outside the law. Morals collapses into law or is reduced to it. On the moderate version, although there is no reduction, nevertheless, law and morals do not overlap[4] except when the former explicitly incorporates norms from the latter.

Just as the rule of recognition is a matter of commitment, so too is the so-called supreme moral principle, be it liberalism or Nazism, in terms of which lower-order principles (such as 'One ought not to persecute homosexuals' or 'One ought to eliminate Jews, Slavs and gypsies') are validated by being derived from it. Just as a legal system is fully autonomous and requires no extraneous underpinning from morals, a moral system too is fully autonomous and requires no extraneous underpinning from so-called facts.

6 THE DEDUCIBILITY-COMMITMENT MODEL LEADS TO THE 'COMMAND THEORY OF KNOWLEDGE'

Both types of positivism implicitly borrow the model of the military to illuminate their own respective natures – a chain of commands involving a pyramidal organisation with the commander-in-chief at the apex and the privates constituting its broad base. An army is a clearly identifiable organisation, with well-defined parameters and an absolutely unambiguous source of authority to sustain it. One could say that the mass of the citizenry who by and large accept and passively obey the law is equivalent to the other ranks who carry out the orders of their superiors; the law-creating and enforcement agencies are comparable to the officer class which actively issues commands and sees to it that they are complied with; the rule of recognition is like the commander-in-chief. Traditionally the common soldier is not supposed or expected to query the contents of a command and judge it to be a sensible or reasonable one; no matter how irrelevant or inadequate it might be to the exigencies of the situation, provided it emanates from the proper superior body, 'theirs not to reason why, theirs but to do and die'. Analogously, no matter how immoral a piece of legislation might be, provided it satisfies the criteria of validity of the system, law is law and is to be obeyed unless and until the sovereign body sees fit to repeal it. The commander-in-chief is by definition someone who does not obey the will of anyone else in his army but who is himself habitually obeyed. From the internal point of view,[5] the soldier is expected and required to be sincerely committed to carrying out the commands of the general; in a legal system, the citizens, as already mentioned, implicitly are committed to the rule of recognition while the officials are overtly committed to upholding it.

It is obvious why the army possesses the structure it does, for the simple reason that, so it is claimed, it could not otherwise be an efficient instrument of winning a war. By concentrating the mind on the validity of the command, and suppressing any critical judgment about its content, from the point of view of its adequacy or relevance to the needs of the situation, authority will not be undermined. Without unquestioned authority, it is claimed, an army and its morale cannot survive intact. The calibre of many a general and the quality of his commands might leave much to be desired; nevertheless, one cannot and must not allow the luxury of critical judgment to flourish as insubordination might ruinously set in. Much the same sort of *raison d'être* is proffered for extending the model of the military to the law. It is claimed too that to allow a citizen to query the content of law (from the moral point of view) is to risk chaos and anarchy. Unfaltering certainty is demanded of the law, as much as of the army, if it is to function effectively and efficiently. The practical desire for certainty, in the case of the law, seems to coincide with the positivist desire for logical certainty *via* logical derivation or subsumption.

Beguiling as the similarities between the army and the law may be, the command theory of the law is not without difficulties when applied to actual existing municipal legal systems, let alone to international law. A legal system, like that of Britain, is not readily susceptible to a straightforward analysis in terms of a chain of commands emanating from an unambiguously identifiable source of authority which is unlimited, absolute and supreme (constituting the principle of sovereignty) or which is habitually obeyed but itself owes no obedience to any other (the Austinian form of the thesis). Parliament is the law-making body but its powers in practice are not unlimited. In theory Parliament, it is said, could commit 'suicide' and make over its legislative function to another body, annihilating its democratic nature by installing a dictator in its place. But the operative phrase is 'in theory' – should such an event occur in normal circumstances (barring possibly wartime conditions), altering the very nature of its unwritten constitution, the judiciary would not wear it. Even short of such a drastic abdication of power, legislation passed by Parliament might not be enforced by the judiciary whose decisions could undermine it should it see fit to do so. The supremacy of Parliament cannot be understood in a naive manner, even if in this legal system, there is no written constitution explicitly setting out entrenched clauses which formally limits its powers. The rule of recognition, formulated as 'What Parliament says is law', is subject to certain unwritten constraints. In a democracy, in theory Parliament is the product of the will of the people. In practice, any Parliament and its legislation is the product of rules, many unwritten, and pressure groups in the electorate lobbying it. All in all, it is immensely difficult if not impossible to obtain a convincing application of the command theory of law in a straightforward manner as required by the model. In other words, legal positivism which tries to make the law autonomous is not really successful.[6]

The point of the foregoing remarks is not to probe into the developments and the ramifications of positivism in the law, but to draw attention to some of its inherent defects in order to make the point that both it and the model of the military upon which it is based do not lead to happy results when they influence moral philosophy.

Hare, following Stevenson, develops a version of the command theory in morals, by using the notion of imperative instead of command. There is, however, no attempt to reduce moral judgments, rules or principles to imperatives but to say that moral language entails imperatives. (In his later book, *Freedom and Reason*, the term 'imperative' is dropped in favour of 'prescription' – moral language entails universalised prescriptions.) The basic deficiencies of the model when applied in moral philosophy are: first, it leads to self-defeat when it is combined, as in Hare's case, with its anti-thesis, namely, conceptual relativism. In the law, the model, when combined with conceptual relativism, at least manages to satisfy the goal that the law be stable and certain. As it is concerned by and large with the outward conformity of human conduct to certain rules, its preoccupation with certainty and efficiency is quite understandable. The citizens' ultimate commitment to the system and its basic rule that whatever is legally valid is law and must be obeyed is conducive to producing order and stability in society. However, an analogous commitment by the individual moral agent to his own highest moral principle, far from producing the moral equivalent of order and stability, produces precisely the opposite effect, namely, anarchy. If the only test of correctness of a moral principle (a lower-order one) is its logical derivability from a higher-order one, and that of the highest principle is the sincere commitment of the individual to it, then, in theory, there may be as many valid or correct but conflicting principles as there are individuals. Any consensus (*pace* Hare in *Freedom and Reason*) is just a matter of fortunate coincidence.

Borrowing from an elitist model of authority (such as the army and through it the law) and then democraticising it to make it do the job in moral philosophy of validating fundamental principles leads to a conclusion contrary to that expected in the light of the original model. While legal positivism may be said to be relatively successful in combining the positivist requirements of logical derivability and logical certainty with the practical desire for certainty and stability in outward conformity to certain rules of behaviour, the attempt in moral philosophy to combine the same positivist requirement of logical derivability with a democratisation of moral authority (which appears to be required by the demands of morality as autonomous, emanating from the consent of the individual and not as an imperative or command imposed from above by an external authority) is not successful as, in the end, it is unable to rescue morals from the original positivist verdict that it is irrational and non-cognitive, as well as failing to achieve uniformity and stability in moral matters.

Second, by adhering to the positivist requirement of logical derivability, it obscures if not suppresses the possibility of justifying moral principles other than validating them *via* subsumption. In the original model of the military, which is an elitist model of authority, by concentrating exclusively on the source of the command for its legitimation, it necessarily and deliberately ignores the critical valuation of the content of the command. To go back to the example of the sergeant major who orders his men to paint coal white. The order may be said to be a valid one in the sense that the sergeant major is competent, that is, acting within his powers to issue such commands, but this does not mean that its content might be incapable of challenge from the point of view of its subject matter, whether it might be a pointless activity and, therefore, a silly way of making people spend their time. It is precisely because the activity enjoined seems to serve no obvious end that the commanded might feel resentful against the order as a pure manifestation of a superior will.

A command may also be criticised because it might fail to achieve the goal it is directed at. Suppose one is given the order to demolish a wall with a slender and fragile bit of stick. The commanded who refuses to carry out such an order on the ground that it would be futile would be correct, even though it could be a clear case of flouting a command emanating from a legitimate source. A command may be valid in this sense but otherwise unsound. A conflict between legitimation by source and authority and legitimation by critical standards of assessment would be analogous to the conflict in law between legal criteria of validity and moral criteria of rightness or wrongness. Just as a legal positivist would say law is law provided the legal criteria of validity are satisfied, so a positivist account of command would confine itself to the problem of legitimation by source and authority and ignore the problem of justification. The logic of commands does not then have anything to say about the latter because to quote one writer on the subject, 'Although a command can patently be justified in this way, it surely cannot be said to *follow* from its justification in the logical sense of the term.'[7] By adhering to the positivist requirement of logical derivability, a whole area of possible investigation is ignored simply on the grounds that a command is not entailed by its justification. This approach is symptomatic of a more general approach to knowledge claims which concerns itself only with validation in terms of source and authority and not in terms of justification through a critical assessment of the content of the claims. Such a positivist approach may be called the 'command theory of knowledge'.

7   TWO SENSES OF AUTHORITY: (i) POWER (POLITICAL AUTHORITY); (ii) KNOWLEDGE (EPISTEMOLOGICAL AUTHORITY)

There are two senses of authority: (a) the sense as understood by the positivist in terms of legitimate authority as it is exercised in accordance with certain recognised rules. This sense pays no attention to the reasonableness, correctness or appropriateness of what is issued and authorised in its name. Power is its basis – in the case of the army and even the law, the ultimate sanction is that of physical force, although the citizens in general might also willingly and sincerely commit themselves to it; (b) the other sense is not based on power but on knowledge. Some people are said to be an authority on a certain subject because they know more than other people about it. Their opinions are deferred to because of their superiority in knowledge and information. Their status as an authority is legitimate and justified because what they claim to know passes certain critical tests of appraisal. If their knowledge claims fail these tests consistently, then they lose their status as an authority. Ultimately, this sense of authority is based on the possibility of critically appraising the content of what is being claimed. Epistemology and not power is its basis. It is easy to confuse these two senses and to mistake the power basis for the epistemological one. The Harean thesis (in *The Language of Morals*) appears to confuse them with the additional twist that every individual is her/his own epistemological authority as far as morals is concerned.

Appeal to authority in the first sense is not appropriate as a justification of a knowledge claim based on authority in the second sense. Sometimes we speak elliptically, giving the erroneous impression that we do precisely what must not be done. For instance, we do on occasions say that the animal is sick and give as justification that the vets say so. We seem to accept it on authority and no further questions asked. But the vets' authority is only acceptable if they in turn can cite (sE), that is, if they can point to certain features and conditions about the animal which can be publicly ascertained and critically appraised. It would not do if they meant their authority to be naked – in the absence of (sE) just simply to say that their authority is sufficient for the truth of (A), the assertion that the animal is sick, or even that other people's firm commitment to their authority is sufficient to guarantee the soundness of their assertion.

Departure from the requirement of serious evidence is sometimes tolerated, however, but one is not satisfied with just mere stopgaps. Suppose that someone predicts that an earthquake will take place at such and such place, at such and such a time. Suppose her/his predictions are confirmed more than they are falsified. But s/he cannot cite any (sE) for these predictions, such as that s/he notices dogs bark incessantly for no obvious reasons on days preceding a quake and that dogs, having more sensitive ears than us, might have picked up seismological disturbances before we do. All that s/he says is, perhaps, that s/he feels it in the bones. If s/he gets a very good run of confirmed predictions, not to be explained by mere chance, then although the predictor cannot cite any (sE), people may still pay attention to the predictions. But this does not mean that it is no longer legitimate to require and search for (sE) for them. The stopgap remains an unsatisfactory puzzle within this framework.

It makes sense to talk of commitment to authority in the first sense but not in the second. But even in the former, the commitment itself is not incapable of rational justification. The army and the law, it is argued, require commitment to its highest source because then only would there be order and stability. This kind of justification is taken for granted and is, therefore, implicit. The suspension of critical judgment is meant to serve a purpose which itself is susceptible to critical appraisal. (Some people might argue, for instance, that if the army were to punish severely flouting of obviously silly and pointless commands, this itself might undermine morale and hence efficiency.) But when authority in this sense is confused with the other, not only is this implicit rational justification for commitment forgotten, but it is assumed *simpliciter* that commitment is in the end all that there is for determining knowledge-claims. But commitment is not the only appropriate standard to use – what the vet says about the medical condition of Ching Ching (the panda in the London Zoo), what the Pope says about the immorality of mechanical forms of contraception, or what the individual says about the morality (or immorality) of chemical warfare is not to be assessed solely in terms of mere commitments to a person playing a certain role or to a set of principles embraced by an individual. To say it is is to subscribe to the 'command theory of knowledge'. Such a theory of knowledge in morality and epistemology in general leads to moral and intellectual anarchy and chaos.

Indeed as arguments adduced in the previous chapter show, intellectual chaos is the conclusion entailed by the thesis of conceptual relativism to which the Naturalistic Fallacy supporters may be driven in their effort to be consistent in the face of the symmetry established between moral and non-moral assertions. The acceptance of this ploy would take the discussion beyond moral philosophy itself. The recognition that moral philosophy is not alone in being vulnerable to the charge of committing the Naturalistic Fallacy would have the wholesome effect of re-integrating moral scepticism with scepticism in general on the one hand, and on the other of re-integrating the possibility of objectivity in morals with the possibility of objectivity in cognitive discourse in general, so that the debate between scepticism and non-scepticism need not be a burden borne by moral philosophers who wish to combat moral scepticism. It then becomes no longer an unfair battle but a better matched all-out war between those who argue for the possibility of rationality and objectivity and those who believe that such standards do not obtain, or do not universally obtain.

III

THE NOTION OF EPISTEMIC IMPLICATION

1 SHIFT FROM STRICT IMPLICATION TO THE TENTATIVE THESIS '(A) REQUIRES (sE)'

In accordance with the positivist criterion of logical derivability as the determinant of 'proper' knowledge or of what counts as 'knowledge', philosophers feel obliged to confine themselves to a safe area of analysis, namely, to the problem of validating knowledge claims from the point of view of hierarchical subsumption, and by and large ignore the epistemological problem of validating knowledge claims from the point of view of their truth (or falsity), or correctness (or incorrectness). From the correct observation that strict implication fails to obtain between assertion (A) and evidence (E), they conclude that moral knowledge claims are pseudo-knowledge claims. But as the last chapter tries to establish, they would be inconsistent to confine the verdict of pseudo to moral discourse alone, for the failure of strict implication obtaining is a general failure and not one peculiar to moral discourse. In the light of the symmetry between (A1), (A2) and (A3), the positivist moral philosopher is faced with a choice: either of retracting the verdict against moral discourse or extending the verdict to (A2) and (A3). The former is impossible so long as one adheres to the positivist *Grundnorm* of what constitutes proper knowledge. In the case of the latter, one is in near danger of abandoning positivism (the thesis) for its anti-thesis, conceptual relativism, and its ensuing intellectual chaos and anarchy, an outcome which cannot be welcome to a positivist. The main thrust

86

of that philosophy is to erect a *cordon sanitaire* around certain sorts of discourse to save them from metaphysical pollution, not to abandon it so that everything eventually becomes contaminated by it; for if conceptual relativism were correct, in the end communication breaks down and everything that is uttered would literally be unintelligible.

The impasse is insurmountable so long as the positivist *Grundnorm* is adhered to. To overcome it requires resisting intimidation by it. If more serious attention were paid to the problem of epistemological validation (lack of strict implication obtaining notwithstanding), then perhaps one might find other relations at work which would be sufficient to warrant some kind of rational safe-conduct between (A) and (E). New light might be shed on the relationship between (A) and (E) if one were to shift the focus (a) from strict implication to other forms of implication and (b) from the thesis that (E) does not strictly imply (A) to the thesis that (A) implies (E) without pre-judging the type of implication involved.

A start in this direction may be made by reminding oneself of the intuitive plausibility of the demand that an assertion seems to require evidence. The last chapter seeks to establish that the sort of evidence required is not (fE) but (sE), that is, that it must not merely refer to the attitude of the speakers towards their assertion or their psychological state of mind regarding it, but to certain features which are public about the situation referred to in the assertion. So at this stage, the intuitive demand may be made more specific to read: (A) requires (sE).

2 THE NOTION OF RELEVANCE: (i) REFERENTIAL; (ii) CAUSAL

This ensures that (A) and (E) share a common term, that is, the subject term. To cite 'this dog has lost weight' as evidence for 'this dog is ill' is at least relevant, from the referential point of view, whereas to say that 'I am fully committed to the view that this dog is ill' does not even begin to be referentially relevant. So the first condition to be met is that (A) and (E) must have the same referent class, that is, they must be referring to one and the same object. In other words, (fE) fails on two counts: (i) on the

objective count by failing to refer to public external features of the situation; and (ii) on the referential count, by not having the same referent as the assertion it is meant to be supporting.

But satisfying referential relevance may not be enough. Consider this example. Suppose someone cites 'oxygen is colourless' as evidence for 'oxygen is necessary for combustion'. There is a shared subject term, namely, 'oxygen'. The (sE) in question satisfies referential relevance, but fails to satisfy what may be called causal relevance. 'Oxygen is colourless' does not appear to be causally relevant to establishing the truth or falsity of 'oxygen is necessary for combustion'. Hence a second requirement must be added so that the original intuitive demand now reads: (A) requires causally relevant serious evidence, for short (c/r sE).

At this stage of play, a potentially thorny problem crops up, namely, that it is not obvious what the criteria of causal relevance are. The notion of causal relevance itself, for a start, seems to have one foot in scientific discourse and another in discourse about ordinary knowledge (which is the concern of this chapter). Furthermore, there is controversy over whether developed science dispenses with the notion of causality altogether.[1] This controversy may itself be coloured by the controversy in the philosophy of science whether the positivist conception is a valid account of scientific theorising.[2] As far as ordinary knowledge is concerned, it seems to recognise four different criteria: (1) controllability;[3] (2) abnormality;[4] (3) statistically significant correlation; and (4) constant conjunction. On the positivist conception of cause in science, only (4) is really relevant, although one often has to make do with (3). On a non-positivist (realist) view of cause in science, (4) and (3) may be regarded as preliminary indicators that cause is at work, because to find the cause is to discover the generative mechanisms which explains why and how (3) and (4) obtain.[5]

The relationship between scientific knowledge and ordinary knowledge cannot be dealt with here; in Chapter Five there will be an opportunity to explore it further. But for the purpose of elucidating the thesis '(A) requires (c/r sE)' in the domain of ordinary knowledge, one may assume that each of these criteria is of importance and contributes towards the mapping of the notion of cause even if none of them singly or even all of them jointly exhaust the content of that notion elsewhere. One need not go into detail about their relative merits or their relations to one another, but to note that these criteria help to identify factors which in a fuller theoretical understanding of the matter may be said to be related to one another. For this reason too, one need not be unduly worried by the fact that certain phenomena not suspected before of being causally related to other phenomena may in due course be discovered to be so; *vice versa*, what is thought to be causally connected may in the light of better theoretical understanding at best be only indirectly thus related. For instance, there may be a very high statistical connection between idiocy and living in a certain village, which suffers from heavy pollution from the production of a certain chemical in a neighbouring factory, so that at least on criterion (3), some would say this indicates a likely causal connection. However, later research may show that the soil in the village lacks a certain vital element, that people eat the vegetables grown locally and that the absence of the vital element in the diet causes the idiocy.

3 CAUSAL CONNECTIONS AND PARTIAL MEANING LINKS BETWEEN (A1), (A2) AND (A3) – ASSERTIONS AND (E1), (E2) AND (E3) – EVIDENCE

What are the semantic assumptions behind causal relevance as understood in the domain of ordinary knowledge? One assumption, we saw, is that (A) and (E) share the same referent class. A further one concerns the predicate variables in (A) and (E), that there should be an overlap, but not identity of meaning between them. Take the two propositions: 'this man is ill' (p) and 'this man has eaten contaminated food' (q). The shared term is the subject term 'this man' and the overlap in meaning between the predicate variables 'is ill' in (p) and 'eaten contaminated food' in (q). These two predicate variables are not identical in meaning; hence they are not interchangeable. In general, 'is ill' may imply 'having eaten contaminated food', 'has vomited', 'loses weight', 'has a bug in the stomach', etc.; and on any particular occasion, one or more of these causal factors may be involved. But no matter how long the list one cares to cite, in principle, one cannot rule out the discovery of more similar factors. Causal relevance is discovered and one cannot anticipate all future discoveries. Since the future is in this sense open, it is appropriate that we retain terms in language which are open-textured and we do not turn such terms into terms of strict definition. 'Is ill' is such an open-textured term. So although it is possible to elucidate the meaning of 'is ill' by referring to 'having eaten contaminated food' (q.1) or 'running a high temperature' (q.2), or 'has a bug' (q.3), its meaning cannot be exhaustively defined in terms of (q.1) or (q.2) or (q.3) or (q.n) taken singly or as a disjunction. The last disjunct really amounts to an admission that an exhaustive definition of the kind proposed is not appropriate and cannot be given.

However, although there is no identity of meaning, this does not mean that there is no overlap in meaning, that the meaning of 'is ill' may not be partially explicated in terms of (q.1) or (q.2), etc. As mentioned earlier, causal relevance is empirically discovered and cannot be linguistically created and guaranteed. But once causal relevance has been established between two processes or things, then a meaning connection is also established between the two terms which refer to the things or processes found to be causally related to another. We first have to find out that eating food of a certain kind can bring about an abnormal physiological condition in the body. People who do not know that oysters may cause food poisoning if they are not absolutely free from impurities may wonder why they are ill (after having eaten some). They might put it down to too much sun, for instance. But we know that shell food in certain conditions and being ill after eating them are causally related. For us, 'is ill' may be partially explicated in terms of 'eating contaminated food', so that you can say to someone 'If you want to know what it is to be ill, then eat these oysters (i.e. contaminated food)'. In the same way, because there is a causal connection between having hallucinations and taking LSD, a meaning connection is set up between 'having a trip' and 'taking LSD'. One can then say to someone who wants to know what 'having a trip' means, in partial explication, 'it is what you experience when you take LSD' and 'if you want to know what a trip is about, then take some LSD'.

What has been said can be put in a slightly different way by saying that the meaning of a term in language may be modified and changed by causal discoveries about things and processes referred to by the term in question. So a term may acquire a new aspect of its meaning or lose an old aspect of it depending on the state of our causal knowledge. (In dictionaries, the latter would be recorded as an outdated or older meaning.) Meanings are not eternally given and immutable, and one of the most important causes of meaning change is causal discoveries and revision of existing causal theories. The old meaning of 'influenza' is now lost to us because we no longer consider the astrological theory behind it as valid. What was once considered to be causally connected but now found to be causally unconnected would destroy the link in meaning between the terms involved; similarly, what was once considered to be causally unconnected but now found to be causally connected would forge a new link in meaning, thereby enriching at least one of the terms which refer to the causal processes involved.

In view of a meaning link being forged between terms through causal relevance, when (c/rSE) is offered to support (A) and when it is about an established causal connection, we understand it and find it intelligible even if on that particular occasion when it was cited to support (A), it happened to be false. For instance, there is an established causal connection between death and arsenic in the body. When a corpse is first discovered, the police might say that the cause of death was arsenic poisoning. Later the pathologist might conclude that was false – the person died of paraquat poisoning instead. But now imagine a case where someone cites as evidence for (A) something which according to current causal knowledge is deemed to be entirely causally irrelevant to (A). Suppose someone asserts 'this animal is ill' and proceeds to give as evidence 'this animal has a black nose'. One would be puzzled. The correct response to it would be to say to the speaker 'I don't really know what you are talking about. What has "being ill" got to do with "having a black nose"?' and dismiss the remark accordingly as a piece of gibberish, not because one wishes to deny that the two expressions each respectively is perfectly intelligible and meaningful. There is no difficulty comprehending their respective meanings. We, however, simply do not understand the meaning of 'having a black nose' being evidence for 'is ill'. In the absence of a causal link between being ill and having a black nose, there is no meaning bridge between the terms 'is ill' and 'having a black nose'.

Take another example, the phenomenon of hay fever. Suppose a certain community has no knowledge about what brings it on or about the wider phenomenon of allergy itself. Suppose it believes that sneezing, sore throat and running nose in the summer are caused by too little exercise. (Suppose that these people do all their hard work in the winter and take to sunbathing excessively in the summer.) Knowledgeable outsiders who know about allergy might predict that someone will soon suffer a bout of hay fever, and cite as evidence that that person has been lolling in the flower-carpeted meadow the whole day. Their listeners would find what they say unintelligible (unless they have already been accepted by them as the scientific expert, in which case they might grant that they have postulated a genuine causal connection upsetting their own explanation), because for them, in the absence of a causal link between the symptoms and the evidence, there is no meaning connection between them either. They too will dismiss the evidence accordingly as nonsense.

Now the more firmly entrenched is the causal connection between two things or phenomena isolated, the more entrenched is the overlap in meaning between the terms which refer to them, so much so that one would have extreme difficulty in under-standing what someone is talking about should s/he offer as evidence for the assertion a completely causally irrelevant piece of evidence. We have no doubt whatsoever about the causal connection between being able to see and possessing an eye (if not a sound eye). Suppose someone does not know a person called Crouzet and has never met him. When asked by that person for evidence in support of my assertion that Crouzet is blind, I reply, 'Crouzet was a French resistance fighter in the last war. The Nazis gouged out both his eyes when they finally caught him.' Suppose a third person proceeds to challenge my evidence by saying, 'No, Crouzet is not blind. He has two ears because the Nazis did not bother to cut them off as well.' Now one cannot even begin to understand what s/he is talking about. I am forced to either deny her/his sanity, or say s/he is making a very sick joke, or (more charitably) that s/he has not grasped the concept of an assertion and its requirements. S/he has not in any mean-ingful and intelligible way challenged my evidence, although no one would wish to deny that the counter 'evidence' is true.

However, if in a case where we do not know the cause of a phenomenon, or where causal understanding of it is at best partial, then suggestions which may sound outrageous or even bizarre are not dismissed as gibberish. We suffer no or little meaning shock and we are prepared to entertain any hypothesis which could in some way make a kind of makeshift causal bridge, and in turn makeshift meaning bridge, between the phenomena and the terms postulated by it. We know something about cancer, but not enough and certainly by no means fully. Suppose someone were to offer as evidence for saying that X is liable to get cancer of the bones that X used to run barefoot in childhood even during very cold weather. Now we may dismiss the claim as being possibly false, especially when the person cannot cite any statistically significant correlation between the incidence of cancer and such childhood experience. (But one could retort that unless research resources were made available for studying the field one has specified, how can one be so sure in advance that no such significant data might be found.) But we would not consider her/ him insane, or pulling our leg (at least s/he is not necessarily pulling our leg) or that s/he does not understand the concept of assertion and its requirements. Even 'cranky' projects might be given funds if funds were endlessly available and if society feels that cancer is a curse that must be expunged at all cost. So we keep an open mind and leave open the possibility of establishing causal connections between phenomena not formerly suspected, and hence of a possible meaning link between terms which does not now exist. In such an area of study and discourse there is both causal and meaning suspense.

So far the thesis has been tested against an ordinary factual assertion and its evidence. Next it will be tested against a non-moral 'ought'. Suppose someone says 'this object ought to be treated with extremely great care' and cites as evidence 'this object is the last surviving great art work of its kind.' There is a shared term, again the subject term 'this object'. There seems also to be an overlap in meaning between 'treated with extremely great care' – a – and 'the last surviving great art work of its kind' – b. The meaning link occurs because there is a causal link between treating something with care and preserving something. Rough treatment is causally incompatible with preservation of things. If someone as an art appreciator waxes enthusiastic about the object and then as an art appreciator (not as a religious fanatic who holds the belief that all art, especially great art, distracts human beings from their spiritual quest and is, therefore, corrupting, or as a political fanatic who holds that art of the past is bourgeois art and, therefore, also corrupting) proceeds to smash it to smithereens, we would not find such behaviour nor her/his verbal explanation of it intelligible – 'one ought to smash it because it is the last surviving great art work of its kind'. 'Treating with care' enters (partially) into the meaning of 'being a surviving (great art) work', so that smashing it is not merely eccentric but implies a failure to understand fully the meaning of 'being a surviving (great art) work'. Again, if as evidence for 'this object ought to be treated with extremely great care' someone were to cite 'this object is called by a name which has three letters in its spelling', we would not be able to make sense of this remark. As far as any one knows, there is not the faintest causal connection between treating something with care and the fact that it is called by a name with three letters of the alphabet in its spelling. Therefore, such a remark is totally unintelligible since in the absence of a causal link, there is no meaning link either.

Finally, it will be tested against a moral 'ought' proposition. Take 'One ought not to torture'. But first let us put it in a form which is similar to 'this object ought to be treated with extremely great care'. The moral assertion now reads 'torture is an activity which ought to be avoided', and the evidence is 'torture is an activity which causes pain'. 'Torture' is the shared subject term. Now is there an overlap in meaning between two other terms in the two propositions? Let's see if it works to say that analogous to the non-moral 'ought' and the ordinary factual assertion, there is an overlap in meaning between 'an activity to be avoided' and 'causes pain'. Is there first of all a causal link? We think so; one finds out empirically that something that causes pain is something that people avoid doing. Thrusting hands into fire causes pain and we naturally (once we find out the causal connection) in future try to avoid doing so. One does not wish to deny that this natural avoidance may, of course, on occasions be overlooked or overcome, if for instance in order to clear one's name, as with the Vikings, one had to put one's hands into cauldrons of boiling water, or in order to save one's soul, one must literally go through flames of purification. The point is that this natural avoidance must somehow be held in check if one wishes to achieve some other goal like religious salvation or re-establishment of one's honour. These other goals, however, do not deny the existence of such a phenomenon, but rather make use of this causal knowledge to test the faith of the participants in such rites and rituals. The causal link creates a meaning bridge so that the meaning of 'avoidance' is partially given in terms of 'causing pain'. To explicate fully the meaning of 'an activity to be avoided' one refers amongst other things to pain-causing talk.

So this type of moral proposition seems to satisfy the formal conditions for causal relevance as explicated earlier. But as a matter of fact, there seems also to be a further overlap of meaning between 'torture' and 'causing pain'. The meaning of 'torture' is itself partially explicated in terms of pain-talk. (Let's confine the example to physical torture and physical pain.) Explaining to those who do not know the meaning of 'torture' would involve telling them about the intentions and motives of torturers, the devices they are likely to use from the point of view of their causal efficacy, etc. as well as referring to the pain to the victims produced by their intentions being executed into action through the various devices already mentioned. The pain aspect is not the sole ingredient but no explanation would be complete without talking about it. The overlap in meaning is based on the causal link between doing certain things to people and making them feel pain. Such a causal discovery enables the would-be torturers to make use of it for the purpose of coercing and humiliating their victims, getting information out of them or for their own sheer sadistic delight. The meaning connection is so strong that someone might want to maintain that 'torture' necessarily involves pain-talk. Although this may be true of some terms which enter into moral discourse, not all terms which do satisfy this strong requirement. So one would not insist on such a stringent meaning connection.

Suppose someone in support of the proposition 'torture is an activity which ought to be avoided' says 'torture is an activity which interferes with flute-playing'. By this one does not merely mean that one, as an individual, would rather not bother to torture people if torturing them on any one occasion interferes with one's playing the flute, and so, on grounds of inconvenience, one foregoes torture (which would then turn the proposition into one about expediency, not morality), but that somehow torture in virtue of the very nature of the activity interferes with flute-playing as an activity *per se*. Again we would not know what such a person is talking about, since as far as anyone knows, no causal relation of any kind exists between the two activities, and hence no meaning bridge or partial overlap in meaning exists between the two terms either. So we rightly find such an utterance unintelligible.

Similarly if someone cites in support of the moral assertion that X and people like X (i.e. whose ancestors lived in southern Africa long before the arrival of the Europeans) ought to be discriminated against solely on the grounds that such people have a black skin, we are equally puzzled. Causally speaking, having a black skin and being discriminated against, say by being paid less than white colleagues for the same job, like mending a broken pipe, are totally unrelated. (What is causally relevant is the lack of the particular skill in question, or the degree of skill in question.[6]) So there is no point of contact in meaning between the two terms referring to the characteristic singled out. But for the fact that we have been anaesthetised as to its real import (or the lack of) by dint of frequent repetition, we should find the utterance as unintelligible as saying that one ought not to torture people because torture interferes with flute-playing. However, this is not to deny that some people as a matter of fact proceed to act as if the utterance were intelligible and in consequence bring into existence certain conditions which obtain differentially between white people and black people, and which in their turn and in their own right may be said to be causally relevant to the original norm of discrimination. But this aspect of the matter will be dealt with in the next section.

4   THE CONDITION OF CAUSAL INDEPENDENCE

So far it has been argued that (fE) is to be rejected in favour of (sE) on the grounds that it fails to refer to public external features of the situation referred to in (A), and that it fails to satisfy referential relevance because its referent is not the same as that of the assertion it is purporting to support. But (fE) also is to be rejected because it does not satisfy the condition of causal relevance. (fE) is causally irrelevant to (A) in the required sense. Sincerely committing oneself to something being the case does not bring it about that something is the case. The two are entirely causally unrelated, at least as far as our world is concerned. There could be another world where sheer belief, sincere commitment to a belief, or other mental states of the speaker could directly cause things to happen, where wanting something to happen would make that thing come about. But in our world, no amount of passion in commitment or in volition could causally bring into existence cows with wings that can fly, if as a matter of fact they have no wings and cannot fly.

Although it is true in the context quoted just now that (fE) and (A) are causally unconnected, what about contexts involving self-fulfilling prophecies where there seems to be a causal link? Suppose a malicious and ruthless business competitor let it be known generally that a certain building society (a body which finances mortgages on houses) is about to be bankrupt. By dint of skilful rumouring, he gets investors and would-be investors to become 'sincerely committed' to the belief that it is about to be bankrupt, and as a result to act accordingly, that is, withdraw funds or refrain from investing new funds in it, thus bringing about the very bankruptcy referred to in his assertion. Is there not then a clear causal link between (A) and (fE)?

Similarly with an 'ought' assertion. Suppose that a cunning dictator asserts that people ought to obey him unquestioningly and then by dint of skilful indoctrination or propaganda gets people to be sincerely committed to the norm of unquestioning obedience. The fact that they are sincerely committed to the norm would in turn make people obey him and feel they ought to do so unquestioningly. So just as the sincere commitment to the assertion on the part of investors that the building society in question is about to be bankrupt may causally bring about the very bankruptcy talked about, so sincere commitment to the norm of unquestioning obedience would bring about actual obedience in accordance with the norm.

There is no point in denying the obvious, that self-fulfilling prophecies do occur. They occur when the assertion if accepted and sincerely committed to (or rejected as the case may be) can, as a matter of fact in causal terms, make a difference to the prophecy being fulfilled (or not). Clearly sincere commitment to the assertion about the bankruptcy or the norm of unquestioning obedience, as a matter of fact, do make people behave in a manner so as to confirm it; whereas rejection of the assertion would bring about a different outcome. But in contexts where neither sincere commitment nor the lack of it makes a difference to the outcome, no such prophecy is possible – that cows have

97

wings and can fly is an assertion whose truth or falsity is not affected by either sincere commitment or the absence of sincere commitment to it.

How much damage does the admission do to the thesis? Not very much, for the causal connection one is looking for is prior to the sincere commitment to (A), so that if it exists, it can be cited in support not only of (A) but also in justification of one's commitment to (A). Sincere commitment to (A), that is, (fE) cannot then do the job of validating (A) itself in terms of the causal link postulated and which comes into existence only posterior to the commitment. The prior sincere commitment to (A) may be procured in several ways; however, the only one of these ways which is relevant to the issue of validating (A) is ruled out *ex hypothesi*. For instance, the cunning dictator or ruthless business competitor may get people to be sincerely committed to (A1) or (A3) by (1) sheer force of personality, (2) indoctrination, propaganda, etc., (3) hypnosis, (4) rumours and other dirty tricks of a similar kind, (5) citing (c/r sE). (1) and (3) are straightforwardly non-rational and non-critical. (2) resorts to half-truths, suppressions of truths, distortions of truths, etc., all deliberately calculated to dull or lull the critical faculty to sleep. Rumour may be of two kinds, verbal and behavioural. The former falls squarely into the category of untruths and half-truths; the latter is performed with the intention of inducing other people to accept the prophecy and thereby making it come true. For instance, the ruthless competitor could by careful and deviously laid plans first invest large sums in the rival's business and at the appropriate moment withdraw them, thus causing a run on the funds. It is something which is rational to do (from the point of view of means/end efficiency) and which may provide rational grounds for others to accept or commit themselves to the belief. But this is not rational justification of the belief itself. Therefore (1) to (4) could not be said to be relevant to the problem of validating (A).

(5) is *ex hypothesi* ruled out, since if such evidence is indeed available, then presumably it would render redundant an attempt to 'justify' the belief in terms of (fE) – the person whose sole concern is the question of validating (A) by providing a rational warrant for it, would no doubt cite it in the first place. The Naturalistic Fallacy supporter, as we saw, is convinced that (c/rsE) is not available because of the lack of strict implication between (E) and (A) and therefore substitutes (fE); those making

(factual) assertions with extraneous motives (or people who simply are panicked into acting in a certain way on the basis of rumours) are not concerned with the problem in any case of the validation of the assertion. Now the availability of (c/rsE) would indeed provide justification for saying that (A) is true or correct and in turn for people's acceptance of it. But this is different from the argument of the Naturalistic Fallacy subscriber that (fE) is all there is to 'justify' (A). And, moreover, just as it is intelligible in the first place to ask for justification of (A), it is equally intelligible to ask why one must accept sincere commitment to a norm or a belief as a reasonable basis for saying that (A) is correct. If the answer is further (fE), this leads to an infinite regress, since one can in turn subject such an answer to a similar treatment.

One way of coping with the requirement that the causally relevant evidence be prior to the commitment is to add explicitly a further criterion to the procedure of validating an assertion, namely, that the evidence not only be first (sE), second (c/rE) but third, that (E) be causally independent of the prior sincere commitment to (A). In this way one can consistently rule out (fE) even if (fE) under certain circumstances may be said to be causally related to (A). So the thesis '(A) requires (E)' if completely specified with regard to (E) amounts to:

(1) that it explicitly rules out (fE);
(2) that (E) is referentially relevant to (A), i.e., that (sE) obtains;
(3) that (sE) is causally relevant to (A);
(4) that (c/rsE) obtains prior to sincere commitment to (A) and is causally independent of such commitment.

If the evidence satisfies the above four demands, then (E), if true, would serve to support (A), and if false, would serve to falsify (A).

5   EPISTEMIC IMPLICATION AND THE ATTEMPT TO AVOID THE PARADOXES OF RELEVANCE INVOLVED IN MATERIAL IMPLICATION AND STRICT IMPLICATION

Epistemic implication is the term chosen to characterise the relation between (A) and (E) thus: A epistemically implies E, if:

(a) (E) is not (fE) but (sE) – thus satisfying referential relevance;

(b) (E) is not only (sE) but also (c/rsE) – thus satisfying both referential and causal relevance;

(c) (c/rsE) obtains prior to commitment to (A) and is causally independent of such commitment;

(d) (c/rsE) is true, then (A) would be supported;

(e) (c/rsE) is false, then (A) would be false.

Logic textbooks as a rule talk about two kinds of implication, strict implication (entailment) and material implication.[7] But epistemic implication is neither. Strict implication is too strict and material implication is too lax to do the job in hand, namely, to provide rational safe-conduct in the passage from evidence to assertion.[8]

Material implication and strict implication suffer from the fallacies of relevance (and for this reason some deny that material implication is a 'kind' of implication[9]). Material implication says any true proposition whatever may materially imply any true proposition whatever ('A cat has four legs' materially implies 'Mozart wrote *Don Giovanni*'); any false proposition materially implies any true proposition whatever ('The earth is four thousand years old' materially implies 'Britain is in the northern hemisphere'); and any false proposition implies any false proposition whatever ('Human beings have wings' materially implies 'The planet Earth has no atmosphere'). It only rules out the possibility of a true proposition implying a false one, and for this reason, has been defended as the weakest form of implication. Clearly material implication is of no help to one trying to establish rational warrant for the passage from evidence to assertion, since it even fails to satisfy the elementary semantical condition of securing referential relevance. (a), (b) and (c) above are designed to avoid the fallacies of relevance which both material implication and strict implication suffer from.

We have already seen in discussing the criterion of causal relevance why the requirement of strict implication is impossible to satisfy, because the assertions contain terms which refer to states and processes which are causally linked (or potentially causally linked) to other states and processes referred to by other terms in language. Causal discoveries are, to repeat, empirically made and are open to revision and modification. Hence the terms used to talk about them remain open-textured. And although it is the case that causal connections may forge a meaning connection between the terms involved, it is only an overlap in meaning and not complete identity of meaning. As a result the meaning of a term 'a' in an assertion may only be partially explicated in terms of the meaning of another term 'b' in the evidence. Term 'a' may as a matter of fact already be (partially) connected in meaning to terms other than 'b' in view of the existence of causal links between the states and processes referred to by the terms involved. For instance, being ill is causally linked to a virus in the bloodstream, a deficient set of kidneys, eating contaminated food and countless other states and processes. The term 'is ill', as we saw, cannot be defined in just one of the terms referring to these processes; nor would it do to define it in terms of a disjunction of such terms. And unless it is so defined, strict implication fails to obtain between (A) which contains term 'a' and (E) which contains term 'b', 'c' or 'd' or 'n'.

However, sometimes, in an empirical inquiry, there comes a point when causal understanding of certain states and processes might reach such a level that the investigators may wish to erect a taxonomic principle based on such understanding. For instance, one's understanding of the phenomenon involved may be such as to warrant the scientists to choose one feature or a set of features as the defining characteristics of the phenomenon in question. Zoologists define mammals as animals the female members of which possess mammalian glands, which are used to nourish and suckle the young. They have created a taxonomic principle for identifying animals which are mammals. As a result of this creation (which is not dictated by whim, sincere commitment, or any arbitrary fancy, but guided by their theoretical understanding backed by empirical observation), the proposition 'this is a cow' strictly entails 'this is a mammal' (although 'this is a mammal' does not strictly entail 'this is a cow' for the class of cows is only a sub-class of the class of mammals).

Taxonomic principles are necessary in empirical/scientific inquiries and this issue will be looked at in greater detail under the problem of classification (see section 7). One may say that strict implication does obtain sometimes in factual inquiry but it is restricted to the creation of taxonomic principles. In such a context, the proposition S_2 such as 'this is a mammal' is not offered as evidence for the proposition S_1 'this is a cow', for it is not a context of justifying an assertion. S_1 is not being uttered as an assertion whose truth or falsity is being determined and S_2 is not offered as evidence for the truth or falsity of S_1. But if S_1 were uttered as an assertion whose truth or falsity (correctness/incorrectness) one is trying to ascertain, then it would be inappropriate to cite S_2 as evidence, since S_1 strictly implies S_2, and what is under consideration is not that one doubts that the creature is a mammal if it were a cow, but that one is asking for evidence in support of the assertion that the creature in question is indeed a cow and not, say, a cat. So S_1 requires citing evidence of the kind 'it moos, but does not meow', 'its genetic material is X whereas that of a cat is Y', etc. But between the assertion and the evidence of this kind, there is no strict implication for the reasons already discussed. So to conclude, if there is strict implication between two propositions, then it is not a context of the justification of assertions; and if that context obtains, then there is no strict implication between the evidence and the assertion.

But if strict implication does not obtain between (A) and (E), the sceptical conclusion would follow if no other type of implication is forthcoming. Epistemic implication *via* (d) and (e) above are meant to stop the sceptic from advancing to the usual conclusion.

6   THE LOGIC OF VERIFICATION, FALSIFICATION AND FALLIBILISM

In Chapter Five, section 4, three senses of the term 'conclusive' will be identified which could be involved when one talks about the conclusive or the lack of conclusive verification or falsification of a claim *via* (d) and (e) above. To anticipate a little, the three senses are: (i) 'conclusive$_D$' – where the truth or falsity of the evidence entails the truth or falsity of the assertion; (ii) 'conclusive$_M$' – where the truth or falsity of the evidence together with certain methodological assumptions about the correctness of scientific, proto and pre-scientific claims enables one *via* (d) and (e) to verify or falsify the assertion; (iii) 'conclusive$_A$' – an assertion which has been 'conclusively$_M$' verified or falsified is not absolutely certain or secure, as future changes in scientific knowledge, proto and pre-scientific knowledge could occur which would yield new evidence that could defeat the assertion as either true or false. An assertion which is 'conclusively$_M$' verified/falsified is, therefore, not 'conclusively$_A$' verified/falsified.

With these distinctions in mind, let us look at (d) – 'If (A) is true, then (E) is true and (E) is true'. If (c/rsE) or (E) for short is true, (A) is verified, corroborated or supported in the sense that the truth of (A) is not incompatible with the truth of (E), and not that the truth of (E) entails the truth of (A). To argue in the latter manner is to commit the fallacy of affirming the consequent. To say that the truth of (E) does not entail the truth of (A) is to say that (A) is not 'conclusively$_D$' verified by the truth of (E).

Although there is no 'conclusive$_D$' verification of (A), there is 'conclusive$_M$' verification of (A) – for details about this argument, see Chapter Five, section 4. But 'conclusive$_M$' verification of (A) is not 'conclusive$_A$' verification of (A).

If (c/rsE) or (E) for short is false, then (A) is falsified. But the falsity of (E) does not entail the falsity of (A) – there is no 'conclusive$_D$' falsification of (A). (A) may, however, be 'conclusively$_M$' falsified – the methodological assumption about the correctness of extant scientific, proto and pre-scientific knowledge together with the *modus tollens*, allows one to do so – for further details, see Chapter Five, section 4. But the 'conclusive$_M$' falsification of (A) is not 'conclusive$_A$' falsification of (A).

(d) and (e) clearly entail fallibilism. But what is fallibilism? Susan Haack rightly says that it is not a single thesis but that it refers to a family of related theses. But the definition she gives appears to be a very general one – fallibilism is the view that no beliefs are absolutely secure.[10] On this account of fallibilism, (d) is clearly fallibilistic – the truth of (A) being verified or corroborated by the truth (E) does not mean that (A) is 'conclusively$_A$' verified, and is therefore not absolutely secure. Later evidence of a different kind could appear, and if it turns out to be true, this new evidence could defeat the claim that (A) is true, correct or justified.

(e) too is also fallibilistic on Haack's definition – although (A) has been shown to be false because (E) is false, yet the belief about the falsity of (A) is not absolutely secure, as (A) has not been 'conclusively$_A$' falsified by the falsity of (E). Future evidence, other than (E) itself, such as (Ei) or (Eii), may be available and cited in support of (A), and if, say, (Eii) turns out to be true, it would then verify (A). The truth of (Eii) supporting the truth (or verifying) of (A) defeats the original not absolutely secure belief that (A) is false. But the truth of (Eii) supporting the truth of (A) defeating the original not so absolutely secure belief that (A) is false is itself not absolutely secure, and so on.

Although (d) and (e) are fallibilistic on the general definition of fallibilism given by Haack, one might be able to give an expanded account of it, which consists of the following elements: (i) there is no 'conclusive$_D$' verification of an assertion if the evidence cited in its support turns out to be true, although there is 'conclusive$_M$' verification of it; (ii) there is no 'conclusive$_D$' falsification of an assertion if the evidence cited in its support turns out to be false, although there is 'conclusive$_M$' falsification of it; (iii) (i) and (ii) imply that no assertions are absolutely secure – there is no 'conclusive$_A$' verification or falsification of (A); (iv) the elimination of error via (e), the *modus tollens* (and certain methodological assumptions) and the verification (corroboration) *via* (d) (and certain methodological assumptions) are essentially open-ended, which gives rise to the impression of what Gallie calls the 'agonistic style' in intellectual activities (see Chapter One); (v) but this does not imply that one assertion is as correct or as justified as another – some beliefs can be shown to be false (incorrect) and others to be true (correct), even though no assertions are absolutely secure or certain.

The thesis of epistemic implication *via* (d) and (e) is put forward as an attempt to capture these elements just described. Clearly, within the domain of ordinary knowledge (which includes moral knowledge – see Chapter Five), fallibilism obtains. The arguments in Chapter Five and in this chapter also imply that fallibilism obtains in the domain of scientific knowledge (but this should not be understood that fallibilism is all there is to scientific method; for a brief discussion of fallibilism in the context of theory testing in science, see Chapter Five, section 4). To achieve the goal set out by this book, namely, to defend moral discourse as part of critical/rational/objective discourse *via* epistemic implication, it would be necessary to argue that fallibilism obtains at least within these two domains. But the question, whether an overall epistemology, in order to be adequate and to combat scepticism, must have fallibilism as one of its features is an issue beyond the confines of this more limited inquiry, and cannot be settled here and now.[11]

7 ' "OUGHT" EPISTEMICALLY IMPLIES "CAN" '

The notion of epistemic implication is not new, least of all in moral philosophy, for the Kantian dictum, which is usually unquestioned even by those who subscribe to the Naturalistic Fallacy, – '"ought" implies "can"' – could be shown, when subjected to analysis, to be a case of epistemic implication. Take the following example. 'He ought to save the drowning person' implies 'He can save the drowning person', that is, he can swim, he is on the spot or near enough to run to the rescue in good time, he is himself at that moment in a fit state to mount the operation (such as that he is not that very minute having a heart attack), etc. 'Saving a drowning person' may itself be accomplished in a variety of ways which is open-ended, for example, by swimming towards the person and dragging her/him to safety, throwing out a life-belt to the victim, stretching out one's hand to haul the victim aboard one's own boat (the last two methods do not even require an ability to swim), etc. In other words, 'He ought to save the drowning person' (A) implies 'He can save the drowning person' (E) which in turn implies 'He is in a position to do a variety of things which has the end result of rescuing the victim'. (EE) Epistemic implication obtains between (E) and (EE); first of all, the fundamental semantic condition of referential relevance is satisfied – the propositions have the same referent, share the same subject term. Next, the activities of swimming and pulling someone ashore, of throwing out a life-belt and hauling the victim out of the water, etc. (activities embodied in (EE)) are causally connected with the activity of saving people from drowning. So the meaning of 'saving a drowning person' is partially explicated in terms of any of these activities. 'He can save the drowning person' (E) is true or is corroborated if he is in a position to do one or more of such activities. But (E) is false or has been falsified if he is not in a position to do any of such activities.

So far one has shown that (E) epistemically implies (EE). But if (A) implies (E) and (E) in turn implies (EE), then one can perhaps also show that (A) epistemically implies (EE). First, (A) and (EE) satisfy referential relevance. Second, the activity of saving a drowning person is causally connected with the activities of swimming and pulling someone ashore, of throwing out a life-belt and hauling the victim out of the water, etc.; so there is a partial meaning link between the term 'saving the drowning person' in (A) and the other terms referring to the various activities listed in (EE). Third, the truth of (EE) understood exclusively or inclusively may be said to determine the appropriateness of asserting 'He ought to save the drowning person' (A); the falsity of (EE) understood exclusively or inclusively may be said to determine the inappropriateness of asserting (A). As all these conditions are satisfied, one may conclude that 'ought' epistemically implies 'can' *via* 'is'.

Clearly the implication in the Kantian dictum is not that of material implication, as it is simply not true that any true 'ought' proposition may imply any true 'is' proposition, that any false 'ought' proposition may imply any false 'is' proposition, or that any false 'ought' proposition implies any true 'is' proposition whatever.

Nor is the relationship between a particular 'ought' proposition and its relevant set of 'is' propositions one of strict implication, for it is possible that the 'ought' proposition is correct and the set of 'is' propositions cited in its support should happen to be false as the set is in principle open-ended. There may be some activity, not mentioned in the set, which may be available to the agent. Such activities would become available, say, in the wake of technological innovations and scientific discoveries. In the past, before one discovered that (and understood why) scurvy may be cured by eating lime (that is food which contains vitamin C), one did not know how to cure scurvy victims of their fatal affliction. The remedies recommended at that time were all useless. But the presence of inefficacious remedies and the absence of knowledge then about eating lime containing vitamin C means that what one is in a position to do to cure scurvy is an open-ended affair. Therefore, what one ought to do is not related to what one is in a position to do by means of strict implication.

The 'ought' in the Kantian dictum does not uniquely entail that there is one specific action or set of actions to be performed, just as the 'ought' in a normal justificatory context does not uniquely entail one fact or set of facts. One could, however, argue that the 'ought' in the Kantian dictum does after all entail 'can' and 'is', by maintaining that the 'ought' strictly implies that some operation or activity is open to the agent to perform, without specifying what it may be. But in the same way, one could also argue that the 'ought' in a normal justificatory context strictly implies some fact or other, without specifying which – on this thesis 'one ought not to steal' will strictly imply some fact about the activity of stealing. However, the point made by the supporter of the Naturalistic Fallacy is not the denial that 'ought' entails facts in this sense, but that no particular fact uniquely entails a particular 'ought' so that compatible with the same fact may be conflicting 'oughts'. The burden of this book is to show that although no particular fact uniquely entails a particular 'ought', it does not follow that compatible with the same fact may be conflicting 'oughts'. If epistemic implication holds good, then an 'ought' is only supported if certain facts obtain and not others. It also implies that the support or corroboration is tentative and open to possible future refutation (and the corollary that its lack of support or corroboration is equally tentative, for evidence may turn up in the future to defeat the present verdict). This thesis, it is argued, holds good for the 'ought' in a normal justificatory context as well as in the Kantian dictum.

8 CLASSIFICATION AND DISTINCTION BETWEEN CLASS AND TAXON

So far it has been argued that (fE) is not an appropriate procedure to adopt for the validation of (A) whether in moral, practical non-moral or ordinary factual discourse, that it seems to be answering a different question from the one originally posed, which is about the truth-or-falsity of (A) as opposed to that about the sincere commitment or the lack of it to (A). We shall now try to reinforce the thesis that (A) epistemically implies (c/rsE) and to exclude (fE) by referring to the problem of classification which may be introduced by talking about (A1) and (A2), i.e., about 'ought' propositions whether moral or non-moral.

'Ought' propositions may be understood as making covert or

overt reference to classifications. An example of (A2) which overtly classifies is the following: 'Alsatians ought to be exercised a great deal more than dachsunds', which explicitly mentions the class of dogs which are alsatians which ought to be treated differently from the class of dogs which are dachsunds. An example of (A2) which covertly classifies is: 'I ought to sort out my old clothes' implying that they may be classified into those which an Oxfam shop may be interested in and the rest to be used as rags, perhaps. An (A1) with covert classification is: 'One ought not to kill' which may be elliptical for (a) 'one ought not to kill members of one's own family, clan or tribe' thereby implying that there is a class of people outside these circles whom one may kill; (b) 'one ought not to kill except in self-defence' implying that there are acts of justified violence as well as acts of unjustified violence; or (c) 'one ought not to kill human beings and other sentient beings', implying a distinction between sentient and non-sentient beings. An (A1) with overt classification is: 'women ought to obey men's will', explicitly referring to two groups, the dominating male and the dominated female.

In the case where the classification is covert but nevertheless implied, one is using 'imply' in the familiar way as when one says that 'there are rotten apples in the barrel' implies that 'the barrel is not totally empty'. It is a straightforward logical implication. The Naturalistic Fallacy supporters would not find this contentious. But what one would like to test is their reaction to the thesis that whenever classification, whether overt or covert, is involved, classification requires that there be certain characteristics possessed by the first group but not by the second (where there are only two categories distinguished) in virtue of which it is apt and appropriate to treat the former in a certain way but not the latter. This is analogous to the earlier thesis that '(A) seems to require (sE)'. For short it may be formulated as: '(C) seems to require (sE).' Would the Naturalistic Fallacy subscribers reject this in the same way that they have abandoned '(A1) seems to require (sE1)' for '(A1) merely requires (fE1.1)'? Again if they were consistent, they must. For them, if someone proposes to classify and treat two separate objects as similar or to classify and treat them as different types of objects, serious reasons for the proposed classification in question are not required. A flippant response will do, namely, that (C1) merely requires (fE1.1). If challenged, in the case of a proposed classification which is contained or implied in a moral 'ought', they would say 'we are sincerely committed to or have chosen this way of classifying people or actions'. In the case of a proposed classification which is contained or implied in a non-moral 'ought' proposition, they would either cite sincere commitment/choice or just pure whim or fancy.

The problem of classification is, needless to say, not peculiar to moral 'ought' or even non-moral 'ought' propositions. It is a general issue. The question one wishes to pose to the Naturalistic Fallacy subscribers is then this: are they prepared to maintain that (C), across the board, merely requires (fE)? Or are they going to hang back from the brink and maintain that it is only in the case where classification enters into moral propositions that (C) merely requires (fE) – that is, '(C1) requires (fE1.1)'? If the latter, one would press for a reason and a justification of their policy of isolating moral discourse from the rest of critical discourse. If they cannot cite any serious reason and in turn rely on (fE) itself, namely that they have sincerely committed themselves to the policy of isolation, then they have committed a *petitio principii*. But if they opt for the former, then they are challenging the whole of serious critical discourse itself. If someone classifies cars and elephants as belonging to one group, namely, animals, and then proceeds to 'justify' it in terms of citing the flippant response 'I am sincerely committed to cars and elephants being grouped together as animals' or more simply that one is doing it only out of whim, then this move is calculated to introduce intellectual chaos. *À la* Humpty Dumpty, words could be made to mean whatever the speaker wants them to mean. This leads straightaway to wider philosophical issues in epistemology, of general names, nominalism and realism, etc.

These are matters one cannot deal with here. But they are worth emphasising, because one aim of this book is indeed to show that it is not fruitful, if not impossible, to discuss the rationality or otherwise of moral discourse without talking about two traditions in wider philosophy itself and their respective assumptions and presuppositions, namely, that tradition which argues for the possibility and necessity of serious critical discourse (of which moral discourse is a part) and the opposing tradition of scepticism which denies its possibility (of which moral scepticism is a part).

As Harré[12] points out the view that classification is ultimately arbitrary is the central and most pervasive (twentieth-century) positivist myth – he calls it 'the myth of Infinite Arbitrariness of Classification'. According to it, classification does not depend on the nature of the objects classified but entirely upon the purposes and the means of the classifier. In the philosophy of taxonomy, this myth goes hand in hand with the doctrine of nominal essence, which refers to those qualities manifested by an object whose appearance is said to justify the use of a particular term in characterising it. In other words, it is part and parcel of the wider positivist outlook which confines science to the study of phenomena, of appearances and manifest qualities.

Harré distinguishes between classes and natural kinds or taxa – the former may be ultimately arbitrary but not the latter. Things which constitute a class may have nothing more in common than a single manifest quality, whereas things which constitute a kind or taxon not only have one or more manifest characteristics in common but also share a similar constitutional make-up (real or inner essence as opposed to nominal essence) which accounts for, amongst other things, the co-manifestation of qualities. (Sometimes, the things in a taxon may not even manifest their common constitution by possessing a single common characteristic; for example, diamond, black carbon and graphite are all carbon as the electronic structure of their atoms are identical although they share no common manifest characteristic; similarly, water, steam and ice are really H_2O even though phenomenally speaking they are different things.) While taxa generally manifest themselves as classes, not all classes are taxa. Harré says, for example, that red entities constitute a class and not a taxon, because the manifested characteristic, their colour, is not a sign of a common constitution; rather their redness may be accounted for in terms of very different constitutions. If things are assigned to classes on the strength of manifest qualities alone, it is possible for there to be as many classes as there are characteristics which an object possesses. If it has no identifiable qualities, then there are no classes to which it can be assigned. Clearly, on this account, there is no non-arbitrary reason for choosing one of these possible classes as the taxon. Indeed, on this view there are simply no natural kinds. But science (as well as ordinary knowledge) does not and cannot operate only with classes, if there is to be knowledge of how things behave because of the kinds of things they are.

This book argues (see next chapter) that a moral theory or moral knowledge claim is to be assessed against the check of scientific assumptions and hypotheses (amongst other checks). In terms of the realist assumption that science uses taxa and not classes, one is able to show that certain moral claims are not admissible because they appear to rely on the nominalist/positivist view that classification is of classes and hence really arbitrary.

Morality is concerned centrally with the conduct of human beings towards one another, less centrally towards other beings than human ones and towards things in general. This presupposes, at the very least, that the classification of certain beings as human beings is not an arbitrary matter, that the manifest different characteristics which obviously exist between individuals or groups of individuals, nevertheless, do not prevent us from assigning these individuals to the same taxon or natural kind, that is, human beings. But if science operates with classes, then there is nothing to prevent someone from devising a morality which is based on excluding beings with a certain pigmentation in their skin, or who do not speak a certain language or share a certain culture, who may lack the very characteristic picked on by the classifier devising the morality and used by him as the defining characteristic of the class of human beings – such a morality cannot then be criticised on the grounds of arbitrariness. But if science uses taxa, we can.

The variation in skin pigmentation, the variations in linguistic and cultural expressions, may be explained in terms of a common constitution (that is, not exactly identical but similar) reacting to very different sets of conditions. Skin pigmentation occurs in all human beings (albinos apart) – how dark or how light depends on the amount of exposure to the sun, as well as on one's genetic make-up which itself is to be explained in terms of evolutionary selection over time of certain factors and their response to solar exposure. Linguistic and cultural differences are naturally due to the different milieu in which individuals are born and brought up. Even beings without language like the unfortunate 'enfant sauvage' cannot be excluded from the natural kind of human beings because the acquisition of language is a social process which must be set in motion at a very early age and continuously sustained. The absence of this manifest characteristic in such a case cannot rule out his membership of the taxon. So certain moralities (like apartheid whose cruder supporters actually claim that black people are not human) cannot escape the charge of arbitrariness precisely because they fall back on class and classification which are determined by the purpose of the classifier, which, in this case, is specifically the intention to discriminate against people whose skin has a darker pigmentation than their own. What counts and what does not count as an entity falling under the particular term, 'human being', when the term refers to a taxon and not a class, is not an arbitrary matter to be decided by the whims, fancies or motives of the person who is proposing the classification. The thesis, that all that is common to things called by the same name is the name, is clearly untenable;[13] but equally untenable is a less extreme type of nominalism which says that things called by the same name are things which happen to share some manifest characteristic.

In spite of the arguments adduced so far for the thesis that classification based on taxa has nothing to do with the attitudes, purposes or intentions of the classifier, a determined critic might still wish to make an objection and it is this: it may be possible to argue that assertions require serious evidence but it is not obvious that a proposed classification does. Assertions may be said to be true or false, correct or incorrect. The concept of assertion seems to indicate that (fE) is not acceptable since (fE) is really about the relationship in terms of attitude on the part of the speaker to (A) itself. But is there anything comparable in the concept of classification to indicate a similar ruling out of (fE)? It is not obvious, the critic would say, that 'truth' or 'falsity' ('correct'/'incorrect') may be used in connection with classification. It is more normal to talk about the usefulness or otherwise of a certain classification, rather than that it is true or false, correct or incorrect.

First, one must concede a point – it is true that we sometimes appraise classifications in terms of their utility. In other words, the classification does serve a purpose, as one cannot assess the utility or otherwise independent of the purpose to which the scheme would be put. To put certain houses and certain trees together as belonging to the same category may be very useful and justified if one is trying to get the Department of the Environ-ment (or some equivalent conservation body) to issue a preser-vation order on them on the grounds that the houses and the trees are several hundred years old. But to admit this does not damage the thesis that the reason for the classification is not (fE) but (sE) – the fact that these objects are very old is a publicly ascertainable feature which can be determined in a perfectly objective manner.

But, second, does the critic wish to maintain that classifications behind moral 'ought' assertions and classifications in purely factual assertions must be assessed only according to their utility and never their truth? Take the latter instance. We classify dogs, lions, whales and human beings as mammals. There seems no obvious purpose involved analogous to the preservation of old artefacts and natural products, which informs the classification behind that 'ought' proposition. At a pinch, in order to conform to the model of purpose/utility, one may convert (C3) into (C2) and say 'One ought to classify dogs, lions, whales and human beings as mammals if we do not want to be misled in our expectations about them'. Now this tortuous and stilted formulation really amounts to an admission that the model is inappropriate. We would be misled in our expectations if the classification is false or incorrect. Utility in other words presupposes truth. Something is useful and works if it is true, and because it is true. Truth is not redundant nor is it reducible to utility. So the critics have not succeeded in making their point.

Although we do sometimes appraise classifications in terms of their utility/inutility, it does not follow that we never do and cannot appraise them in terms of truth or falsity, correctness or incorrectness. And in any case even appraisal in terms of utility/inutility requires (sE) and not (fE). However, one must concede the point that it is possible for some people on some occasions to indulge in classificatory activity for which no (sE) is available – occasions when the persons concerned tell you that they are merely classifying objects in the way they do as the fancy takes them, just to while away the time. If the purpose is mere distrac-tion, then a flippant response would do. But not all classification is indulged in to keep boredom at bay. Often classification is done in the context of trying to understand the objects and their behaviour (in scientific contexts) so that one may not be misled in our expectations about them when the classification of them is applied to practical contexts. It would not do to classify sweet chestnuts and horse chestnuts as belonging to the same taxon because they happen to share the same manifest characteristics; otherwise, one would be badly misled in one's expectation about horse chestnuts if they were to be regarded as no different from sweet chestnuts. In the same way to exclude black people from the taxon of human beings could also mislead one in one's expectation about them.

9 DISTINCTION BETWEEN EPISTEMIC IMPLICATION AND EPISTEMIC OR DOXASTIC LOGIC

Epistemic implication which constitutes the logic of justification in the domain of ordinary knowledge must not be confused with what is called epistemic logic. Epistemic logic is concerned with formulae, such as, 'a knows p', 'a knows that p', 'a believes p', or 'a believes that p', which are symbolised by 'Kap' or 'Bap' where 'K' stands for the relationship of knowing, 'B' for that of believing, 'a' is the knower or believer, and 'p' is the proposition known or believed. Epistemic logic is also known as doxastic logic.[14]

Epistemic implication and doxastic logic differ in two ways: in their ontological and semantical implications. With regard to the first difference – epistemic implication serves to establish that critical arguments are possible within the domain of ordinary knowledge. Critical arguments are constructed and advanced by human beings. But this does not imply that their contents refer to the subjective mental and volitional processes of their producers. Their logical content must not be confused with the objects they could be talking about, which could well be about subjective mental processes on the part of conscious and self-conscious beings. For instance, a psychologist could put forward the argument that children deprived of maternal love when young could grow up to be emotionally unstable on the basis of certain studies s/he has made of the correlation between adult emotional deficiencies and childhood maternal deprivation. The logical content of that theory must be distinguished from (i) the subjective mental processes of the psychologist during the period in which s/he was formulating the thesis, and from (ii) the subjective mental processes of the people who are the subjects of the investigation – such subjective processes are, for the theorists, objective matters of their own study. (This point will be considered further in Chapter Four.) Epistemic logic, on the other hand, deals with states of mind of subjects involved, of believing and knowing, etc.

Epistemic implication involves the following semantical demands: (i) that the *justificandum* and the *justificans* are talking about one and the same object, that is, they satisfy referential relevance; (ii) that there is a partial meaning link between the terms used in the *justificandum* and the *justificans*, to refer to certain processes which are causally linked, either in accordance with well-established scientific hypotheses or theories or with pre-scientific assumptions and generalisations.[15] In other words, it presupposes semantic objectivity. By contrast, epistemic logic does not involve semantic objectivity. It is not, indeed, concerned with semantics at all but with pragmatics.[16] A belief or knowledge statement of the form 'a believes p' or 'a knows p' really concerns two different things – persons who hold the belief or who are said to know that . . ., and propositions. 'a' may refer to an individual or community of individuals. They are statements with two referents. As such they are hybrids, whose nature may be made clear by considering the following statements:

$$p = \text{'apples are good to eat'}$$
$$q = \text{'children believe that } p\text{'}$$

The truth value of q is not a function of the truth value of p, the subordinate statement. q may be true or false independently of whether p is true or false. q depends not merely on p, but also amongst other things on individuals (namely, children in the example cited) and the state of such individuals. So the belief function (or the knowing function) is not a truth function – it is a 'non truth preserving pragmatic function'.[17] Terms like 'believes' and 'knows' designate relations between a person(s) and a proposition. They are propositional attitudes which are pragmatic concepts and not semantic ones.

In the light of this, it is obvious why the Subsumption/Deducibility-Commitment model in moral philosophy and elsewhere can only yield a pragmatic and not a semantic account of truth. 'Committing oneself to' like 'believes' designates a relationship between a person(s) and a proposition – it too is a propositional attitude. It yields truth for someone, namely, personal subjective truth, if the person is an individual, and collective intersubjective truth if the persons involved form part of a group. If p = 'killing Jews, Slavs and gypsies is morally right' and q = 'John Doe (or the Nazis) sincerely commits himself (themselves) to p', the truth value of q is independent of the truth value of p and *vice versa*. 'Sincerely committing oneself to' is a non-truth preserving pragmatic function. An epistemology which rests on such a function can only yield a subjective view of knowledge, and is incompatible with the possibility of rational and objective knowledge.

10   CHISHOLM'S 'CRITICAL COGNITIVISM'

One attempt to account for the epistemic principles of evidence that obtain between (A1), (A3) and (E1), (E3) which is close to the approach pursued by this book is that by Chisholm in his *Theory of Knowledge*.[18] So it would be relevant to look at the similarities as well as the differences between these two attempts.

Like this book, Chisholm maintains that the problem of characterising the relationship between an ordinary factual assertion (A3) and the evidence (E3), between, for instance, 'There is a cat on the roof' and 'I take something to be a cat on the roof' (he calls the former the 'indirectly evident' and the latter the 'directly evident') is the same as that which obtains between a moral assertion (A1) and its evidence (E1).[19] He also says that the relation between the assertion and the evidence is neither a deductive nor an inductive one. By a deductive relationship, he presumably means one of strict implication. On this, clearly, both views agree. Nor does this book wish to disagree with him about the lack of an inductive relationship between assertion and evidence, as there clearly is.[20]

Just as it is argued earlier that the failure of strict implication and material implication obtaining between (A) and (E) does not necessarily lead to a sceptical conclusion, so Chisholm argues that the failure of a deductive or an inductive relationship obtaining between (A) and (E)[21] does not necessarily lead to scepticism. His positive characterisation of the relationship is in terms of what he calls 'critical cognitivism'.

Critical cognitivism (a) rejects what he calls a 'reductivist' account,[22] that is to say, to translate sentences about moral beliefs into sentences about the feelings of people. ('Mercy as such is good' does not mean 'I approve of mercy' or 'Most of the people in our culture circle approve of mercy'.) In the same way, sentences about ordinary factual assertions cannot be reduced or translated into sentences about the ways in which something is appeared to; (b) argues that there are 'principles of evidence, other than the principle of induction and deduction, which will tell us, for example, under what conditions the state we have called "thinking that one perceives" will *confer evidence*, or *confer reasonableness*, upon propositions about external things.'[23]

Applied to moral discourse, critical cognitivism says:

> We do know that mercy is good and that ingratitude is bad.
> The sentences in which such truths are expressed are not
> inductive or deductive consequences of sentences expressing
> our perceptions, our memories of our perceptions or our own
> psychological states; nor can they be translated or paraphrased
> into such sentences. Yet we have no moral intuitions; experi-
> ence and reason are our only sources of knowledge. Hence
> there must be some empirical truths which serve to make known
> the facts of ethics. And these truths can only be those that
> pertain to our feelings for what is good and what is evil.[24]

As Chisholm sees it, there are three arguments which could be constructed out of three different propositions and their negations.

The 'intuitionist' will reason in essentially the following way:

(P)	We have knowledge of certain ethical facts.
(Q)	Experience and reason do not yield such knowledge.
▶(R)	There is an additional source of knowledge.[25]

The 'sceptic', finding no such additional source of knowledge, reasons with equal cogency in the following way:

(Not-R)	There is no source of knowledge other than experience and reason.
(Q)	Experience and reason do not yield any knowledge of ethical facts.
▶(Not-P)	We do not have knowledge of any ethical facts. . . .

The logic of the two arguments reminds us that there is still one other possibility. For if P and Q imply R, then not only do Not-R and Q imply Not-P, but also Not-R and P imply Not-Q. Hence, one could also argue in this way: (this is critical cognitivism)

(Not-R)   There is no source of knowledge other than experience and reason.

(P)   We have knowledge of certain ethical facts.

▶(Not-Q)   Experience and reason yield knowledge of ethical facts.[26]

The ethical sceptic's position may be enlarged as follows:

(Not-R)

(Q)

(D)[27]   Ordinary factual claims are deducible from claims about subjective experience. (This is implied rather than stated.)

(Not-D/E)   Ethical claims are not deducible from claims about subjective experience or factual claims in general.

(Not-P)   Ethical claims are not knowledge claims.

The critical cognitivist's position may also be enlarged as follows:

(Not-R)

(Not-D)   Ordinary factual claims are not deducible from claims about subjective experience.

(Not-D/E)

▶(Not-Q)

(Not-Q1)   Claims about subjective experience are relevant to justifying ordinary factual knowledge claims; claims about subjective feelings of what is good and evil are relevant to justifying moral knowledge claims.

The thesis of epistemic implication agrees with critical cognitivism in respect of (Not-R), (Not-D), (Not-D/E)▶(Not-Q). To the list of premises it adds (Not-M), that is, ordinary factual claims and moral claims are not related to the evidence cited in their favour by means of material implication. But it differs from critical cognitivism by rejecting (Not-Q1), for it maintains that the evidence must satisfy referential relevance, causal relevance, that the causally relevant evidence is prior to and itself causally independent of the acceptance of the claim to be justified; and that such evidence, if true, would support (corroborate) the claim, and if false, would falsify the claim. It is not obvious that Chisholm's (Not-Q1) satisfies the demand that the evidence be serious. And it does not mention the other demands.

(Not-Q1) not only does not satisfy the demand that the evidence be serious, it also seems to involve circularity. When applied to moral claims, the feelings referred to by the assertor as being relevant to justifying the claims, must already be recognised as feelings for what is good and what is evil before they can 'serve to make known the facts of ethics'. In other words, we already know that 'mercy is good' before we can recognise those feelings of approval as pertaining to our feelings for what is good. If we already know that mercy is good, the feelings of approval, even if they exist, are superfluous in justifying that we know. Similarly, if we already know the states of mind of other people (when the thesis of critical cognitivism is applied to the problem of other minds which Chisholm claims can be done), then perception, memory, self-awareness, etc., even if they exist, are superfluous in justifying that one knows other minds.

Critical cognitivism starts off by saying that we have knowledge of moral facts, that we know the states of other people's minds, etc. From this premise (P) and the premise (Not-R), it argues to (Not-Q1). But surely, this is precisely what the sceptics are challenging. They claim we have no knowledge of such matters. The basis for their saying this is that the relationship between the claim and its evidence is not that of strict implication. To resist the sceptical conclusion, one must argue that strict implication is not the logical relationship one needs but that some other type of logical relationship obtains between (A) and (E), in virtue of which we can critically assess the claim in question to determine whether it is a proper knowledge claim. To assume that the claim is a proper knowledge claim and then to argue to (Not-Q1) is to put the cart before the horse.

11 TRUTH/VALIDITY; THE ARGUMENTATIVE AND THE DESCRIPTIVE USES OF LANGUAGE

Popper (i) correctly reminds us that in argumentation, one is interested in establishing good arguments, that is, not merely that they be valid, but also that they be true; (ii) makes the novel point that the argumentative use of language presupposes the descriptive use of language (see Chapter Six, section 4). These two points may be deployed to support the notion of epistemic implication.

Take the first point. Logic books, particularly those dealing with classical logic as 'deductive logic', claim that logicians are only interested in the validity of an argument and not in its truth. This enables the logicians to concentrate on the pure form of an argument without reference to its content. However, in real life arguments, one cannot be as cavalier as textbook logicians in dismissing truth as being relevant to one's concern, as the notions of truth and validity are of equal importance in establishing good arguments. But even in the deductive logic exercises beloved of logic textbooks, it is not the case that truth is entirely irrelevant, the protestations of the authors notwithstanding.

Sellars brings out the point well. He says:

In the case of 'deductive logic', the concept of a sound argument is that of an argument which is such that if its premisses are true, its conclusion *must* be true. A *good* deductive argument is one which is not only sound (valid) but has true premisses, and hence a true conclusion. An argument purports to be 'deductive' if its conclusion is qualified by the parenthetical adverb 'necessary', thus:

All men are mortal.   All Texans are rich.
Socrates is a man.   Getty is rich.
So (necessarily) Socrates is So (necessarily) Getty is a
mortal.   Texan.

Although both these arguments *purport* to be deductive, the former is correct (valid) and indeed sound, while the second is incorrect (invalid). Notice that the parenthetical comment 'necessarily' does not mean that the conclusion by itself is a necessary truth. The necessity indicated is *relative* necessity;

the conclusion (if the argument is sound) is necessary
relatively to the truth of the premisses. . . . In the conclusion
of an argument which purports to be deductive – So
(necessarily) p, – the conclusion *asserts* 'p' and *signifies* by the
parenthetical comment that 'p' is the conclusion of a deductively
good argument; i.e., one which is valid and has true
premisses.[28]

In real life discourse, we are interested in *good* deductive arguments, not in bad ones. By analogy with Sellars's account of a
good deductive argument, a bad deductive argument is one which
may be sound (valid) but has at least one false premise, and hence
a false conclusion. An example would be: all men are immortal,
Socrates is a man, so Socrates is immortal.

If someone were to cite, in support of the assertion that Socrates
is immortal (A3), evidence of the sort that all men are immortal,
one would conclude that it is unjustified to assert (A3), because
the evidence is false. This demand of epistemic implication is no
more than the demand that one is interested in establishing good
arguments and not bad ones. One succeeds in making a point
with a good argument; one fails to make a point with a bad one.
Bad ones are useful in sharpening the mind, alerting it to the
distinction between validity and truth, as a pedagogical device.
But the goal is to get someone to spot such bad arguments in real
life discourse and to reject them, and in turn to avoid putting
them forward in defending a case oneself. They are to be avoided
at all cost when trying to argue a point in critical discourse.

As for Popper's second point, it is supportive of the claim that
epistemic implication obtains across the board with (A1), (A2)
and (A3), that is to say, whenever arguments occur in the domain
of ordinary knowledge. (Of course arguments occur outside this
domain but it is not the concern of this book to consider them.)
Popper says that arguments in the end are about what is and
what is not the case. When one argues with another whether
Chernenko/Reagan is a wife-beater (A3), both sides argue
whether it is the case or not the case that, for example,
Chernenko/Reagan has been observed in public hitting his wife
across the face with his bare fists, or kicking her in the legs with
his boots or shoes, or that neighbours have heard Mrs Chernenko
or Mrs Reagan scream in the middle of the night during an attack,

or that the first lady of the land in question is seen with bruises and black eyes usually on the morrow following those audible nocturnal assaults, etc.

Similarly, when one argues with another whether one ought to swim in the sea (A2), one is arguing about the strength of the current, its direction, the force and direction of the prevailing wind, the temperature of the water, the proficiency and health of the swimmer, etc.

So too when one argues with another whether one ought to permit euthanasia (A1), one is eventually, amongst other things, arguing about the nature of certain sorts of illnesses, the physical consequences of pain and the degree of its intensity, the psychological effect on the human psyche, the curtailment that pain and suffering could bring to one's normal activities, the dangers inherent in an over-hasty or ill-considered decision to end one's life, the risk of abuse on the part of avaricious relatives and friends, and in some contexts, whether there is a god in whom is vested the ultimate right to end a life, etc.

Now, of course, the critic could attempt to drive a wedge between (A3) and (A2) on the one hand and (A1) on the other, and claim that while the former two categories involve genuine arguments, the latter involves pseudo arguments. However, if the reason given for this division is simply that the evidence in an (A1) argument does not entail the conclusion, then, as shown in Chapter Two, by the same token the other two categories must also be considered to involve pseudo arguments.

The rudiment of an argument begins with a denial of what is the case. X asserts that p; Y denies that p is the case. This is the start of an argument. But an argument proper must go on to assert something else, q, to be the case in support of p which in turn prompts the denial that q is the case, and so on. A dispute which is confined solely to the bald assertion that p by one side and its denial by the other, and not carried on further by citing evidence, does not constitute a proper argument. It is in fact a pseudo argument. When parties behave like this, then they are being 'argumentative' in that pejorative sense of the word which means being 'pointlessly quarrelsome', and not in the relevant sense of advancing arguments. When Popper says that the argumentative use of language presupposes the descriptive use, he is using the term in the second sense. In that sense, it implies that evidence may be critically assessed. The notion of epistemic implication tries to explicate what is meant by 'evidence may be critically assessed'.

12   DISTINCTION BETWEEN THE ONTOLOGICAL STATUS OF VALUES/NORMS AND THEIR EPISTEMOLOGICAL STATUS

Epistemic implication, it is argued, is the logic of justification within the philosophical domain of ordinary knowledge (see Chapter Five), which includes ordinary factual assertions (A3), non-moral 'ought' assertions (A2) and moral 'ought' assertions (A1). The thesis is least controversial, one would expect, when it is applied to (A3) but most controversial when it is applied to (A1).

Only the most determined sceptic, that is the cognitive sceptic, would wish to deny that (A3) requires (E3) and (E3) provides rational warrant or support for (A3), even if s/he might not agree that epistemic implication correctly characterises the relationship between (A3) and (E3). Epistemologically speaking, the thesis is relatively unproblematic, especially to a positivist-minded philosopher, as it falls into the category of facts in the fact/value dichotomy.

To a positivist-minded philosopher, (A2) is also relatively unproblematic, for the 'ought' in question is the 'ought' of technical efficiency. Twentieth-century positivism holds that while ends (values) cannot be objectively and rationally argued for, and hence are irrational/non-rational, means are objectively and rationally determinable, once the end is given or chosen. This conception of rationality is that of means/end efficiency. Such a conception has no difficulty in accepting Kant's technical imperative of skill – a hypothetical imperative – as a principle of practical reasoning. It assumes that efficiency is an end or value which is universal, because if agents fail to adopt it or act upon it implicitly, they do not survive for long. Given such a predisposition, such philosophers again might not wish to deny that (A2) requires (E2), and that (E2) provides rational warrant or support for (A2), even if they might not agree that epistemic implication, as characterised, obtains between (A2) and (E2).

But to a contemporary positivist, the claim that (A1) epistemically requires (E1) is anathema, for it directly challenges the thesis which crucially follows from its understanding of the fact/value distinction, namely, that ends/values/norms are irrational. But that understanding is a misunderstanding. To see why it is so, we need to retrace some steps.

Chapter One dealt with the intellectual roots of twentieth-century positivism in moral philosophy – there, we saw that the main impulse is provided by logical positivism and its aftermath.[29] In the main, logical positivists (with the exception of a small minority like Schlick who regarded moral 'ought' propositions as disguised empirical propositions, reducible to factual propositions about feelings of approval/disapproval) held moral values/norms to be non-cognitive but affective in nature. As far as their ontological status is concerned, they are expressions of emotions. Epistemologically, their status is one of irrationality/non-rationality, and this is taken to follow from their ontological status *via* the principle of verifiability understood as a theory of meaning.

The second wave, represented by Hare's *The Language of Morals*, also regards values/norms as non-cognitive but differs from the first wave by saying that they are conative in nature. As far as their ontological status is concerned, they are products of the will (imperatives proceed from the will; later in *Freedom and Reason*, prescriptions replace imperatives, but prescriptions too emanate from the will, the conative side of the human agent). Epistemologically, they are deemed to be irrational. It is simply assumed without further argument that the will is not susceptible to rational persuasion, so that its products are necessarily irrational. This, however, did not deter Hare, unlike other positivists, from constructing a positivist science of morals. In doing so, as pointed out in Chapter One, he appears to combine the thesis of positivism with its anti-thesis to yield a Deducibility-Commitment account of moral values.[30]

Popper (whose views will be examined in Chapter Six) lived in Vienna and in many ways associated with the logical positivists before the advance of Nazism drove them away from Western Europe. Although he distanced himself from the Vienna Circle and did not see himself as a logical positivist, it remains that he is a positivist.[31] And on the question of values, he appears to agree with Hare (and Weber) that ontologically they are products of the will. As far as their epistemological status is concerned, he comes down in the end on the side of those who regard them as irrational. However, he differs from Hare in that he does not go on to build a positivist science of morals. As Popper is an influential philosopher of the post-war English-speaking philosophical world, it is justifiable to treat him (as well as Hare of *The Language of Morals*) as an important contributor to the formulation and the sustainence of the general twentieth-century positivist view with regard to values/norms.

Such a view embodies one confusion and one dogma. The confusion is the failure to distinguish between the ontology and the epistemology of values/norms. The dogma, already mentioned, is that the will is necessarily incapable of being rationally persuaded to adopt certain values and not others. However, Kant's moral philosophy is a quick reminder that the confusion is unnecessary and that the dogma is not unchallengeable – Kant agrees with twentieth-century positivism about the ontological status of moral values/norms, namely, that they are the products of the will; but he does not accept that necessarily such products are irrational.[32] Kant's arguments may not, upon critical scrutiny, be sound arguments; but that is a different matter.

As mentioned already in Chapter One, the history of positivism reveals at least one other alternative to the twentieth-century version of the fact/value distinction which avoids both the confusion and the dogma. This is Mill's fallibilism.[33] It is therefore deeply ironical that this book, which pursues the thesis of fallibilism as epistemic implication, should in the end find much in common with Mill's positivism,[34] and that his basic insight could be developed to overcome the inadequacies of twentieth-century positivism. Moreover, Chapter Six argues that this insight provides a more satisfactory ideological underpinning for liberalism than the contemporary positivism based on the Hare/Popper view of values/norms. Mill, like Kant, implies that their ontological status as products of the will does not entail that they are irrational products of volition. And it is their very rationality which dictates a free and liberal society.

Like Kant and Mill, this book seeks to combat that confusion and that dogma. It is not in the main concerned with the ontological thesis; it accepts the ontological status assigned to values/ norms by contemporary positivism (as well as by Mill and Kant).

The burden of the book lies in resisting the epistemological thesis which contemporary positivism claims is entailed by their ontological status.

Contemporary positivism relies in the main explicitly on the Naturalistic Fallacy to bridge the gap between its ontological and its epistemological theses. But if the arguments in Chapter Two and in this chapter succeed, then the verdict will be that it cannot be relied on to yield the desired epistemological conclusion. And if support is not forthcoming elsewhere other than from this traditional quarter, then twentieth-century positivism is indeed left holding the dogma, the unargued assumption that the will is essentially and necessarily irrational/non-rational.

However, the acceptance of this extreme assumption could have implications which not all moral philosophers sympathetic to the twentieth-century positivist fact/value distinction might wish to embrace. For instance, it might undermine even that conception of rationality as means/end efficiency; for efficiency too is a value/norm, which the will could opt to adopt or not as the fancy dictates. And worse still, even rationality itself may be optional, as it is a value/norm (though an intellectual value, but its ontological status is not different from that of so-called moral and non-moral values), which the will could adopt or reject according to whim.[35] This should have a sobering effect on those who do not wish to rush headlong into the intellectual abyss of total voluntarism, and should make them realise that it is not as easy to confine irrationality to the realm of moral values/norms as it has been made out to be. The fate of moral discourse is part and parcel of the fate of ordinary knowledge discourse in general. If the latter is intelligible, critical and rational, so is the former. If the latter is not intelligible, beyond the critical and the rational, nor is the former.

It is hoped too that the distinction between the ontological and the epistemological theses would remove the unease felt by philosophers like Mackie, who use the so-called argument from queerness to resist any attempt to re-integrate moral discourse with critical discourse in general. Mackie says: 'If there were objective values, then they would be entities or qualities or relations of a very strange sort, utterly different from anything else in the universe. Correspondingly, if we were aware of them, it would have to be by some special faculty of moral perception

126

or intuition, utterly different from our ordinary ways of knowing everything else.'[36]

Take the epistemological side of the queerness argument first. Mackie says that 'the central thesis of intuitionism is one to which any objectivist view of values is in the end committed: intuitionism merely makes unpalatably plain what other forms of objectivism wrap up.'[37] Either the faculty of intuition is a mysterious faculty or talk about ethical intuitions is merely a euphemistic way of talking about the individual's own responses, attitudes, feelings or the reflections of one's upbringing within a certain kind of society. The first possibility leads nowhere and obscures, rather than illuminates, the problem of how human beings come to hold certain moral values which they regard to be correct. The second is then the only plausible interpretation of what ethical intuition is and indeed of what it is for anyone to claim that he knows certain values to be correct. Mackie comes to this conclusion because he holds that 'none of our ordinary accounts of sensory perception or introspection or the framing or confirming of explanatory hypotheses or inference or logical construction or conceptual analysis, or any combination of these, will provide a satisfactory answer'[38] to the epistemological problem about moral values. It is indeed the burden of this book precisely to challenge this claim, to show that there is a domain of discourse, to which moral discourse belongs, the domain of ordinary knowledge in which the logic of justification obtains. If this account is tenable, then there is no need to resort to the unsatisfactory faculty of intuitionism; nor is there any need to regard the claim that there are objective values as involving epistemological queerness.

As for the ontological side of the queerness argument, by admitting that they are the products of the will (conative and not cognitive) they could be rendered unmysterious. At least philosophers on the whole have not found difficulty with the processes of deliberation, of making up one's mind to do something, and announcing that decision by words to the effect 'I/we will do X' or 'I/we/one ought to do X'. Values/norms are indeed human-made products. A world without people is a world without values/norms; a world without people is still a world with objects in it which we now call 'trees' and 'rocks'. A world without people possessing language in the way we do is clearly a world without moral 'ought' propositions. In this sense, values/norms are not part of the furniture of the world in the way trees, rivers and volcanoes are part of the furniture of the world.

Values/norms inform human conduct – we, as human agents, have to make up our minds (or will) how we act. They are not the products of God's will; nor are they to be discovered by us in the same way as Christopher Columbus discovered America. Moral discovery, if that term is used, should not be represented as something similar to a geographical discovery.

Christopher Columbus during his voyage came across a continent not formerly known to the Western world (if one discounts the hypothesis that the Vikings got there centuries earlier because it is unsubstantiated by the evidence available); this continent is North America even though Columbus thought that it was some other place he was hoping to get to. Such discoveries logically presuppose: (a) that there exists a chunk of land somewhere on the planet Earth whose location could be accurately specified; (b) that Columbus, the first Western discoverer of it, looked out of his porthole one morning and saw it there confronting him (at least part of it) whether he liked it or not and whether he was actually looking for it or not. (a) is metaphysically unproblematic – continents are material objects and exist in the same way as other material objects such as chairs and tables (although some philosophers dispute that material objects exist); (b) is epistemologically unproblematic – we know that a continent exists by seeing it, touching it, walking on it, digging it and nowadays taking aerial photographs of it, etc. (again, some sceptics might challenge that we know in these ways, of course).

But these presuppositions should not be applied to values/norms. One 'discovers' or finds out that certain values are supported/unsupported, justified or unjustified by assessing the evidence cited. The 'discovery' is not, therefore, like the discovery of a hitherto undiscovered continent or island. Continents and islands are part of the fabric of the world. They exist even if no one has ever set foot or set eyes on them or ever will (even under Berkelian phenomenalism, they exist because God is looking at them). The discovery that abortion in the early stages of pregnancy is morally justified (at least for Mackie) is an intellectual process of critically sifting arguments. This is, however, not to deny that there may be purely subjective and emotional considerations at work which may prompt an individual to seek for an objective justification of the stance s/he finds her/himself inclined to take; but whether such a justification may be found is independent of her/his inclination and emotions towards the issue in question.

Although the process is an intellectual one, it must not be assimilated to another well-known intellectual process, that of mathematical discovery. In mathematics, strict proof is available. Positivists and others make the mistake of elevating strict proof to be the only paradigm of a wholesome logical relationship between evidence and conclusion. The outcome of this ill-matched assimilation is full-scale scepticism not only in moral discourse but in areas where scepticism appears to be unwelcomed.

The discovery that a moral claim is justified/unjustified is no more and no less mysterious than the discovery that an ordinary factual claim (like, that I am not the biological offspring of my mother's husband) is justified/unjustified. Both involve critically assessing evidence cited in support of the claims.

To say that values/norms are non-cognitive is ambiguous – ontologically, they are conative, and therefore, non-cognitive. Epistemologically, they are part of our cognitive/intellectual operations. We come to know that it is right or justified to adopt certain values/norms/ends by means of our intellectual prowess and faculty. To speak pictorially, it is our intellect (the cognitive side) which persuades our will (the conative side) that it is rational to adopt certain values or to commit ourselves to certain courses of action and not others.

By clarifying the distinction between the ontological status of values/norms and their epistemological status, it is also hoped that one further possible misunderstanding that can militate against the acceptance of the thesis that moral discourse is part of critical discourse may be removed – in arguing that it is possible to justify values/norms rationally and objectively in terms of evidence which contains no 'ought', one is *not* arguing that propositions about moral values/norms are reducible to or translatable into propositions about facts. The thesis has nothing to do with reductionism whatsoever. On the contrary, it clearly recognises that they are normative in character. They are standards which inform and guide human conduct; as such they involve prescriptions.

The logical difference between prescription and description

remains intact. 'Critical dualism' as such is upheld.[39] The crucial point of difference, as the foregoing arguments try to establish, between those prescriptivists who are non-cognitivists and those who maintain the possibility of rationality/objectivity (including Hare from 1963 onwards) lies not in the latter's denial of the thesis of prescriptivism *per se*, but in the fact that for non-cognitivists, prescriptions are ultimately not capable of rational justification; whereas for their opponents, they are susceptible to such treatment.

Here one can suitably combine two insights, namely, the distinction between the ontological and the epistemological statuses of values/norms with the Popperian view, examined in the last section, that the argumentative use of language presupposes the descriptive use of language. The force of these two insights in the context of justifying moral 'ought' statements must be appreciated in two ways: (a) while moral propositions are clearly recognised to be prescriptive, it remains true that if they enter into an argument, they must be supported by other propositions which are not themselves necessarily prescriptions but are descriptions; (b) while realising that moral propositions are prescriptions, this does not mean that such propositions have no descriptive content or meaning whatsoever.

Point (a) has already been discussed. So let us turn to point (b). To say that 'it is morally right to kill in self-defence' implies that, for instance, if I perceive someone approaching me with a sawn-off shotgun, the fingers on the trigger, with every intent on the face to kill me, I will (other things being equal) throw my poison dart at him before that person presses the trigger. Unless we can give an intelligible account of such and similar situations *via* a description of them, that is to say, use language descriptively, we cannot begin to make prescriptions of the sort 'it is morally right (or wrong) to kill in self-defence'. Prescriptions entail certain courses of action. We cannot begin to carry out such actions unless we can describe such courses of action. The same goes for non-moral prescriptions such as 'One ought not to run financial risks, which are plainly foolish'. That implies that, if I have a sum of money available for investment, and I see an advertisement in the local papers which promises to give investors a phenomenal rate of return, I do not straightaway despatch my money to the advertiser in question without looking carefully into the credentials of such an operator. Unless we can give an intelligible account of such and similar situations by describing them, we cannot begin to make sense of the prescription in question.

The prescriptive use of language presupposes the descriptive use of language. This insight is indeed not lost on the positivist moral philosophers. Hare, following the Stevensonian tradition of regarding moral language as a combination of two sorts of meanings – emotive and descriptive – tries to incorporate the descriptive element in *Freedom and Reason via* what he calls weak descriptivism. He believes that weak, unlike strong descriptivism, will enable him to get the results he wants without falling into the trap of committing the Naturalistic Fallacy. For Hare, the problem of the possible rational justification of moral norms/prescriptions by reference to 'is' propositions, to descriptions, is transformed into the problem of combining prescriptive meaning with weak descriptive meaning. This venture into dual meanings which he feels obliged to embark upon in order to avoid committing the Naturalistic Fallacy, but yet to bestow some semblance of rationality on moral thinking, does not, however, succeed, for in the end the theses of weak descriptivism, universalisability and prescriptivism, together with the application of the logical principle of consistency, only yield at best a fortunate consensus of moral norms/prescriptions, which clearly is not the same as showing the possibility of procuring agreements in the long run by arguments which can be rationally and critically assessed. (See also Chapter One, Section 9.)

The thesis of epistemic implication which claims to be able to secure this possibility is able to preserve this insight of Hare – weak descriptivism – as well as to preserve critical dualism, but without falling prey to the Naturalistic Fallacy, because it does not maintain that 'ought' propositions are entailed by 'is' propositions.

IV

APPLICATION AND TESTING
OF EPISTEMIC IMPLICATION

The preceding chapter argues for the thesis '(A) epistemically implies (E)' – that (i) the truth-value of (A) is not independent of the truth-value of (E); (ii) that if (E) is true, (A) is true or corroborated; (iii) if (E) is false, then by *modus tollens*, (A) is false or refuted (but there is neither 'conclusive$_{D/A}$' verification or 'conclusive$_{D/A}$' falsification); (iv) that (E) must be serious and not flippant in order to satisfy the conditions of referential relevance and objectivity; (v) that (E) must be causally relevant to (A); (vi) that (E) must be causally independent of prior commitment to (A). This thesis will now be tested against (a) moral 'ought' assertions (A1) in order to establish that moral discourse is part of rational critical discourse; (b) against non-moral 'ought' assertions (A2) to show that there is no hiatus between (A1) and (A2) as far as their logic of justification goes; and (c) against ordinary factual assertions (A3) to establish that there is symmetry between (A1), (A2) and (A3) as far as the logic of justification is concerned.

1 FALSE (BUT CAUSALLY RELEVANT) EVIDENCE
DEFEATS ASSERTION

Consider the case where the evidence may be causally relevant but happens to be false, so that *modus tollens* occurs. Take two instances in which moral 'oughts' might be involved. The first concerns the Kantian dictum 'ought' epistemically implies 'can' *via* 'is'. Bartley cites the following argument:

> On our assumptions, the following argument is valid.
>
> Premise: <u>Jones ought to be a genius.</u>
>
> Conclusion: Jones can be a genius.
>
> And suppose that we have evidence indicating that the conclusion is false. We might learn, for instance, that Jones is suffering from extensive organic brain damage, or that he has an 'I.Q.' unusually below normal. Whilst one might reasonably question the results of an I.Q. test, one probably would accept sound evidence of massive damage as proof that it is false that Jones can be a genius. But then, by *modus tollens*, it is false that Jones ought to be a genius. And so we have used a factual consideration in evaluation and criticism of a moral statement.[1]

The next example does not involve the Kantian dictum. Take the doctrine of male chauvinism formulated as 'Women ought to obey men's will' (p). What serious causally relevant evidence might be offered in support of (p)? Suppose the upholder of male chauvinism cites as (c/rsE) that women are less intelligent than men. (Let us grant that 'being intelligent' is causally relevant to (p)). But it happens to be false. The truth of the matter is that the incidence of intelligence is about evenly divided between the sexes. So *modus tollens* obtains to defeat or refute (p). (p) fails to be supported by this particular piece of evidence, and the proponent of the doctrine would have to try again to make another case.

Now take a non-moral 'ought', of (A2/C2). Suppose I am sorting buttons, putting some into a box painted green and others into another painted red. Unless I am doing this to pass the time in a mindless fashion, then 'I ought to put some into the green box and others into the red' epistemically implies that, for instance, I believe that the green box buttons would sell at 30 cents or pence each, while those that go into the red box are worthless. This difference would be causally relevant to the way I treat them. But suppose I am wrong about the price those green box buttons would fetch; maybe they too are worthless. If so, I ought not to classify them any longer in the way I have been doing. *Modus tollens* operates here as well. I would not be justified in classifying the way I do unless some other reason is forthcoming which passes the test of being true as well as being causally relevant.

One need not linger long over (A3) as the last chapter has dealt with it at length. But here is one very brief example: 'this child is very short-sighted' may be supported by evidence such as 'this child wears very thick glasses'. But if it turns out that the child's glasses are fun glasses which have no lenses to them, then the assertion has been defeated, and unless another piece of causally relevant evidence is cited in its place which is true, the assertion remains uncorroborated or unjustified.

2 CAUSALLY IRRELEVANT (EVEN IF TRUE) EVIDENCE LEADS TO *NON-SEQUITUR* AND THEREFORE RENDERS THE ARGUMENT INVALID

What if the evidence cited is not so much false as causally irrelevant to the assertion. Suppose the reason cited in support of male chauvinism is that women do not have penises or that physically they bear children. As it stands the reason or evidence is plainly causally irrelevant to the issue whether women should be dominated by men. It is as irrelevant as saying that one must obey Z in whatever Z commands because Z plays the double bass. It is just a *non sequitur*. Upholders of the doctrine would have to look elsewhere for a different set of evidence if they want their 'ought' to be seriously justified. If the evidence cited is to be made relevant to the assertion, then it would have to be reformulated as follows: 'the sex without penises or which has to bear children physically is soft in the brain or cannot concentrate on anything more than two minutes at a time.' One could see how the possession of such attributes might render one a natural object of domination. But the reformulated evidence happens to be false. Once again in virtue of *modus tollens*, its falsity entails the falsity of the assertion.

In the case of the non-moral 'ought', suppose someone says that s/he ought to redecorate the living-room because the living-room is on the ground floor, we fail to understand what s/he is really talking about, unless s/he can convince us somehow that there is a causal link somewhere which no one else has perceived as yet. In the absence of such an explanation, the reason or evidence remains causally irrelevant to the assertion, although true. The evidence, again, is *non sequitur*.

3 TRUE AND CAUSALLY RELEVANT EVIDENCE MAY STILL BE RULED OUT BY THE CONDITION OF CAUSAL INDEPENDENCE

And what if the evidence cited is neither false, nor causally irrelevant to the assertion, but may yield results in the case of moral 'ought' assertions which seem intuitively unacceptable to some people? This, as we saw, can be ruled out by the requirement that the causally relevant evidence be causally independent of the prior commitment to the norm embodied in the assertion. There is, therefore, no need to deny the fact that moral norms are part of social norms which if taken up and practised within a given society could causally bring about certain consequences, which in their turn might be cited by those who wish to maintain the norms in question as justifications of the norms themselves. Since this point has already been dealt with in the last chapter, one may be brief here. Before black consciousness took roots in America,[2] the dominant social norm was that negroes ought to be treated in an inferior manner because as a matter of fact they are inferior in every way compared to their white counterparts. Here the evidence cited appears to be true and causally relevant. But although true and causally relevant, if it can itself be shown to be a causal consequence of accepting and acting upon the norm referred to in the assertion, then to postulate the norm on grounds that the evidence obtains is to beg the very point at issue, to commit a *petitio principii*. The backwardness of the inferior orders being the result of long years of domination by the higher orders, so the system produces the effect and the effect is used to justify the system. This may be said to be a case of special pleading which logic textbooks tell us vitiates an argument.

Take a parallel from a non-moral 'ought'. Suppose someone says: 'One ought not to sell houses to coloured people' not because they are inferior or despicable but for economic reasons. The presence of coloured people in a neighbourhood brings down the

135

value of houses. Such reason or evidence is both true and causally relevant but the evidence is itself the product of a prior commitment to the norm that coloured people are somehow inferior, undesirable and lower the tone of the area. If so, the non-moral 'ought' as it stands is all right but if pressed beyond it to the moral 'ought' of discrimination, it would not do to cite such evidence.

4 TESTING THE THESIS *VIA* THE PRACTICAL SYLLOGISM

Next the problem of validating moral 'oughts' will be dealt with from a slightly different aspect and the arguments will be re-cast in a different logical mould – this time in the form of the traditional syllogism. The doctrine of male chauvinism, for instance, now reads:

> All unintelligent persons ought to obey intelligent persons who are male.
> All women are unintelligent persons.
> All women ought to obey intelligent persons who are male.

The above syllogism is undoubtedly valid. However, one may challenge a syllogism on two grounds: (a) that the conclusion is invalidly derived; and (b) that its premises are false or unacceptable in some ways. A critic of male chauvinism confronted by the above valid syllogism would straightaway rebut it by pointing out that the minor premise is false. Therefore, the syllogism which the upholders of the doctrine of male chauvinism are really deploying in their argument is the following:

> All unintelligent persons ought to obey intelligent persons who are male.
> It is not the case that all women are unintelligent persons
> (or there are just as many unintelligent persons amongst males as there are amongst females).
> All women ought to obey intelligent persons who are male.

This clearly is invalid. By challenging the minor premise, the critic has succeeded in showing that the exponent of the doctrine has argued and is arguing in an invalid manner. The 'ought' in the conclusion is not entailed by the major premise and the particular revised minor premise in question. The use of deductive logic together with the demand of truth have shown that the argument actually deployed is an invalid one. The upholder of male chauvinism would need again to produce a different and better syllogism. In its absence, one is permitted to conclude that the case for male chauvinism has not been made.

What if the defender of sexual inequality refuses to admit that the minor premise is false? A standard tactic adopted in the face of counter-evidence is to turn an empirical proposition into a tautology – in this case, by making it true as a matter of definition that only males are intelligent and the only intelligent persons are males. When black swans were first discovered in Australia, the proposition 'all swans are white' became falsified. The proposition was amended to 'some swans are white'. This means that the original proposition is held as an empirical proposition (part of scientific discourse) which could be falsified or has been falsified. However, it is conceivable that upon the discovery of such black creatures, that someone in refusing to admit the counter-example would be prepared to turn the proposition into a tautology, so that anything which is anatomically like a swan, looks and behaves like one, but is not white is not a swan.

Extreme white racists might claim in the same spirit that black people are not human beings since in their usage no one who is black counts as a human being no matter how like a white person s/he may be in other respects. This move would be in keeping with the Myth of the Infinite Arbitrariness of Classifications which, as we saw, Harré says is part of the positivist thesis of deductivism. In this way, it is claimed that the proposition may be saved from falsification, but the price paid for it renders it trivially true. Unlike a taxonomic principle (like the one which says that swans, both black and white, belong to the same taxon) which is based on a complicated understanding of these creatures about their anatomy, physiology, ethology, evolutionary history, etc., this kind of definitional legislation and creation is *ad hoc* based on a single difference in manifest characteristics and introduced in the face of knowledge about a whole range of other similarities, turning it into an arbitrary matter about what counts and what does not count as belonging to the same taxon. The syllogism might remain valid, but its conclusion is suspect since it follows as a result of special pleading.

Suppose the minor premise to be true and the argument is valid. Can one still challenge the conclusion by challenging the major premise? Not on the orthodox view as purveyed by Hare who tries to combine the positivist criterion of deducibility with the thesis of conceptual relativism based on the form of life argument. A major premise containing an 'ought' when challenged may be defended by subsuming it under a more general premise also containing an 'ought'. But the process of subsumption and justification comes to an end when a complete specification of a way of life is given by the most general major premise that can be formulated. When this stage is reached, in *The Language of Morals*, Hare says justification comes to an end. The matter is simply sealed by a commitment or decision to adopt or abide by the way of life encapsulated in the most general major premise. Hence morality is ultimately irrational and subjective. According to him, it is no good trying to justify a whole way of life by appealing to consequences, since these are purely factual matters, and no 'oughts' or imperatives are entailed by factual premises.

Hare reaches this impasse because he supports the Naturalistic Fallacy which, although correct in maintaining that 'is' cannot strictly entail 'ought', is, nevertheless, wrong in concluding that morality is irrational. His blind adherence to the positivist *Grundnorm* has prevented him from seeing the possibility that 'ought' epistemically implies 'is'. If this thesis obtains, then 'oughts', as we have argued, may be supported or may fail to be supported by evidence which do not themselves contain 'oughts'.

We have already seen how such justifications may be challenged. But to labour an important point, take the following example:

All people under six feet ought to be bossed by those over six feet tall.
All Jews are under six feet tall.
All Jews ought to be bossed by those over six feet tall.

For the sake of the argument, let us grant that the minor premise is factually true. To challenge the conclusion which is validly derived, one must, therefore, challenge the major premise. Whoever advances such an argument must give serious and causally relevant evidence for classifying and treating two groups as belonging to different types. But if s/he simply refuses to supply reasons containing no 'oughts' because of the Naturalistic Fallacy, then the refusal either commits a *petitio principii* or amounts to a simple determination to exclude morality from serious critical discourse. The former, because the issue here is precisely whether the logical gulf entails irrationality or not. To insist that it does is simply to invoke the very thing that is at issue. The latter, because in the absence of further reason why morality is to be excluded from critical discourse, its exclusion can only be arbitrary. But if such reasons are given, then one can in the ways already discussed assess them in a critical manner. In the case of the reason being false, then *modus tollens* operates to defeat or falsify the major premise, etc.

On Hare's view in *The Language of Morals* (actually the historical Hare is irrelevant to the point that will be made. One is merely using his position in his earlier book as an instance of this kind of anti-rational meta-ethics), even the most eccentric and whimsical principle may become a moral principle simply because someone decides to commit oneself sincerely to it. Suppose someone says: 'I ought to kill every third person I meet each morning.' Now according to the thesis of epistemic implication, even such a person is not exempt from the requirement of providing a serious causally relevant reason for this 'ought', as the proposal is based on (a) maintaining a difference between the speaker and those s/he intends to kill, and (b) maintaining a difference between 'every third person s/he meets in the morning' and others who do not happen to fall into that slot in the sequence. With regard to both (a) and (b) one doubts if s/he could produce evidence which satisfies at once the criteria of truth, causal relevance and causal independence. In the absence of such evidence, s/he can but cite flippant evidence. But as it has already been argued, (fE) is not an answer to a moral 'ought' question, since it has nothing to do with the correct/incorrectness of (A1) but has to do with the attitude on the part of the speaker towards (A1).

But what if in regard to (a), s/he cites spatio-temporal differences between her/himself and others, 'because I am born on such and such a date, etc.'? This can be ruled out by the check of causal relevance. Spatio-temporal characteristics *per se* do not directly enter into causal matters. Of course, for instance, we do say 'Monday morning brings on the gloom'. We do not, however, mean that the mere fact that Monday is the day in the week which comes between Sunday and Tuesday can have causal effects. What we do mean is that people have to go back to work and the thought of that brings on the depression. Similarly, if we say that people who live above latitude 60° north are more prone to suicide than those who do not, again we are not assigning causal effects to spatial characteristics *per se*. It is an elliptical way of saying that above that latitude, one hardly sees the sun for months on end, and it is cold, etc., which (supposing all this to be true) make people unable to face life any more. Again suppose a Muslim tells you that s/he ought to try to be good on a Friday whereas s/he may be a 'lapsed' Muslim on other days of the week. What s/he says would be unintelligible if s/he is understood to refer to Friday simply as the day that stands between Thursday and Saturday. Friday has significance for Muslims because it is the Muslim 'sabbath', the day set aside specially for godly and morally laudable pursuits.

5 APPLYING EPISTEMIC IMPLICATION TO MACKIE'S ARGUMENTS ON ABORTION

So far the examples cited to test the thesis of epistemic implication are ones formulated by the author of the thesis. As such the charge could be made that even if these examples pass the tests proposed, they could do so because they have been specially selected and tailor-made to fit the thesis. As such they might be suspect and the thesis remains 'non-proven', as it were. To overcome this objection, an example will now be examined which is not provided by the author at all but by J. L. Mackie in his book on ethics. His arguments on behalf of the claim that abortion is morally justified will be analysed in the light of the thesis and they will be shown to satisfy the criteria laid down. So notwithstanding Mackie's own meta-ethical position, which is one of moral scepticism (he believes in the 'error theory' about the thesis of moral objectivity), his arguments for abortion may be shown to conform to the logic of fallibilism when enriched as suggested.

It would be advisable to quote him in full so that the reader can be assured that there is no deliberate distortion of his arguments to suit the thesis being pursued:

There are three main grounds that are held to justify abortion: it may be needed to prevent a grave risk to the mother's life or health; there may be good reasons to expect that if the child is born it will suffer from some serious permanent defect; or the mother simply may not want a child – or another child, or this particular child, for example if it has been conceived as a result of rape – and it may be held that she has a right not to have her body used by or for what she does not want. . . . The basic argument against abortion, on which all others build, is that the unborn child is already a human being, a person, a bearer of rights, and that abortion is murder. This is essentially a continuity argument. Given that we want to regard a newly-born baby as a person, and to forbid the killing of it as murder, it seems arbitrary to distinguish between this and the killing of an unborn child almost at full term, and then the argument can be carried back step by step until immediately after conception. It is, of course, quite implausible to carry it back any further. Though ova and sperms are, taken in pairs, potential human beings, nature is far too lavish in its production of them, particularly the latter, for us to accord them a right to life. But why should conception or fertilisation be taken as the point of distinction? It is true that it is the only salient point, the only discontinuity between the ovum and sperm that have no right to life and the baby just before birth, which has. (Birth itself is, of course, another salient point.) But this discontinuity is a very inadequate ground for the required moral distinction. It would be more reasonable to think of the right or claim to life as growing gradually in strength, but as still being very slight immediately after conception. Then we might well conclude that the third ground for abortion is valid early in pregnancy – the mother's right to the control of her own body then outweighs the child's right to life – but not late in pregnancy. The first ground, however, according to the graveness of the risk to the mother's life, might be valid at any time up to birth. The second ground, the likelihood of serious permanent defect, also seems to be valid at any time up to birth. In saying this I am relying on the presumption that not only is it much against the interests of the parents (or whoever else will have to look after it) and the other members of the family that

141

the child should survive, but it is also against the child's own interest. Of course this brings us back to the question of euthanasia: if a child is born with such a severe defect, should it then be killed? The view that it should is supported by the reflection that it is only by a fiction that we regard a newly-born child as a person. It is surely not yet conscious of itself as itself, as a distinct and potentially continuing being. It cannot be seen as making even an unspoken demand that it should continue in existence which would need to be weighed against any other presumptions about its interests. Nor can we appeal against this view to what was said . . . about a humane disposition: in this case reflective humanity would require that the child should be killed. What does tell against this view is that this rule cuts across the classifications that are most natural to us and very well established in ordinary thought: this would be seen as the deliberate killing of an independent human being, not at his own request. Here birth is a salient point, a popularly acceptable ground of distinction: abortion is seen as different from the killing of what is now a separately existing human being. In principle, therefore, I think that a baby born with a very severe permanent defect should not be allowed to survive; but recognition of this principle must be conditional upon widespread appreciation of what makes this distinct from other cases of killing – that is upon its being seen and felt why this is not murder.[3]

Now to the analysis of Mackie's arguments. First: the basic thesis contested by anti- and pro-abortionists – whether an unborn child is already a human being, a person, a bearer of rights. If the evidence available supports the conclusion that it is, then it can be shown that abortion is murder. The construction of such an argument may take the usual unproblematic form of a syllogism: killing (innocent) human beings is murder; an unborn child is a human person; therefore, killing an unborn child is murder. It is assumed by both sides that the moral claim 'killing innocent human beings is murder' is not contentious. The major premise is common ground. What is crucial is the minor premise: an unborn child is a human being (A).

Reformulating Mackie a little, he may be said to have advanced two arguments for saying that (A) is incorrect: (i) an unborn child has a foetal existence usually of nine months during which very dramatic developments take place. The process starts off with ovum meeting sperm, the ingredients for producing human beings. But they are only the ingredients for the potential production of human beings. They are not themselves human beings and therefore the bearers of rights. (Mackie's argument here is actually that they are too lavishly produced by nature to be accorded a right to life – this is not a good argument for surely, Mackie would not want to say that abundance is an excuse for extinction, otherwise, his argument could be consistently used by a racist to exterminate an ethnic group which is considered to be breeding too fast altogether); (ii) after fertilisation, life begins. But the claim to life is very weak at the beginning of conception but grows as the embryological processes become more and more advanced, so that in the early stages of pregnancy it is unjustified to talk of the unborn child as a human person but justified in very late pregnancy.

Mackie in these arguments is not relying on methods, modes of procedure, etc. which are mysterious in any way or peculiar only to moral controversy. He is basically making distinctions which he justifies in accordance with the thesis that classification requires serious and causally relevant evidence, by appealing to certain salient facts of the case and to a certain body of scientific knowledge and empirical assumptions and claims, as well as to logical methods of assessment which are accepted elsewhere in critical discourse.

Reformulated argument (i) above (a) relies on the same logic as is used in the following non-moral example: a cake is a mixture made up of the basic ingredients like flour, milk (or water), egg, butter (or fat of some kind), sugar, etc. The separate ingredients do not constitute a cake – a cake is the result of mixing them together and then baking the mixture. If I have only the ingredients sufficient to make ten cakes sitting in the larder or the refrigerator, I do not say nor am I entitled to say that I have ten cakes in there. To do so would be very misleading indeed. Neither am I justified to charge you the price of ten cakes if I were selling the ingredients to you or to claim that the local cookery class should award me with a certificate for having produced the required number of cakes. The human foetus is analogous to the cake; the sperms and ova to the cake ingredients. Argument (ii) above rests on the sciences of embryology, gynaecology, physiology, biochemistry, etc. From these two arguments, Mackie concludes that legitimate distinctions may be made between the different stages of foetal development: (a) sperm and ovum before fertilisation do not and cannot count as human beings; (b) neither does the foetus in its early stages of development count as a human being; (c) in its late stages of development, one would be justified to regard it as a human being. Hence the minor premise – an unborn child is a human being (A) – is only true in late pregnancy.

Mackie uses the conclusions arrived at above to support and justify abortion in early pregnancy but not in late pregnancy only when it is a case of the mother simply not wanting a child (the third ground). This argument involves a conflict of rights – the right of the mother to the control of her own body and the right of the unborn child (in late pregnancy) to life, and the priority rule that the latter takes precedence over the former. The priority rule is asserted by Mackie and not argued for, which could be explained by the fact that Mackie is engaged with a fragment of a moral viewpoint and not with the systematic defence of a more comprehensive theory which would indeed have to try to justify such a rule. But the beginning of a defence of the rule might be made in the following way: the mother's life and the life of the unborn child are both innocent; to argue that the former should take precedence over the latter on the ground that the child's existence would interfere with and cause great changes in the lifestyle of the mother is unacceptable because the general principle it involves is unacceptable – accepting it would mean in consistency condoning the killing of any individual or classes of individuals whose very existence causes great inconvenience and disruption to the lives of other individuals. Consistency then demands that abortion of an unborn child in late pregnancy who counts as a human being for the convenience of the mother would be morally wrong. If an extreme pro-abortionist wishes to challenge this conclusion, then to be successful, s/he must be able to produce evidence which satisfies the demands of being serious, causally relevant and consistent with what s/he accepts elsewhere in other areas of argument.

Mackie, however, argues that the conclusions are not sufficient to justify the condemnation of abortion even in late pregnancy up to the time of birth if it is to prevent a grave risk to the mother's life or health (his first ground for abortion). He does not again spell out the distinction between this case and the case just discussed, but it may be said to rest on the following point: while the third ground for abortion rests on grave inconvenience or disruption to the adult life, the first ground for abortion rests on grave risk to that life and its health. In this sense, the child's continued existence may not be said to be entirely 'innocent' as it might cause death or very severe damage to the mother, albeit not intentionally. This then makes the case at first sight to rest on the doctrine of necessity – namely, a case where the first party cannot itself survive without the death of the second. For example, those on a life-boat already fully loaded having to push off and drown those struggling to climb on board.

However, the law itself does not condone necessity although it recognises the very special circumstances involved. In 1884 the case of *Stephens* arose which concerned three men and a boy shipwrecked 1600 miles off the Cape of Good Hope. Food would sooner or later run out. There was virtually no hope of being rescued before then. The three men conferred and decided that in the eventuality of starvation, the weakest amongst them would be killed and eaten by the rest. In the event, they killed the boy who was the weakest and ate him. Contrary to all expectation, they were later rescued, returned to civilisation, were tried and found guilty of murder, but were later pardoned. So Mackie must distinguish between such a case from the first ground for abortion. Necessity in the latter may be morally justified (even if one, like the law, regards necessity in the former not to be so) because the unborn child at even a very late stage of pregnancy is unlike the young boy, not a properly and fully developed human person. The young boy had language, was self-conscious, probably knew what was going to be his fate, had memories, etc., whereas an unborn child even in late pregnancy is not a fully developed human being. This we know because of our understanding of not only neuro-physiology, biochemistry or whatever of the human organism but also of psychology and of human life, involving the acquisition of language, the formation of notions of the self, of social institutions, etc. In the light of this understanding, it is not

145

arbitrary to distinguish an unborn child who is regarded as a human being from a developed human being.

Finally Mackie justifies the second ground for abortion, which comes close to euthanasia, of an unborn child, even up to the time of birth or at birth itself, if there are good reasons for believing that the child if born will suffer from permanent and serious disability on two grounds which operate jointly: (1) consideration of the child's own interest (not so much those of the family and those who have to care for him); and (2) the fiction, as he puts it, that a newly born child or an unborn one at a very late stage of pregnancy is a fully developed person. The second ground may be passed over since it is really the same argument as the one used in the previous paragraph. The first involves a consideration of the so-called 'quality of life' argument employed in justifying euthanasia.

To succeed, this argument must (i) show that medical opinion is convinced that the damage is both very grave and permanent; (ii) establish that there is virtually no likelihood in the foreseeable future of a medical breakthrough and cure; (iii) show that the defect would render the child utterly dependent on others or machines for survival, that the range of possible activity open to such a defective human being, both mental and physical, is extremely limited, that these defects would prevent a proper development of the child's potentiality, etc. Again Mackie would be appealing to extant scientific knowledge and assumptions, making distinctions which are not arbitrary but in accordance with our understanding of human development and of the conditions under which agents could perform certain actions and not others. If the unborn child suffers from extensive and severe brain damage, such damage can be shown to be causally relevant to the impairment of the ability or capacity for development. It is, therefore, not arbitrary to maintain that it would not be in the child's own interest to lead an existence which could not be said to be consonant with that possible for normal persons as the potentiality for development in the case in question has been so drastically and so unfortunately curtailed.

The evidence or reasons which Mackie gives in support of his views on abortion are perfectly amenable to critical assessment. They are arguments, which can be criticised from the point of view of the truth of the claims made and of their validity. He cites serious evidence (not flippant ones); evidence which is causally relevant to the assertions he is making. His evidence is in accordance with extant scientific knowledge and assumptions. He also abides by the normal logical principles of avoiding inconsistencies, self-contradictions (and detecting them in the arguments of his opponents), by the rules of reasoning such as the *modus tollens* – that false evidence defeats the assertion and the rule that true evidence verifies or corroborates it, etc. As such, through the actual arguments he puts forward, he has shown that moral discourse is part of rational critical discourse and not, as his overt meta-ethics would lead him to say, that moral scepticism prevails, and that it is a mistake to believe in the possibility of objective moral values.

6   MORAL PHILOSOPHY AND META-ETHICS

The main opponent to the thesis about the possibility of moral discourse being rational' and critical is assumed to be the subscribers of the Naturalistic Fallacy. The strategies, positive and negative, pursued in meeting the challenge they present consist of making clear the inconsistencies and absurdities to which they would be led by the meta-ethics which they hold. But might there not be another kind of moral philosopher who wants nothing to do with meta-ethics but nevertheless attempts to build up some kind of a moral system? Someone might maintain that, for instance, a moral philosophy could be built round the moral vision of the superman, by simply maintaining that moral superiority consists in being ruthless and aggressive (amongst others s/he deems desirable), that anyone possessing them is morally superior and ought to have superior rights. (This example should not be understood to imply that Nietzsche held such a view.)

It is fair to say that a plain person moralising might not necessarily be led into the murky waters of meta-ethics. But such a plain person who is never led at some point to reflect on the nature of one's assertions and how they can be validated (or not) must be a mere creature of moral habits. But the moment one starts to reflect and ponder about the source, origin and *raison d'être* of the moral prescriptions one adheres to, one would sooner or later be involved with the central preoccupations of moral philosophy, which include the nature of moral discourse and the justification of moral values. In fact the moment one's moral values are challenged by another and one finds oneself forced to defend them, one would stop being a plain moraliser and start to engage in doing moral philosophy. If so, then it is difficult to see how anyone can claim not to be involved with issues in meta-ethics if they were trying to build up a moral system. If people were simply to make assertions and make no pretence whatsoever at justifying them, but at the same time maintain that they are enunciating very important insights or truths, then they should be rightly dismissed as moral *gurus* and need not be taken seriously as moral philosophers. To avoid the risk of being disregarded by philosophers, they must be prepared to give some kind of justification.

They could say (in the case of someone who believes in the correctness of the superman philosophy), 'I just do approve of such qualities, and approve of people with such qualities, and I approve of giving people with such qualities superior rights.' Clearly, they are citing a flippant reason, in which case they are in the same position as the Naturalistic Fallacy subscriber who produces (fE) because one cannot derive 'ought' from 'is', in which case the arguments deployed against (fE) would be relevant against them. But if they fall back on ethical relativism and the form of life argument, by saying that in their society what counts as moral superiority is precisely the possession of such characteristics like aggressiveness which are deemed desirable, and that for such a society moral 'truth' consists in maintaining this, then one would indicate to them the drawback of this move from their point of view, namely, that they cannot claim universality for their norms, since other alternative forms of ethical life are just as valid as their own. This might not be palatable to those who believe in the superman morality as they would not be noted for their spirit of tolerant (new) liberalism and benevolence to all moral norms, regardless of their content. If they wish to eradicate 'evil' in the form of humility, gentleness or kindness in the name of what is 'right' and 'good', accepting the form of life position would modify their thesis to such an extent that it would become no longer recognisably theirs – it will now read: for us, moral 'good' consists of naked self-assertion; for others, it is love or whatever; but that view is just as right and just as valid as ours. It is doubtful if they would find this tolerable.

But suppose they do. One then points out to them that ethical relativism is a species of cognitive relativism – accepting the former consistently leads them to embracing the latter (in virtue of the form of life argument being a general epistemological argument), and its implications. Suppose upon reflection they do not want to buy relativism at all in view of its implications, then they might actually even fall into the trap that is being laid for them – they might indeed try to justify their position in terms of serious evidence which can be critically appraised and assessed, in which case they would have conceded that moral discourse is part of rational critical discourse. Then there can be genuine discussion. The discussion may be endless and endlessly complicated but they would be sharing the same ground rules as their opponents who challenge their substantive views as to what counts as a cogent argument, what is relevant evidence and what is not.

7 DO TRANSCENDENT MORAL THEORIES FAIL TO SATISFY THE CONDITIONS FOR EPISTEMIC IMPLICATION?

There is, however, yet another kind of moral theorist who might be said to elude the net – the theorists who use transcendent (i.e. theistic) arguments. But do they? First, it is important to bear in mind that the thesis that moral discourse is rational critical discourse should not be misunderstood as implicitly maintaining what amounts to logical positivism, which throws out theological discourse from the domain of intelligible meaningful discourse, or simple-minded empiricism, which throws it out from the domain of the real, because it is not directly verifiable. Any discourse counts as part of serious critical discourse provided it abides by certain criteria which govern the validation of assertions. So what is relevant here is the question, whether theological discourse satisfies these criteria. If it does, then this is fine. But if it cannot, as some theologians themselves seem to admit, then it cannot do the job of justifying moral 'oughts' in a rational manner. These theologians explicitly claim that theology falls on the side of the irrational,[4] by relying on sincere commitment to their belief in

God, and on cognitive relativism based on the form of life argument. As a result they may maintain that the criteria of 'validity' governing theological discourse may be different from those obtaining elsewhere like in science, but they are equally valid. But the irrationality implicit in such a theory of rationality which lays down the limits of rationality has been already discussed and there is no need to go into it again here.

Second, one could point out, as it has often been done, that deriving morality from God is really putting the cart before the horse, since we need to have a prior notion of what is morally good and right before we can identify them as commands from God and not another theological entity like the devil. Those who base their morality on theology do not simply rely on an appeal to naked authority, but on the argument that God's authority is worthy of human submission precisely because God is by definition a being who is good and perfect. So the whole argument involves circularity, since morality is derived from God and God is implicitly derived from morality, as God is defined in moral terms.

Third, one could also point out to them that they are in danger of committing the Naturalistic Fallacy, that it is not possible to derive 'ought' from 'is' even if the 'is' is not about empirically verifiable matters but transcendent matters.

Fourth, moreover, many conflicting accounts of God's commands exist and therefore, not all of them could be true – appealing to one's own conception of the deity cannot solve the problem of distinguishing the true from the false. If an attempt at such distinction can be shown to abide by the critical criteria normally employed, then theology too would be shown to be part of critical discourse, and a morality validated in terms of it would also be part of such discourse.

8 THE LOGIC AND CONTENT OF DISCOURSE

However, a determined critic of epistemic implication could still mount the following objection: even if one grants that moral discourse is part of serious critical discourse and that its logic follows by and large the outline sketched, have you then not abolished all differences between moral and other forms of discourse? For you, a moral 'ought' is no different from a non-moral 'ought' or indeed from an ordinary factual assertion, since all these assertions are to be validated by the same procedure.

Now one must admit that this book is confined to establishing a similarity in the validation of (A1), (A2) and (A3). But this does not mean that the logic of moral assertions or of moral 'oughts' is all that one can legitimately be concerned with. The formalists (the label which supporters of the Naturalistic Fallacy sometimes wear) have to maintain that the logic alone is relevant, for to talk about the content of moral norms runs the risk of committing the Naturalistic Fallacy. But the goal here is different from theirs – the object of the exercise of laying bare the procedure of validation of the 'ought' is to prepare the ground for fruitful exploration into the building of substantive moral theories, and the critical appraisal of them, an enterprise ruled out as logically impossible, so long as one cannot overcome the Naturalistic Fallacy.

The position is analogous to someone who maintains that a variety of different discourses all fall under the rubric of scientific discourse. But this is not to deny that there are no differences between geology, astronomy, botany or any other scientific subject you care to mention. Geology studies rocks, astronomy the stars, planets and other heavenly bodies, etc. The domain of each is clear as far as the subject matter is concerned although there may be overlaps, and even sometimes the incorporation of one by the other. Similarly, ordinary factual claims are about the world of physical events, processes and things, of sensory experience and of other possible worlds (of extra-sensory experience, mystical experience, etc.); non-moral 'ought' claims, some maintain, can be reduced to the rule of means/end efficiency which yields a rationality norm in practical reasoning which governs human conduct in matters of expediency; moral 'ought' claims lay down norms which govern human conduct in personal and inter-personal relationships, but without the benefit of reliance on physical sanctions which legal norms require or on religious sanctions. Nor are they to be reduced to expediency claims. One obeys a moral 'ought' not because one is afraid of being punished by an external authority if one did not, nor because obedience would be instrumental in promoting some such goal as getting rich or securing eternal bliss or temporal comforts, but because it is right. And the question what constitutes right is indeed what sets in motion the whole subject called moral philosophy.

9 CHECKS OR TESTS OF ADEQUACY

If epistemic implication were a tenable account of the logic of justification, then Popper[5] notwithstanding, it might not be too far-fetched to suggest that the process of eliminating errors through criticism of hypotheses in the natural sciences may be said to be paralleled by an analogous attempt to eliminate error in the value sphere. Bartley has proposed four ways of doing so in the sciences:

(1) The check of *logic*: Is the theory in question consistent? (2) The check of *sense observation*: Is the theory empirically refutable by some sense observation? And if it is, do we know of any refutation of it? (3) The *check of scientific theory*: Is the theory, whether or not in conflict with sense observation, in conflict with any scientific hypotheses? (4) The check of the *problem*: What problem is the theory intended to solve? Does it do so successfully?'[6]

Analogously, a moral claim may be checked by the following tests: (1) the check of *logic*: is the claim in question consistent? Is the conclusion of such a claim supported by the evidence cited, that is, (i) is the evidence relevant (referentially and causally) to the putative knowledge claim? (ii) if so, and if such evidence actually obtains in the case in question (that is, if it passes the check of facts), then the claim is supported or justified; if the evidence does not obtain, then by *modus tollens*, the claim is defeated, not justified or incorrect; (2) the check of *facts*: is the causally relevant evidence cited true? (3) the check of *empirical/ scientific assumptions and claims*: does the claim conflict with well-established scientific hypotheses and commonly accepted empirical generalisations (such as, people will die if they do not have air to breathe or sufficient food to eat, people will decline in mental alertness if they live in a non-stimulating environment); (4) the check of the *problem*: what problem is the claim trying to solve? Does it do so successfully?

A moral claim may have to be rejected because of the faulty logic between its conclusion and the evidence cited in its support. The claim that people ought to be treated badly because they have black skins is to be rejected because it fails to pass the test of causal relevance; the claim that good is what God commands is to be rejected because it commits circularity; the claim that male homosexuality is immoral while, say, maintaining that lesbianism is not is to be rejected because it violates consistency.

A moral claim may have to be rejected because it is based on or implies false factual claims or claims which conflict with well-established scientific theories and empirical generalisations. The claim that women are men's inferiors because they are less intelligent than men is to be rejected because the evidence cited is false. The claim that it is morally all right to impose summary decisions on children because they are not in a position to appreciate one's reasons is to be rejected because it is not true that children, even very young ones, are thus incapable. The claim that it is morally permissible to subject animals to painful experiments for the purpose of advancing medical research because there is no other way of achieving the same objective is to be rejected because it is not true that it is the most efficient and the only way.

A moral claim may have to be rejected because it does not do the job adequately to which it seemingly addresses itself – suppose the moral problem is the perennial one of how to get hold of a principle of just distribution. Utilitarians seem to think that they are trying to solve this problem. However, their familiarly formulated principle – the greatest happiness of the greatest number – fails to be a proper policy guide because it requires the decision-maker to maximise two different functions at the same time.[7] One may maximise the greatest happiness, irrespective of distribution, or one may maximise the greatest number, even if it may fall short by the first function. But one cannot do both at once. In practice, the utilitarians in general maximise the former while hoping that it will not be too unfair in the distribution. This leads them to concentrate on growth and not on distribution, without realising that promoting the former is not necessarily promoting the latter. To say that the cake has grown to a larger size so that everyone's slice is larger relative to the slice they had when the cake was smaller is not the same as saying that at any one moment in time, one person's slice in relation to that of another is bigger

153

or smaller than it. Utilitarianism is generally wide off the mark and cannot be taken as a theory to meet the problem posed by just distribution.

Take another theory which is also designed to meet the distributive problem. This time it fails because it makes assumptions which violate the check of empirical/scientific claims and assumptions. This is Nozick's distributive theory. In reformulating Locke, he puts forward the following principles of just distribution:

> The subject of justice in holdings consists of . . . the *original acquisition of holdings*, the appropriation of unheld things . . . the principle of justice in acquisition. The second topic concerns the *transfer of holdings* from one person to another. By what processes may a person transfer holdings to another? How may a person acquire a holding from another who holds it? Under this topic come general descriptions of voluntary exchange, and gift. . . . The complicated truth about this subject . . . we shall call the principle of justice in transfer. . . . If the world were wholly just, the following inductive definition would exhaustively cover the subject of justice in holdings: 1. A person who acquires a holding in accordance with the principle of justice in acquisition is entitled to that holding. 2. A person who acquires a holding in accordance with the principle of justice in transfer, from someone else entitled to the holding, is entitled to the holding. 3. No one is entitled to a holding except by (repeated) applications of 1 and 2.[8]

In order for this theory to work, it has to, amongst other things, assume that every member of the human race on this planet earth (or at least within the boundaries of any one national jurisdiction) appears fully grown at the same time and will die at the same time. It has to assume that there will be no overlap of generations. A theory with such assumptions cannot be a solution to the problem it sets out to grapple with, namely, 'what are the correct principles of distributive justice in a world in which not only is there generally scarcity of resources,[9] but also where human beings have life cycles, the different stages of each may overlap with those of others?' The world as we know it does not consist of people who appear fully grown and developed from nowhere, who then acquire certain bundles of hitherto unheld goods, who will then work upon these bundles to turn them into other bundles of goods which they can then exchange with other people for other bundles. Nor is it true that after living the biblical three score and ten years, people will all die at once and a new lot appear fully grown and developed from nowhere to take their place.

Human existence is messier and more complicated than that. Every individual goes through three well-defined stages – infancy/ childhood, mature adulthood and old age. (This does not mean that all societies at all times have drawn the boundaries between these stages at precisely the same point, or, for that matter, that all societies at all times manage to reach a life expectancy beyond the middle stage for the majority of its members, as in quite a lot of societies people are killed off by disease, famine or war well before they reach what is normally termed 'old age'.) It is at best only during the middle phase that human beings approximate to the ideal of the able-bodied agent which the principles of just distribution by and large presuppose. During the other two stages it is not obvious that we human beings are capable of the kind of acquisitive activity envisaged under principle (1). And even during mature adulthood, not all of us may be fortunate enough to be the strong unblemished specimens of acquisitive agency required by principle (1). Some may be born handicapped or become handi-capped through accident, misadventure or disease. The infantile, the senile, the ill and the handicapped are facts of life and would have to be taken into consideration unless one succeeds in arguing why they should be left out. And even if one were to use a crude utilitarian argument to dispose of the last three categories, that they are a drain on the economy, the first cannot be so readily disposed of. Given human beings to be the biological and social organisms that they are, the young have to be nurtured for a fairly long period of time; otherwise, the survival of the society is endangered. Nozick's theory takes the continuity of society for granted; yet it assumes that the reproduction of that society is effected in a manner which is hard to reconcile with the facts of human reproduction as we know them to be. While some members of a society are dying, others are being born; while death is offset by renewal, that renewal would bear no fruit unless labour, physical and emotional, time and resources are directed to the nurturing of these lives. To the infantile, principle (1) is irrelevant to them.

To put it in another way, in the principles of justice Nozick has enunciated, it is not clear what the term 'a person' refers to. If 'a person' refers to a hypothesised idealised theoretical entity which possesses the characteristics of being a physically and mentally normal adult without an infantile past nor a senile future, and if such entities are assumed all to have the same birthdays and deathdays, that they are reproduced in a manner which is not consonant with human reproduction, then it is conceivable that his principles would count as just principles of distribution. But if 'a person' refers to a human individual as we know him/her to be and if such individuals are at varying stages of growth, maturity and decay, then such principles cannot begin to be principles of just distribution. Indeed they may even begin to look like unjust principles of distribution, for some real persons are not in a position to acquire holdings 'in accordance with the principle of justice in acquisition', nor are they in a position to acquire 'holdings in accordance with the principle of justice in transfer, from someone else entitled to that holding'. (Those with no original acquisitions, not even their labour, would not be in a position to enter into voluntary exchange with another.) Such real persons would be excluded, yet Nozick's theory is meant to apply to all 'human persons'. The defect in his formulation lies in the failure to specify the referent of his key term.

Now it may be argued that theorising requires abstraction and simplification in order to devise a manageable model. However, in Nozick's case, the abstraction and simplification amount to a sleight of hand, which conjures away some of the most intractable problems facing distributive justice, namely that the capacities for productive activity do not necessarily match with the capacity for consumption even for survival, the overlap of generations, the processes and states of growth, maturity and decay in human beings.

Nozick says his theory may be said to be a 'fundamental potential explanation', fundamental because he wishes to explain the political (moral) in terms of the non-political (non-moral), and potential (after Hempel) because it would only constitute a correct explanation 'if everything mentioned in it were true and operated'.[10] But it may not be correct because it could be (a) process-

defective, if 'some process Q other than P produced the phenomenon' in question; (b) law-defective if it deploys a false law-
like statement; (c) fact-defective if it involves a false antecedent
condition. As is obvious, Nozick adheres to the positivist account
of explanation in terms of the D-N model.

First of all, he is wrong in thinking that moral theorising is
explanatory. But let that pass. What is to the point here is that
the theory fails to pass even the tests laid down by his own account
of a correct explanation. Our criticism made above is that he fails
to pass the check of empirical/scientific assumptions and claims
as well as the check of facts. These checks are analogous to his
test that an explanation should not be law-defective and his test
that it should not be fact-defective. However, Nozick maintains
that 'A *fundamental* potential explanation . . . carries important
explanatory illumination even if it is *not* the correct explanation.
. . . Fact-defective fundamental potential explanations, if their
false initial conditions "could have been true" will carry great
illumination; even wildly false initial conditions will illuminate,
sometimes very greatly!'[11]

The operative phrase in that argument is 'could have been true'.
Nozick does not go into any detail about it. But there are several
ways in which it could be understood. First, it could mean 'X did
not happen but Y happened instead, although given the situation
X could have happened'. Second, 'X did not happen but Y
happened as a matter of fact, because given the situation, X could
not have happened'. Third, 'X did not happen but Y happened
because for X to have occurred would involve envisaging the
world to be quite other than we know it to be'.

The assertion of a falsehood in the first context could be illuminating. For instance, human beings could have got together to
create a social pact even if they never did. The point of saying
that it could happen although it never did is precisely that it could
conceivably happen. It is not so obvious that the second context
is at all illuminating. Take, for instance, the legal fiction of the
'reasonable man'. It could be helpful if the defendant in question
possesses the qualities of mind presupposed by the fiction, that
is, that s/he has an average I.Q., etc. But if the defendant is
severely abnormal, the fiction applied to her/him would not
produce illuminating results. On the contrary, the results would
be obfuscating for the purpose of assigning responsibility. (See R.

v Ward, 1956, in which a severely mentally subnormal defendant was found guilty of murdering a subnormal 18-month-old child who died as a result of the defendant shaking her so hard because she would not stop crying. Ward was convicted because it was said that he could have foreseen that such violence would lead to death, on the grounds that a reasonable person could have foreseen it.) The third context is even more obviously unilluminating, since the problems which arise because the world is as we know it to be would be conjured away by imagining a world totally different from what it is here and now. And it is this type of 'could have been true' that is implied in his principles of just distribution. For instance, it is not illuminating to argue that human society need not place such great stress on the prohibition (legal and moral) against causing bodily injury on the grounds that, although it is not true but it could have been true, that human beings could grow another arm immediately an existing limb had been lopped off. To imagine a human organism possessing the capacity for instant total organ renewal (as opposed to tissue renewal) is to imagine a world where the laws of human physiology and biochemistry, etc. are totally different from those we know to obtain.

10   UNENDING MORAL CONFLICTS AND CONTROVERSIES

In spite of all that has been said, there may still be plenty of resistance to the idea that moral discourse is part of critical discourse. It seems clear from the standpoint of objectivity and rationality that the flat-earth theory is to be rejected in favour of the theory that the earth is roughly orange-shaped, given the evidence we have today. The claim that one moral theory is justified or is superior to another runs against deeply engrained resistance, so much so that the very claim itself has to be interpreted as a misleading linguistic form of expression or that the objective claim embodied in certain linguistic forms (such as 'murder is wrong') is simply false. For instance, Mackie says that 'although most people in making moral judgements implicitly claim, among other things, to be pointing to something objectively prescriptive, these claims are all false'.[12] That is why he calls it an 'error theory' which explains the apparent objectivity of values.

Objectivity and rationality are implausible while subjectivism is eminently plausible, because it is so obvious that fundamental moral conflicts (Popper, we shall see, goes so far as to say that a society without conflicts is a society of ants, not of human beings, which amounts to using their existence as a defining characteristic of what counts as a human society) have occurred in the past, occur today and will occur in the future. By contrast, in the history of science, excepting periods of revolution when allegiance was being canvassed on behalf of what Kuhn calls competing and conflicting paradigms, during periods of normal science, the scientific community as well as the lay world accept the dominant theory. Fundamental conflicts do occur but they do not come daily. Long periods, even centuries, may occur without serious challenge to the dominant paradigm. Witness the long reign respectively of the Aristotelian and Newtonian theories and world-views. This cannot, it is claimed, be said of human history in general and of the history of moral ideas in particular.

It seems to follow then that the very undeniable existence of such continuous and interminable conflicts is an obvious explanation of why conflicts are of the essence of human society. However, their existence need not be taken to entail the non-objectivity and non-rationality of the claims at stake. The conflicting views may all be wrong, or one of them may be more correct than the others. A view may be wrong or inadequate on several grounds as we have tried to show. But in general to show that it is wrong or mistaken may not be a brief, simple and easy matter. Whole books may have to be written, full of counter-arguments, in order to display its inadequacies. If theory is to progress, in morals or elsewhere, continuous criticism is indispensable. This may give rise to the impression that nothing is ever settled, nothing can be shown to be supported or unsupported, justified or unjustified. It may also account for the 'agonistic style' that Gallie talks about, except that in Gallie's case, he does not subscribe to the view that the continuous, open-ended defence/ challenge/defence is a precondition for the discovery of truth *via* the elimination of error; for him, as we saw, it is a compulsive neurotic activity, an occupational disease of philosophers and theorists in general.

Apart from the epistemological justification for interminable continuous criticism, there are undoubtedly other reasons which may account to some extent for the existence of such seemingly interminable disputes in morals. First, if moral 'oughts' entail prescriptions, to be sincere about those prescriptions which one maintains can be shown to be right or correct, then one must translate such correct norms into action. But to do so may sometimes require yielding up vested interests, both personal and class, readjusting attitudes to oneself and others which may be all very painful and traumatic. When such interests and emotions are at stake, is it any wonder that people fall prey to irrationality and display a singular lack of enthusiasm in prosecuting their premises to their proper conclusions?[13] Even scientists, as Kuhn has amply demonstrated, do not readily give up their theories in the face of adverse evidence and criticism. But the conclusion drawn from this observation need not be the Kuhnian one that therefore, ultimately, there are no rationality criteria (for in the last resort they simply are the criteria the scientific community has decided to adopt or committed themselves to) for adjudicating between theories.[14] In the same way, the fact that people will be attached to certain moral ideas or theories, and that their emotional commitment to them may produce a powerful impulse behind ever renewing attempts to defend them, does not necessarily lead to the conclusion that there are no rationality criteria for adjudicating between rival moral ideas and claims.

One should distinguish between the psychology behind the impulse of theorising, of supporting certain theories and not others, from the possibility of critically assessing the arguments produced in their defence. Perhaps, the motive behind a particular defendant's defence of the flat-earth theory is that such a belief is an integral part of the religion to which s/he subscribes. But this motive does not itself vitiate the nature of the arguments adduced – whether these are good or bad, correct or incorrect is an independent matter.

Similarly, certain philosophers like Duhem, a leading name among French conventionalists, openly admitted the ideological intention behind his conventionalist philosophy. In his *Physics of a Believer*, he revealed that his motive was, to quote Kolakowski on this point, to give a critique of scientific methodology so that his interpretation of science forestalls all scientific objections to the Catholic faith and Church. For since natural science makes no statements about the real world (as his criticisms of the laws of physics shows) it cannot come into conflict with religious dogmas that are statements about real existents – the soul (that it is immortal), man (that his will is free), the Pope (that he is infallible). For instance, unbelievers say that man's freedom is incompatible with the principle of conservation of energy. There is no such incompatibility, Duhem replies: the principle of conservation of energy is an artificial schematization of experiences and permits no inference to real objects, and hence by definition cannot conflict with the content of the dogma in question. Consequently spiritualist metaphysics retains its cognitive status and its claim to provide reliable information about the world, since scientific laws have lost that status.[15]

Duhem's ideological motive to defend and protect Catholic dogma is one thing; whether the thesis of conventionalism is correct or true as an account of scientific theories is a matter which can be independently and critically assessed.

Second, one must not forget that a moral/social theory is part of those beliefs which are at the very core of society's existence if not of its identity, or to change the metaphor, they are woven into the very fabric of society. To challenge these beliefs is often construed as a threat to the continued existence of a particular social/political/economic order. Very elaborate and sophisticated intellectual defences could be erected around the challenged thesis. For instance, when the Church felt its authority threatened and undermined by a realist understanding of the new astronomy, it did not hesitate to advance an instrumentalist view of science (akin to Duhem's conventionalism which says that scientific theories are merely computational devices or instruments for prediction and do not say what the world is really like) in order to neutralise the heliocentric view, and to protect the biblical geocentric picture of the universe. Again the passion on either side of this dispute is understandable, but whether the new astronomy is correct or not, and whether the Church's instrumentalist understanding of it is correct or not, can be rationally assessed and determined: the first as an issue in astronomy, the second as an issue in the philosophy of science.

The Catholic Church in the seventeenth century reacted violently to the threat posed by heliocentrism to its authority; Christianity in general (but the Protestants in the English-speaking world in particular) in the nineteenth century reacted equally violently to the threat posed by the theory of evolution to its authority. While seventeenth-century Rome adopted instrumentalism to avoid the uncomfortable confrontation between two conflicting and competing conceptions of cosmological reality, nineteenth-century Christianity by and large eventually came to terms with the Darwinian theory of evolution by relinquishing its claim to scientific reality and to re-interpret the Bible to stake a different and autonomous claim to religious reality. Fundamentalists apart, people today no longer find it impossible or even difficult to accept a peaceful co-existence between science and religion. This is precisely because the latter saw fit to re-define its own significance, relevance and intelligibility in the face of such a powerful paradigm of rationality and objectivity. The point is this: whenever a theory, whatever its content, whether pertaining to science or to values, is perceived to be a threat to the existing social or scientific fabric, then much intellectual effort and energy would be devoted to criticising it and attacking it, which in turn will generate an equally intense amount of counter-criticism. In the process of defence/challenge/defence, theories on either side would be reformulated, modified and refurbished in an attempt to meet what are acknowledged as genuine defects in their original form. This kind of critical activity is not at all alarming but indeed is quite indispensable if there is to be truth through the elimination of error by means of criticism. It is only alarming to those who do not share this epistemological requirement and postulate.

11 MORAL PROGRESS

Those who maintain that moral judgments are ultimately no more than subjective preferences or attitudes would find the idea of moral progress bizarre. 'Progress' for them is merely the replacement of one set of values by another which in the opinion of the individual (or group) is regarded to be superior to an earlier set.

But the notion of progress would not at all be bizarre if one can establish the possibility of rationality and objectivity in moral discourse.

Although one has to admit that there has been slow advance unfortunately since the beginning of recorded history, it is not true that there has been none whatsoever. To take one example, so obvious that no one would dream of querying it – the elimination of human and animal sacrifices in burial rituals. The ancient Chinese of the Shang Dynasty (1500 BC to c. 1100 BC), for example, used to bury their king and other important members of his family and court, not only with beautiful objects which could be of use to him in his next life, but also large numbers of people and animals as well, who were expected to serve him as they had done in his life time. Sometimes his attendants and slaves were beheaded first and then buried. But sometimes they were buried alive. In one grave up to two hundred bodies have been discovered. Horses and chariots with the charioteers beside them, were also found in these tombs. After the Shang period, the ancient Chinese gave up this practice and instead buried pottery models of humans and animals. History did not record that the humans who were sacrificed went willingly and happily to serve their master in the next. Neither did it record why this ritual of human sacrifice was superseded by what later Chinese considered to be a morally superior substitute (except that the Chou dynasty which succeeded the Shang evolved a very different ethical code which Confucius later appealed to in his own formulations).

But a critical reconstruction could be made: (1) the deliberate killing of innocent lives is a clear case of harm to others; (2) the king was undoubtedly superior to his subjects; yet the hypothesis that he survived death and that the world to come was a replica of the social order of this world remained only as speculation. (1) and (2) would account for the alternative custom of using clay models – harm would be avoided and an expression of faith that the social order would continue intact in the next world could be said to be satisfied. (1) satisfies the test of causal relevance as well as of causal independence; (2) satisfies the check of empirical assumptions and claims. (1) and (2) satisfy the check of the problem, namely, how to honour dead rulers.

It may be said that this reconstruction is excessively rational (although a study[16] of ancient Chinese philosophy would show that Chinese philosophers were 'critical' and 'rational' in the same way that ancient Greek and contemporary human beings are said to be 'critical' and 'rational') and that the ancient Chinese could never have argued in such a way. However, the point that is being made is not so much the historical plausibility of such reconstruction but that critically speaking, one is justified in saying that substantial moral progress was made by the early Chinese when they abandoned the custom of human and animal sacrifice as part of burial rituals. Or to put it in another way: suppose a modern dictator (unfortunately not so far-fetched a conception, judging by the Hitlers, the Stalins and the Idi Amins of this century) were to maintain that it is morally right that his subjects be slaughtered and buried alive to serve him in the next world, the arguments advanced against the claim would be cogent regardless of whether the despot or his indoctrinated subjects believe them to be so, and regardless of whether such moral reasoning would be effective in stopping him from carrying out such a barbarous practice. Such a claim could not be simply characterised as an expression of personal preference for or commitment to the norm that it is right to inter live servants and subjects, but could be said to constitute moral retrogression of an abominally enormous order. Similarly, the counter-claim that it is wrong to inter live subjects is not a mere irrational commitment.

In the same way would one regard any attempt on the part of orthodox Hinduism today to return to the practice of suttee. The British Raj, in prohibiting it, no doubt rested their belief in its wickedness on the superiority of Christian values. But one does not have to rely on Christian revelation to show that it is wrong to require widows to kill themselves in order to continue serving their dead husbands in the after-life. These arguments may include the following (boring though it may seem to have them set out): if it is right for widows to commit suttee, what is the basis for discriminating against female spouses in this way? Ultimately, it rests on the superiority of the male in such a society. But in what ways are males superior to females? If characteristics like intelligence, physical toughness, strength of character, etc. are cited, then they may be subjected to the checks of logic, of facts and of empirical/scientific assumptions and claims. These putative characteristics may then be shown to fail either the test of causal relevance or/and the tests of truth and of causal independence, etc. If the reason or evidence cited is that male superiority is divinely ordained, the discussion shifts to the assessment of Hindu religious claims as well as religious claims in general, to the objections in deriving morality from religion, etc. If the reply is that Hindus regard suttee as right because they are sincerely committed to the Hindu way of life under which suttee is a morally correct norm, then they are vulnerable to the arguments against relativism in general.

One dimension of moral progress may be said to be the progressive realisation in human history that the scope of morality includes (at least) the whole human race (some argue that the limit should not be drawn there, otherwise, it is mere speceism). Societies appear to have evolved moral codes whose scope of application initially was confined to certain male members only or just members of the tribe – for instance, ancient Greek democracies excluded barbarians, slaves and women; and for certain tribes, while it was wrong to kill a fellow tribesman it might be morally right or neutral to kill an outsider. Moral growth consists of realising that the distinction resting on tribal or sexual or legal membership might be said to be a matter which does not affect the basic constitution of being a human being. To kill someone even if s/he were not a member of one's tribe is, nevertheless, to kill a human being. If it is wrong to kill one such member it is *ipso facto* wrong to kill another who happens to be an outsider. To justify discrimination against the outsider on the grounds that s/he is not a human being is to indulge in arbitrary classification which ignores the fact that insiders and outsiders all belong to the same taxon or natural kind. Or to argue, as Aristotle did, that slaves and women were to be excluded from the privileges and duties of citizenship because they were inferior, less intelligent beings, would not do since the evidence is either false, and if not false but causally relevant, nevertheless would violate the test of causal independence.

V

THE PHILOSOPHICAL DOMAIN OF ORDINARY KNOWLEDGE

The preceding chapters seek to establish that (A1), (A2) and (A3) are all subject to the same criteria of justification. These similarities suggest that there is a domain of knowledge which may be called 'ordinary knowledge' of which these three sorts of assertions form part, and to which philosophers in the main have not paid much attention. This chapter will try to make good to some extent this neglect – to specify the boundaries of such a domain in some detail and to work out the conditions which must obtain if such knowledge is said to exist.

1 ORDINARY KNOWLEDGE AS PART OF A NORMAL AGENT'S COGNITIVE APPARATUS

That ordinary knowledge exists is taken for granted by people at large. It is part of ordinary knowledge that rhubarb leaves are poisonous (A3), that, therefore, they ought not be eaten (A2), and that one ought not (morally) to urge the unsuspecting to eat them (A1). It is part of ordinary knowledge that fire burns (A3), that one ought not to play with naked flames (A2), that one ought (morally) not to burn down a shack while knowing that someone is in it (A1). It used not to be part of ordinary knowledge but has since become so, that driving under the influence of alcohol is highly dangerous (A3), that one ought not to exceed a certain amount if one does not wish to be maimed or killed or get into trouble with the police (A2), and that one ought not (morally) wittingly to imbibe it in such quantity so that it is likely that one would endanger the lives of others (A1).

In order to cope adequately with nature and other people, one must be equipped with so-called ordinary knowledge. Someone who is devoid of it systematically over a considerable area is likely to be assigned to an institution, or to care, both for their own protection and for the protection of others. Someone who is not incapable of appreciating that such knowledge exists, but is merely ignorant because of deficient opportunities would have to be explicitly taught to acquire the ordinary layperson's cognitive equipment, before s/he could be safely let loose to fend for her/himself in society at large. For instance, children brought up all their lives in homes or orphanages may not know that bread not eaten up within a few days would go stale. On reaching the age of majority when the local authorities are no longer legally required to look after them, they are left to cope on their own, but without the basic cognitive equipment that is usually painlessly absorbed in more normal contexts of upbringing. Such unfortunate persons have been known to spend most, if not all the week's wages or supplementary benefits on perishable foods, which they could not possibly consume before they go bad, no doubt in accordance with the sound fundamental principle that to stay alive, one must have food.

2 ORDINARY AND SCIENTIFIC KNOWLEDGE

It is natural to contrast ordinary knowledge with scientific knowledge. The former is supposed to be non-specialised, non-esoteric, available to all (or nearly all) agents and hence democratic in nature. The latter is specialised, esoteric, generally highly abstract and systematised, accessible only to those initiated into its methods, the contents yielded by its methods after long and arduous training, and hence elitist in nature. There is a great deal of truth to the contrast, which, however, must not be overplayed, for to do so might give the wrong impression that these are two watertight compartments of human knowledge without points of contact or mutual exchange and enrichment. Ordinary knowledge is not static – its greatest source of growth, refinement and revision comes from the sciences. Some might even go so far as to say that ordinary knowledge is simply hand-me-down scientific knowledge, and because of the time lag involved in the hand-me-down process, necessarily outmoded scientific knowledge. Just as, for instance, it is beginning to form part of ordinary knowledge that contraceptive pills can produce dangerous and highly undesirable side-effects in certain women, scientific research has gone one step ahead to show (at least it is claimed) that such pills may also have desirable side-effects like being correlated with a lower incidence of cancer of the breast. While scientific knowledge may itself be partial and subject to revision, ordinary knowledge is even more partial, being at one remove from the fountainhead of knowledge, as it were, and precisely because it is more remote, it is also less sensitive in responding to revision. Science is concerned with the attempt to increase knowledge at a deeper and deeper level of understanding, that is, breaking new grounds and making new discoveries about processes and inter-relationships between them not suspected of before. Ordinary knowledge, by contrast, simply absorbs and assimilates these claims rather than advances any.

However, this account of ordinary knowledge in terms of second-hand scientific knowledge passively received and accepted does not quite fit the picture in two respects: (1) it is unfair to overlook the fact that the goal of the former is different from the goal of the latter. Science[1] seeks primarily to understand how the world works in the way it does. It aims to provide explanations for observed phenomena. Its theories are basically explanatory although in some cases, and in some contexts, they may also be predictive. They may also on occasion be enlisted for the purpose of controlling and modifying phenomena. For instance, if we had adequate explanatory theories in terms of the nature of nicotine, of our organ tissues, the process of combustion, of cell growth and development, and numerous other processes which could be involved, then we would be able to make successful predictions about the incidence of lung cancer and the incidence of smoking, and also to use them to warn people of the dangers of smoking, thereby hoping to lower the incidence of lung cancer among the population. But one might be able to provide a satisfactory explanatory theory without being able either to make successful predictions or to generate a recipe for controlling the phenomenon in question. We might know and understand how fossil fuels were formed in the earth's crust, but such explanations might not enable us to predict exactly where such deposits might be found,[2] nor would they enable us to facilitate (or retard) the formation of such fuels.

The goal of ordinary knowledge is not primarily theoretical but practical. As such, it is not basically concerned with explanation or prediction or even with control. Its main preoccupation is with justification – unless what is put forward as a knowledge claim is justified in terms of the evidence cited in its support (or validated from the epistemological point of view and not simply *via* subsumption), the agent is not required to take it into account and act upon it. Unless there is evidence of a certain sort to back up the claim, that, for instance, alcohol in drivers causes motor accidents, the agent may rightly ignore it in coping with the world and other agents. If s/he were intending to go to a drinks party, one would not need to arrange for a non-drinker to drive the car home. Nor would one need to upbraid oneself or tolerate others to upbraid one for being foolhardy, stupid and immoral for trying to drive after an evening of steady drinking. Unless there is evidence of a certain kind to support the claim that this dog is suffering from rabies, then again the agent need not act upon it as if it were justified, that is, immediately inform the police and the public health authorities. And if the claim were justified, then it would follow one ought not to hide the animal and try to treat it oneself, or to pretend it is not infected and let it roam at will.

Since the fundamental goal in determining whether an ordinary knowledge claim is justified is a practical one, the lay agent, in the main, relies on existing evidence, whether provided by current science (up-to-the-minute latest discoveries), or what has been established a long time ago by scientific investigation for which there is no new evidence to challenge its truth, or by what may be called pre-scientific evidence. The agent is not likely to go out of the way to actively seek to establish such evidence. In that sense it is true to say that the agent makes use of what there is available. Unlike the scientist, one is usually not in a position to provide the strongest type of evidence possible, namely, an adequate explanatory theory which could account for the phenomenon occurring in the way it does. One does no theorising and no experimenting in a systematic way which can be called scientific. If such a theory does exist, one would no doubt invoke it to justify the claim one has made.

Before scientific knowledge could become available as evidence to back up (or query) an ordinary knowledge claim, some concerted effort is usually required to publish it and to present it in a manner which the lay agent could comprehend in broad outline if not in detail. For instance, in assessing a claim such as 'This child is the offspring of Mr X and not Mr Y', the lay agent must at least know of the existence of blood tests, know that there is a genetic theory behind such a test which renders it reliable, even if one is ignorant about and at a loss in understanding the technical details of, the test and the theory, not to mention that one must know that conception requires genetic material from the male and the female. (This last piece of scientific knowledge is of such long standing that it has become absorbed entirely by ordinary knowledge in the same way as the scientific discovery by Harvey in the West that blood circulates is now so thoroughly assimilated by ordinary knowledge that neither would require any effort of publicity.) In assessing the claim that 'abortion is morally wrong', the lay agent must know in outline the process of conception, the formation and development of the foetus, etc. In assessing the claim that 'nuclear energy is safe' and the accompanying claim that we ought to develop it as a form of fuel, the lay agent again must be able to grasp in general the processes involved in the production of nuclear energy, the nature of the material used, the state of technology from the safety point of view, etc.

But often in determining whether an ordinary knowledge claim is justified or not, the lay agent does not have the highest possible type of scientific evidence available in the background to support or discredit the claim. One has to make do with what may be called pre-scientific and proto-scientific evidence. For instance, even in the absence of a scientific explanatory theory which accounts for death through cancer, the lay agent could rely on evidence yielded by using criteria like that of constant conjunction, high statistical correlation and controllability to back up the claim that smoking cigarettes is highly undesirable and can cause lung cancer, and that, therefore, it is morally incorrect for tobacco companies to lure teenagers to start the addictive habit through glossy advertisements in magazines which they read. In the same way, the lay agent would maintain even in the days before the theory of photosynthesis was available that the claim that plants need light to grow was justified given the evidence yielded by the criteria mentioned above. Similarly, one would say, even in the absence of any satisfactory explanatory psychological theory about personality development in children, that the claim that children require affection and attention is justified in terms of the evidence available, and one would, therefore, reject as unjustified any claim (moral and non-moral) that children should be denied love and affection on the grounds that they do not need such care for their proper development. We do not at the moment have a satisfactory explanatory theory in science to know precisely the causes of homosexuality; but this does not necessarily preclude the lay agent from assessing the claim, for instance, that homosexuality is wrong because homosexual practices cause earthquakes. (The emperor Justinian is reputed to have advanced such an assertion.) The assertion may be rejected or held to be defeated or unjustified because the evidence cited is just simply false (not that it is causally irrelevant to the claim). Since it is false, *modus tollens* obtains to defeat the assertion.

So far it looks as if that ordinary knowledge is parasitic upon scientific knowledge. But this image of one-sided dependence has to be corrected by the reminder that the former may sometimes suggest fruitful research programmes to the latter. If the research in the end confirms the original claim, then that claim is reinforced and entrenched. If it does not, then it is undermined or modified or destroyed. One notable instance of success which may be cited in the history of science is the discovery of immunisation. Jenner worked upon the ordinary knowledge claim prevalent in rural communities that milkmaids did not appear to catch smallpox because they had already caught a mild dose of cowpox. He experimented and investigated systematically this claim; as a result techniques of immunisation were developed which in turn led to the theory of immunology. Another example would be the knowledge, ordinary and pre-scientific, which was/is involved in domestic breeding of animals and plants. Genetic selection and manipulation in this area led Darwin to, among other things, the theory of evolution. It used to be part of ordinary knowledge that teething in infants caused all sorts of ailments, from diarrhoea to pneumonia. This claim was justified by evidence in terms of high statistical co-relation or conjunction between teething and such illnesses. But scientific research has since established that there is no causal connection between the two in spite of the high co-relation. As a result, this particular claim is now considered to be without basis and dropped out of the cognitive repertoire of the lay agent. At any moment, there are scientific programmes engaged in looking into various ordinary knowledge claims, the most socially pressing of which just now is the claim that the increase in the incidence of cancers of various sorts amongst all ages is possibly linked to the increase in the use of chemicals in our industrialised technological lifestyle. But until science is able to specify and identify which substances are carcinogenic and which are not, to gain greater understanding of the phenomenon commonly described as cancer, the verdict upon the claim, whether in the end justified or not, remains open.

There is in fact a healthy interchange between scientific and ordinary knowledge. Neither is static and the growth of the one benefits the growth of the other. The extent of the co-operation between the two domains is itself a matter open to political influence, in the sense that a society which is wedded to 'grassroots' participatory democracy in general, and which believes that information and knowledge should not succumb to elitist pressures and inclinations, might consciously set about to involve the ordinary people in scientific research and development. A notable example of this sort of co-operation concerns the efforts of the Chinese government, scientists and citizens in seismological investigations. The hunch provided by ordinary knowledge is that earthquakes in an area are often preceded by unusual behaviour on the part of animals. Dogs bark incessantly for no obvious reasons, for instance. The speculation underlying this observation is that seismic activity, while rumbling underground as it were, might have been picked up by the more sensitive organs of animals. Citizens in this project were asked to make and report observations of such strange animal behaviour. This together with other more orthodox indicators led to accurate prediction about the then imminent Haicheng earthquake in 1975. The government was able to mount a successful evacuation of the endangered population. But unfortunately, this method of prediction, upon further investigation, turns out not to be universally valid, as there are numerous types of earthquake activities not all of which could be monitored in such a way.

However, in spite of such possible co-operation, the differences which exist between them and which serve to delimit their respective domains may be briefly summarised as follows: that they vary in their goals, one is theoretical, the other practical; that the primary task of science is to produce explanatory theories (which may also be predictive in some cases, and may too, provide the basis for techniques of control), which can give an adequate account of the phenomena under study, while the primary concern of ordinary knowledge is justificatory, to ensure that the claim in question is supported by the evidence cited – if it is justified, then the lay agent would take it into account in coping with the world, and if it is not justified, one would ignore it; that in assessing an ordinary knowledge claim, acceptable evidence may be pre-scientific (although it would be hospitable to scientific evidence), but in assessing scientific knowledge-claims, pre-scientific evidence is not enough.

3 HOW POSITIVISM OBSCURES THE DOMAIN OF ORDINARY KNOWLEDGE

This characterisation of ordinary knowledge is dependent upon rejecting the positivist account of scientific knowledge and its domain. A key tenet of positivism is the abolition of the difference between appearance and reality, between phenomena and essence. This when applied to philosophy purged it of meta-physics. Applied to science, it leads to the view that the primary task of science is to give an ordering of individual observable facts, phenomena or events. Science admittedly makes use of theoretical constructs which are not themselves observable facts, phenomena or events, but their justification lies in their utility – they are convenient tools or devices for making calculations, and they help one to order the facts into a system. But the test of the system lies ultimately in its ability to make predictions which are checkable. In other words, on this conception of science, explanation is not fundamental; prediction based on an ordered description of phenomena is. That is why it cavalierly assumes that prediction and explanation are symmetrical. Explanation, as a result, is forced into a framework moulded by the goal of prediction like a kind of afterthought. By keeping to appearance, and abolishing hidden or occult entities and qualities, it reduces scientific laws to laws of constant conjunction or high statistical correlations. Hume's analysis of cause may be regarded as a paradigm of this genre – that cause is a redundant notion in science since whatever experiential content it might have is reducible to the notion of uniform sequence. Its excess content might be psychological, but he would not allow that it could have excess theoretical content over and above uniformity of sequence. By reducing a theoretical term to a psychological dimension, he outlawed the attempt to seek for explanatory theories which might account for the 'necessity' (natural, not logical) of the constant conjunction obtaining between process a and process b. The theoretical dimension of science is itself reduced to the function of producing an ordering system, of for instance, subsuming a constant conjunction between 'a's and 'b's under one between 'A's and 'B's, and that in turn under another where the terms refer to more and more general types or classes of events or phenomena.[3]

As a result, it mistakes the pre-scientific or proto-scientific for science. Detecting constant conjunctions or high statistical correlations and ordering them is not the be-all and the end-all of science. The task of science is above all to go beyond these observations to determine whether they are accidental correlations or not. If accidental then they are not part of scientific knowledge, and for that matter not part of ordinary knowledge any more. But by appropriating the pre-scientific and then misconstruing it to be scientific, it leaves no room for the domain of ordinary knowledge, at least of (A3) which forms part of it. By decreeing that to be scientific, a statement must deal with empirically observable states of affairs, and if it does not, it would only be legitimate provided it is entailed by one which does (*via* correspondence rules linking theoretical terms to experiential ones), it rules out normative ordinary knowledge (A1), since the statements belonging to its domain are neither about empirically observable states of affairs, nor are they entailed by statements which refer to such phenomena. By displacing the explanatory goal from the centre of the scientific enterprise, and by reducing truth to utility (so that theories are successful instruments of prediction[4]), by reducing the theoretical to the pragmatic (in Peirce's original sense, that is, the meaning of a statement is exhausted by its practical consequences), and then by confusing the pragmatic with the practical ('pragmatic' is simply what works; 'practical' in the sense that the agent, before s/he can act sensibly, must know what the world is like, as opposed simply to what one thinks it is like. If one were to act on the latter, one would sooner or later run into trouble. It is easy to see how one would run into trouble – if one did not accept the claim that fire burns as justified and proceeded to put one's hands into a fire; or if one did not accept the claim as justified that one ought to avoid cigarettes if one did not wish to risk getting lung cancer as justified and proceeded to smoke regardless; similarly if one did not accept the claim that one ought not to kill another whose face one did not like as justified and proceeded to kill according to whim, then one would find oneself the object of moral condemnation and legal sanctions), it obscures the fact that the goal of ordinary knowledge ((A1), (A2), (A3)), both normative and factual, is neither explanatory nor predictive but justificatory.[5] And in ignoring it, it also ignores that there is a logic even if it does not consist of enacting the relationship of strict implication between the *justificandum* and the *justificans*, and in spite of the fact that the former (in the case of (A1)) may not refer to matters of observable fact, but are norms which are not empirical and cannot be reduced to statements which are.[6]

4   THREE SENSES OF 'CONCLUSIVE' VERIFICATION/ FALSIFICATION IN THE CONTEXTS OF JUSTIFYING ORDINARY KNOWLEDGE CLAIMS AND OF TESTING A SCIENTIFIC THEORY OR HYPOTHESIS

Chapter Three has argued that the logic of justification employed in the domain of ordinary knowledge is the logic of fallibilism (though suitably enriched). In contemporary philosophy, this logic has become much celebrated through the Popperian thesis of falsifiability as the hallmark of a scientific theory. It has generated widespread controversy,[7] an evaluation of which is not the concern of this book. However, there is an aspect of this mode of inference as used by Popper which is of relevance to the discussion of a logic of justification in the domain of ordinary knowledge. As applied to scientific theory, Popper relies on the relation of logical derivability or deducibility to do the job for him – if q is derivable from p (p stands for statements which consist of a hypothesis (H) and initial conditions (I)), and if q is false, then p is false. It is also further specified that q is a singular existential statement – it satisfies the formal requirement for basic statements as well as the material requirement by being testable intersubjectively by observation.[8] But this account borrowed and applied straightforwardly to ordinary knowledge would not do.

Popper grants that singular statements may themselves be regarded as hypotheses capable of falsifiability. So let us see if the Popperian model would work in the case of a statement belonging to ordinary knowledge like 'this dog is ill' (A3). The hypothetico-deductive construction would be as follows: Ill dogs vomit; this dog is ill; this dog vomits. It looks at first that 'this dog vomits', q, satisfies the requirements of being a basic statement, and if it turns out to be false, then p (the universal hypothesis (H) as well as the singular hypothesis (I)) is false. Either both components of p are false, or one may be false and not the other.

In the Popperian account of scientific theories, when p turns out to be false, it is logically possible to determine independent of the hypothesis that is being tested (that is for Popper in the main the universal one (H)) and of the prediction itself whether the statement of initial conditions is true. If the statement of initial conditions turns out to be true, then the offender must be the hypothesis that is being tested. So one may conclude that the hypothesis under testing is false. Suppose one is trying to test the hypothesis 'wood conducts electricity'. In conjunction with 'this object is wood', it entails 'this object conducts electricity', q. Assuming there is inter-subjective testing of q and if q is false, checks can be made to ensure that the object in question has been properly identified as wood, the identification of which is done independently of the truth or falsity of 'wood conducts electricity' and of the prediction, q, itself. So is the truth or falsity of the hypothesis tested ('wood conducts electricity') independent of the truth or falsity of the statement of initial condition.

However, in the case of (A3) no such independence exists. Unlike the testing of scientific theories which Popper avows is for the purpose of increasing scientific knowledge, in the case of ordinary knowledge, one is merely justifying the hypothesis 'this dog is ill' in terms of the proferred evidence 'this dog vomits'. We already know as a matter of fact that dogs which are ill may vomit (amongst other things which they may also do or suffer), so that what we are really entitled to say is merely 'ill dogs sometimes vomit' and not 'whenever dogs are ill, they vomit'. Put thus in a less than universal form, the falsity of 'this dog vomits' does not falsify either 'this dog is ill' or 'Ill dogs sometimes vomit' or both. It is because we already know that there is a causal connection between 'being ill' and 'vomiting' that we can say that 'this dog is ill' is supported if 'this dog vomits' is true and not supported if 'this dog vomits' turns out to be false. The causal connection also ensures that the state of being ill cannot be identified entirely independently of the process of vomiting, as well as enables a partial meaning link to be built between the terms 'being ill' and 'vomiting'. This then reinforces the point that logical derivability (or what Popper calls analytic implication[9]) does not do justice to the 'if-then' relationship within the domain of ordinary knowledge, and that it can only be adequately characterised in terms of epistemic implication, where the verifying/falsifying modes of inference exist even though logical derivability does not obtain.

Popper assumes that logical derivability obtains *tout court* in the context of testing a theory. In this, he may not be as clear as he ought to be. This unclarity leads to the controversy between himself and his critics about the asymmetry between verification and falsification. It may be helpful to distinguish between three senses of the term 'conclusive' when one talks of conclusive falsification but the lack of conclusive verification. Popper himself now talks about two aspects of conclusive falsification – its logical and its methodological aspects.[10] But the distinctions pursued here do not altogether coincide with that of Popper.

It may also be helpful to distinguish between different steps in the process of applying the logical formula (H.I) Ω q to the test situation. First, Popper says that this formula enables one to derive logically a testable statement containing a prediction q from p (that is, a statement about the hypothesis (H) and a statement(s) about initial conditions (I)). It is true that q follows necessarily from p. This is because that argument is assumed to be not merely a valid argument but also a good one, that is, its premises are assumed to be true. If (H.I) is true, then q is true, but (H.I) is true, therefore q is true. In this context, the truth of (H.I) entails the truth of q.

The next step consists of assessing the evidence in the light of testing when that evidence turns out to be positive, that is, q is true. If q, in the light of testing, indeed turns out to be true, Popper correctly points out that the truth of q does not entail the truth of (H). The reason is that logically speaking, a finite set of singular observational statements does not entail a universal statement or law. 'All Xs are Ys' is not entailed by 'X_1 is Y_1', 'X_2 is Y_2', 'X_n is Y_n' . . . this is the well-known Humean gap in inductive logic between premises and conclusion. For this reason, Popper says that there can be no conclusive verification logically speaking, and hence prefers to speak of corroboration rather than verification or confirmation of the hypothesis. Call this sense 'conclusive$_D$' where the truth of the conclusion entails the truth of the premises. In this sense, there is no 'conclusive$_D$' verification of (H). Moreover, to say that the truth of q entails the truth of (H.I) is to commit the fallacy of affirming the consequent.

However, there is another sense in which the truth of q may be said to 'conclusively' verify (H). Logically speaking, in the test situation, as we have seen, the truth of q verifies (corroborates) the truth of (H.I), not (H) alone. To say that the truth of q verifies (corroborates) the truth of (H) is to assume that (I) is true. As (I) is true, the truth of q may then be said to verify (corroborate) the truth of (H). But the truth of q verifying (corroborating) the truth of (H) only works in conjunction with the methodological presupposition that (I) is true, is unproblematic. Call this sense 'conclusive$_M$', where the truth of the conclusion together with certain methodological assumptions enable one to arrive at the truth of the hypothesis that is being tested. In this sense, there is 'conclusive$_M$' verification (corroboration) of H.

In the light of testing, if q turns out to be false, logically speaking, $-q \, \Omega \, -(H.I)$. As the original argument in the pre-testing stage assumes the truth of (H.I) in order to deduce q, the falsity of q then entails the falsity of (H.I). It is in this sense that there is 'conclusive$_D$' falsification of (H.I) by the falsity of q. Here there is no logical gap between premises and conclusion – the falsity of (H.I) logically follows from the falsity of q, given that one has assumed the truth of (H.I) in order to deduce the testable

178

statement q. Confined to this context, one may say with Popper that there is a logical asymmetry between verification and falsification – in the former, the truth of the conclusion does not entail the truth of (H) but in the latter, the falsity of the conclusion does entail the falsity of (H.I).

However, on this view of 'conclusive$_D$' falsification, Popper is entitled to say that the conjunct (H.I) is false, and it is not (H) alone that is false. In order to arrive at the conclusion that (H) has been falsified, he must make certain methodological assumptions. Strictly speaking, −q can mean (i) both (H) and (I) are false; (ii) (H) is false, but (I) is true; or (iii) (H) is true but (I) is false. When Popper argues that −q implies −H, this piece of 'strict deductive logic' only works if he rules out (i) and (iii) above on other grounds. But logical derivability on its own cannot do this for him. As a matter of fact, he takes it for granted that (I) is true, which then enables him to infer the falsity of (H). But the falsity of (H) only follows logically from the falsity of q if the truth of (I) is presupposed on the methodological grounds, that for the purpose of testing a hypothesis, one holds the statement of initial conditions to be unproblematic, that is, true. So although there is 'conclusive$_D$' falsification of (H.I), there is no 'conclusive$_D$' falsification of (H).

Although there is no 'conclusive$_D$' falsification of (H), there is 'conclusive$_M$' falsification of (H), just as there is 'conclusive$_M$' verification of (H). We saw above that to arrive at the conclusion that (H) has been falsified, one needs to assume on methodological grounds that (I) is true. But once the assumption is made, one can conclude that (H) is false.

Indeed, the methodological complexities are even greater than the assumption that (I) is true or unproblematic. The Popperian philosopher of science must also hold to be unproblematic other background assumptions or auxiliary hypotheses. For logically speaking, −q can mean not only the three possibilities mentioned above, but also a fourth, namely, both (H) and (I) are true, but some other auxiliary hypothesis is false. An illustration of this last possibility – suppose one is testing the hypothesis 'metals expand when heated' (H). Together with 'this is a piece of metal' (I), it entails the testable conclusion 'this will expand when heated' (q). But the failure of the metal to expand when heated may not necessarily mean that (H) is false and/or (I) is false. Rather it could be that the instrument that is used to measure the expansion is too clumsy to measure the degree of expansion that has taken place when the substance was heated. In other words, one normally assumes that the instrument is an adequate one for the purpose in hand. But sometimes one may have reason to suspect that it is not adequate, and if further investigation confirms the suspicion, then one no longer accepts that (H) has been falsified. In testing a hypothesis, the scientist must also subscribe to the methodological assumption that auxiliary hypotheses are unproblematic. To say baldly that the falsity of q entails the falsity of (H) because of the *modus tollens* is to grossly oversimplify matters, and to gloss over crucial matters of methodological propriety. That is why it is misleading to claim that falsification is a logical weapon *simpliciter* which demolishes a theory with one mortal blow. And it is false to claim that a hypothesis can be 'conclusively$_D$' falsified (although the conjunct (H.I) may be said to be thus falsified). But it is correct to claim that (H) can be 'conclusively$_M$' falsified.

Popper is, therefore, correct in maintaining that there is a logical asymmetry between verification and falsification, in so far as no finite set of true singular statements entails a universal statement (the form a hypothesis takes) – q does not 'conclusively$_D$' verify (H). (And to say that it does, is also to commit the fallacy of affirming the consequent.) As the falsity of q entails the falsity of (H.I), (H.I) may be said to be 'conclusively$_D$' falsified, but not that (H) alone has been 'conclusively$_D$' falsified. However, there is no asymmetry between verification and falsification as far as 'conclusive$_M$' is concerned. In conjunction with certain methodological assumptions, deductive logic enables one to say that (H) is both 'conclusively$_M$' verified or 'conclusively$_M$' falsified.

In the light of the analysis above, the focus of the differences between Popper and his critics shifts somewhat. His critics presumably do not wish to deny that the truth of q does not entail the truth of (H) and that it does not 'conclusively$_D$' verify (H). They differ from him in saying that the lack of 'conclusive$_D$' verification does not prevent one from constructing a logic of confirmation. This issue is connected with the long-running controversy between those who accept inductive logic and those who reject it, as Popper does on the grounds that it is both unsound and irrelevant to science. While 'conclusive$_D$' falsification does obtain, it does not obtain in quite the way Popper has envisaged, for he is entitled to claim that there is 'conclusive$_D$' falsification of (H.I) but not of (H) alone. He is, however, entitled to say that (H) is 'conclusively$_M$' falsified; but then, so is he entitled to say that (H) is 'conclusively$_M$' verified or corroborated. Those critics of Popper who deny that there is conclusive falsification are not necessarily denying that deductive logic in conjunction with certain methodological assumptions enables one to 'conclusively$_M$' falsify (H) provided it is understood that the 'conclusive$_M$' falsification of (H) is not an absolutely certain or secure belief.[11] An absolutely certain or secure belief may be said to be 'conclusively$_A$' verified or falsified. It follows that (H) is not 'conclusively$_A$' falsified. And for that matter neither is (H) 'conclusively$_A$' verified (corroborated).

To conclude, there is no asymmetry between verification and falsification as far as (i) 'conclusively$_M$' verification/falsification of (H) is concerned; (ii) 'conclusive$_A$' of (H) is concerned. There is asymmetry, it is true, between verification and falsification as far as 'conclusive$_D$' is concerned; however, in this case, 'conclusive$_D$' does not obtain in the verification of (H), but obtains in the falsification of (H.I), though not of (H) alone.

An analogous degree of methodological complexity surrounds the application to the domain of ordinary knowledge of the formula 'p implies q and q is true/false' involved in epistemic implication.

It has already been pointed out that if q is true, as far as epistemic implication is concerned, the truth of q does not entail the truth of p – there is no 'conclusive$_D$' verification of the assertion if the evidence turns out to be true.

However, there is 'conclusive$_M$' verification of the assertion (A) if the evidence (E) turns out to be true. For the purpose of justifying one's beliefs and actions in the domain of ordinary knowledge, one takes to be unproblematic the corpus of extant scientific knowledge and/or proto-scientific knowledge and pre-scientific knowledge. One is not critically challenging these. Instead one takes the truth of such matters for granted in order to get on with the business of critically assessing the assertions made within the philosophical domain of ordinary knowledge. The acceptance of this methodological assumption enables us to use 'p implies q and q is true' to consider certain claims to be correct or justified.

Although there is 'conclusive$_M$' verification of (A), there is no 'conclusive$_A$' verification of (A). As scientific knowledge increases or alters (what was once considered to be acceptable common-sense pre-scientific knowledge is no longer acceptable if it turns out not to have the backing of science; scientific investigation may also discover causal connections not before suspected by pre-scientific knowledge), what has been 'conclusively$_M$' verified could be defeated or refuted by later evidence.

If (E) turns out to be false, the falsity of (E) does not 'conclusively$_D$' falsify (A). The falsity of the evidence does not entail the falsity of the assertion. There is no 'conclusive$_D$' falsification of (A).

However, there is 'conclusive$_M$' falsification of (A). Again one assumes the correctness of current scientific, proto-scientific and pre-scientific knowledge in order to get on with the business of eliminating false claims put forward as evidence for assertions in the domain of ordinary knowledge. This methodological assumption allows one to ascertain in certain cases that the (E) cited is false. In other words, the acceptance of the assumption enables one to use the *modus tollens* to reject certain assertions as incorrect, unjustified or false.

Although there is 'conclusive$_M$' falsification of (A), there is no 'conclusive$_A$' falsification of (A). If the scientific, proto- and pre-scientific claims are themselves successfully challenged in any way, the 'conclusive$_M$' falsification of (A) would itself be overturned or defeated.

Compared with the Popperian context of theory testing, where asymmetry exists between verification and falsification in the following aspect, namely, that there is no 'conclusive$_D$' verification of (H), but there is 'conclusive$_D$' falsification of (H.I) though not of (H) alone, the context of the justifying of assertions (A1), (A2) and (A3) yields symmetries between verification and falsification in all the three senses of the notion 'conclusive' identified above.

Paradoxically, the formula 'p implies q and q is true/false' as used in the justification of an ordinary knowledge claim may be said to possess greater 'logical tightness' than when it is used in the scientific context of testing a theory. First, in the former, we need only to hold scientific/proto-/pre-scientific knowledge in general to be unproblematic; whereas in the latter, we have seen how one needs to hold several things to be unproblematic without knowing in advance which of these things may turn out to be not unproblematic. Second, in the former, the context of critical assessment is given by the party with whom one is contending, that is to say, the party making an assertion goes on to cite (if not spontaneously, at least when prodded) the evidence for it. By so doing, s/he is laying down the scope of the critical inquiry. The assertor as well as the inquisitor are both agreed that if the evidence given is causally irrelevant, or if causally relevant false, and so on, the assertor would have to withdraw the assertion, or put forward another piece of evidence which could then be similarly assessed. The conditions of relevance, referential and causal, predetermine the sort of evidence that would be admissible, so that the falsity of such evidence has the effect of rendering the assertion false. In contrast, in the context of testing a scientific theory, one does not and cannot admit that the testable conclusion alone is crucial and relevant to the correctness or otherwise of the theory – other things may also be relevant and may also be crucial, although one does not know in advance of further investigation what they are.

5   THREE DOMAINS IN EPISTEMOLOGY – THE SCIENTIFIC, ORDINARY KNOWLEDGE AND THE PERCEPTUAL

In the preface to the 1958 English edition of *The Logic of Scientific Discovery* (1961), Popper said that the problem of epistemology may be tackled as the problem of ordinary knowledge or as the problem of scientific knowledge. The first tends to regard science as itself writ large, so that whatever insights gained in studying it may be appropriately applied to the second. The latter tends to regard itself to be in possession of an epistemological imprimatur, so that anything outside it which does not come up to its requirements would simply be written off as beyond the pale of knowledge. We have seen how the powerful tradition of positivism regards scientific knowledge as a structure with theory at the top but eventually resting on an empirical base, with a deductive thread linking one level with the next until such a base is reached.

Under its influence, we have seen that ordinary knowledge as delimited and characterised by the thesis of epistemic implication does not exist in its own right. But neither does it exist even when approached by those who study epistemology of so-called ordinary knowledge, and this for several reasons: (1) by concentrating on perceptual knowledge as the paradigm of ordinary knowledge; (2) by trying to provide a secure basis for perceptual knowledge immune to sceptical attacks by trying to meet the sceptic's criterion of certainty; (3) by the discussion being dominated by the two grand over-arching theories of Empiricism and Rationalism.

One does not wish to deny that the problems in the domain of perceptual knowledge are of fundamental epistemological significance, but it would be misleading to regard them as identical with those in the domain of ordinary knowledge as characterised in this book. A statement of the kind containing perceptual knowledge that 'this grass is green' is very different from a statement expressing ordinary knowledge of the kind 'this man is reputed to be a wife-beater' or 'one ought not to commit arson' (both morally and non-morally). The former is sometimes said to be immediate knowledge; the latter mediate, that is, mediated *via* evidence. It would be inappropriate to ask for evidence to support or back up the claim that this grass is green – one just *sees* this grass to be green (provided the grass in question has not died or turned brown during a period of drought, that there is suitable daylight, the observer's eyesight is not impaired, etc.) It is odd, as Harré points out, to say that this grass being green is evidence for the truth of the claim that this grass is green. This brings up the question at the most fundamental epistemological level of how a certain grouping of words may be used to give a correct account of states of affairs or how things are in the world, a question which the present enterprise cannot hope to deal with.[12] But it is appropriate to ask for evidence in support of the claim that the man in question is reputed to be a wife-beater, because one does not establish this alleged fact in the same way that one can observe the alleged fact that grass is green, for in support or challenge of it, one might have to cite other facts whereas the 'evidence' for 'grass is green' is simply the fact that grass is green. The claim for the former is an inference from something else which is observed to be the case, such as what his wife has to show for after such a session, and even other people's observations of his actually

184

thrashing her in public. As Harré puts it, there is a logical distance between the alleged fact and the evidence cited in its support.[13] But although the logical distance exists, it should not be inferred from it that there can be no warrant for rational safe-conduct in the passage from evidence to alleged fact. To do so is to fall into the error of supposing that logical distance, if it exists, can only be bridged by logical entailment or strict implication.

At the level of perceptual knowledge, philosophical scepticism, by asking for indubitable and certain knowledge, appears to have driven a logical wedge between the perceptual knowledge claim and its so-called 'evidence'. One like the empiricist who tries to resist the sceptical attack, instead of arguing that the notion of evidence is inappropriate, accepts the sceptical thesis that a wedge could exist between the claim and its 'evidence', and then tries to overcome the obstacle by translating the claim into a form which one thinks is immune to the sceptical challenge. The claim that this grass is green is conceded to need 'evidence' of the kind that this grass appears to be green to the perceiver. This salvage operation, however, does not bestow immunity to attack, for the sceptic could persist in arguing that even the reduced claim, that grass appears to be green to the perceiver, does not entail that grass is green. To prevent this further wedge from being driven, some Empiricists end up by reducing the claim to its so-called 'evidence', by saying that 'grass is green' means no more than 'there appears to be a green patch in my visual field' (or words to such effect). This, unfortunately, brings with it the familiar difficulties of phenomenalism and of sense-data as the foundations for our knowledge of the world.

While Empiricism retreats into the 'given' of sensory experience in meeting the sceptical challenge, the Rationalists retreat into the mathematical mode of reasoning to get at indubitable truths which are necessary, and from which all other knowledge claims may be deduced and thus secured. The Cartesian *cogito* is *par excellence* a product of this mode of procedure. While the Empiricist is trying to provide a foundation by securing a rock-bottom base in the given of sensory experience upon which an ascent may be made, the Rationalist is busy doing the same by securing self-evident first truths from which a descent may be made. But both, without hesitation, accept the sceptic's paradigm of knowledge, that nothing counts as knowledge unless it is certain, that nothing is certain unless proof (strict implication) is available, and that mathematics (and logic) which satisfy that condition is really knowledge. On such a view of knowledge, the prime and only proper logical relationship between propositions is that of strict implication.

Traditional epistemology has gone wrong on two counts: (i) its insistence on getting hold of foundations of knowledge; and (ii) its demand that such a foundation must be logically certain. Popper rejects both these goals – certain knowledge is neither available nor is it necessary for knowledge (outside mathematics) to be possible and obtainable.[14] He approaches epistemology from the standpoint of scientific knowledge, and claims that although there is a continuum from ordinary to scientific knowledge, to concentrate on the former at the expense of the latter is to miss out 'the most important and most exciting problems of epistemology'. In this contention, Popper is correct because as he himself emphasises, scientific knowledge is concerned with the critical growth of knowledge, whereas, as we have seen, ordinary knowledge may at best contribute to the preliminary stage of this process of systematic critical growth. Indeed once freed from the task of providing for a logically certain foundation, epistemology may usefully consider problems which cluster around three loci: (a) the Popperian one about science and the critical growth of this kind of knowledge, whose basic concern is to provide satisfactory and adequate explanatory theories about observed phenomena; (b) the domain of ordinary knowledge (including moral knowledge) as identified by this book and whose main concern is to provide justifications for knowledge claims by relying on scientific or pre-scientific theorising; (c) the domain of perceptual knowledge which raises in a most urgent manner the semantical link between language and the world of which it purports to give a correct description. This book focuses on the second of these three domains, and argues that even if Popper were mistaken about the logic of fallibilism including that of falsification being the logic of scientific discovery, this does not mean that that logic suitably edited and enriched, could not be the logic of justification which obtains in the domain of ordinary knowledge.

6   *LOGICA UTENS* AND THE NOTION OF 'RELEVANCE' IN THE DOMAIN OF ORDINARY KNOWLEDGE

Traditionally logic is said to apply to reasoning irrespective of its subject matter, because it is concerned with the form of arguments and not with their content. It is said to determine their validity, that is, whether the premises and the conclusion are linked in a suitable way. In this way, one would be able to distinguish between a conclusion which is valid but false from one which may be true but invalidly derived. This view of logic leads to it operating at the very highest abstract level – the collection of marks is susceptible to interpretation of a very minimal kind, to the extent that one regards the variables as sentences, and their operators to be negation, conjunction, etc. And one assumes that variables have truth-values. Logic systematically investigates the relationships between variables when the operators are made to bear on them. As such it is a formal system.

Logic is not primarily undertaken for its own sake (although it may be so indulged), for its rationale is to enable one to assess the validity of arguments in actual discourse. Or to put it in another way, it is to enable us to think clearly so that eventually one may act effectively. Although it is acknowledged that logic as a formal system might begin by being guided by what intuitively appears to be valid or invalid in informal arguments, and developing what is vague and implicit to become precise and explicit rules of inference, it is also the case that these rules once formulated are used as arbiters of what is valid or invalid in informal arguments. *Logica utens* is to be distinguished from *logica docens* – the former referring to the intuitive judgments of validity or invalidity of informal arguments and the latter to rigorous and precise rules of inference developed by formal logical systems.[15] This then raises the question how well *logica utens* is served by *logica docens*, for the latter is necessarily abstract, while the former employs not propositional variables but actual propositions. The 'p' and the 'q' have to be further interpreted – we need to know what they stand for. Actual informal arguments take place within specific domains of discourse – it is taken for granted that in a mathematical argument, 'p' and 'q' stand for mathematical propositions. To try to prove p which may be a

187

mathematical proposition of the kind '2 + 2 = 4' in terms of q, a proposition like 'Beethoven wrote the Eroïca Symphony' would be to commit an absurdity or perhaps even a category mistake. And even if p and q stand for propositions within the same domain of discourse, such as factual discourse, an informal argument relying on *logica utens* would be ruled out of court if q, that Beethoven wrote the Eroïca Symphony, were offered as the conclusion based on the premise p, that Britain in August 1983 had a Tory government.

Logica docens is like logic *in absentia* – like an absentee landlord who insists on his tenants paying him in Deutschmarks when the local economy is based on cowrie shells. Such a landlord would say cowrie shells do not constitute a valid form of payment and claim that the terms of the contract have not been fulfilled. To the natives, cowrie shells are perfectly valid as a form of payment. *Logica utens* is like logic *in situ* – it tacitly recognises that not any p and not any q would do. It is like the more sensitive landlord who is aware of local conditions and who, therefore, would not reject outright cowrie shells as a form of payment, but instead endeavour to use those shells to purchase goods which can eventually be sold elsewhere for Deutschmarks. In this way Deutschmarks would still in the end be relied upon as the mode of payment in his own accounting books, but the cowrie shells would not have to be rejected provided they can be transformed into an intermediary. This roundabout method of economic transaction might mean fewer Deutschmarks in the bank account (or it could mean more if he is lucky), but it would not have the disastrous effect of ruling cowrie shells as an invalid mode of payment without ado.

Logic *in situ* would require the recognition of relevance, and this is what 'relevance logic' attempts to do.[16] Some logicians are appalled by the paradoxes of strict as well as of material implication. The latter, as we saw in Chapter Three, only rules out the possibility of p being true and q being false. In accordance with the former, (i) a necessary proposition is strictly implied by any proposition whatever, and (ii) an impossible proposition strictly implies any proposition whatever. Anderson and Belnap argue that strict implication, by ignoring the demands of relevance, is defective: 'the fancy that relevance is irrelevant to validity strikes us as ludicrous, and we therefore make an attempt to explicate the notion of relevance of A to B.'[17] Classical logic regards the lack of relevance not as a logical defect but at best as a rhetorical one.[18] But at the level of informal argument and logic *in situ*, clearly irrelevance renders an argument invalid and not merely plain boring or uninteresting to an audience. An audience may find irrelevance a waste of time but this is precisely because what is looked for here is a *valid* argument and not an *invalid* one. Someone who collects originals would no doubt find the vendor of reproductions trying to sell him *ersatz* goods a waste of one's time; but this is not because one finds the salesman's techniques not persuasive or hard-hitting enough or amusing, but because he is hawking *ersatz* objects which one is not interested at all in getting. It is not plausible to maintain that lack of relevance is merely a piece of rhetorical inefficiency, and if classical logic so categorises it, then classical logic appears to be mistaken.

Indeed one would go so far as to say that if someone in assessing a flesh-and-blood argument were to insist that it is valid (according to classical logic) in spite of the absence of relevance (both referential and causal) between assertion and so-called evidence, and proceed to act upon the assertion, then one would consider such a person to be a suitable case for treatment. To take an example – suppose X is told that the nut s/he is about to eat is poisonous ('this nut is poisonous'), and is next told that another proposition, namely, 'the moon is made of cheese' materially implies 'this nut is poisonous'. Following material implication (a false proposition may materially imply any false proposition), X considers the above to be a valid argument, and refrains from eating the nut. Should s/he systematically reject all foods because similar 'valid' arguments may be constructed, s/he would soon die of starvation. Such a victim of the demands of material implication would be a comic-tragic figure. Fortunately in real life, the common sense of *logica utens* prevails; and even classical logicians themselves implicitly accept that relevance matters in real life although in their professional moments, they rather cavalierly assign it to poor rhetoric. No classical logician would be prepared to act like X, in accordance with such conclusions 'validly' inferred from the premises. Logicians might justify the discrimination between those arguments which pass the relevance tests and those which do not, on pragmatic grounds – that acting on the latter could lead one to come a cropper. But unless one accepts that the pragmatic justification happens to obtain by accident or coincidence, an explanation is forthcoming, namely and precisely, that relevance fails to obtain in those cases which have led them astray. The belief that events just happen to occur together is but a variant of Hume's thesis of constant conjunction. So here it looks as if that classical logic may join hands with Humean positivism to reinforce the view that there is nothing to distinguish non-accidental from accidental generalisations. It appears then that classical logic has gone astray on this point, since to follow it would not enable one to act effectively, and the inability would be brought about by a failure to think clearly in the first place.

It is said that classical logic shuns relevance because it is notoriously difficult to formalise. However, the recent efforts of relevance logicians have shown that the task is not impossible, even if the systems they have so far produced are not without flaws or above criticism.[19] Most importantly, what they have done is to draw attention to an area in logic where work needs to be done. Such work would be of help in certain issues in epistemology. Susan Haack[20] mentions one such issue, the Quinian thesis that the whole of science faces 'the tribunal of experience'. In Quine's view, it is impossible to test a single sentence in isolation from others. Haack thinks that the dilemma – either a single sentence or the whole of science is the unit of verification or falsification – may be traced to the notion of material implication governing the relationship between any two sentences.

However, the systems of relevance logic devised by logicians like Belnap and Anderson[21] are not relevant to the preoccupation of this book. But unfortunately, to provide a *logica docens* of relevance with respect to the problem of justification in the domain of ordinary knowledge, is beyond the aim of this book and without doubt beyond the competence of its author. What one hopes to do here is merely to go one or two small steps beyond *logica utens* as it operates in such a domain. Chapter Three tries to do this by rejecting both strict implication and material implication on the grounds that the former is too strict and the latter too lax. It argues for epistemic implication which takes precautions against the paradoxes of relevance involved in both strict and material implication, by maintaining that the *justificandum* ((A1), (A2), (A3)) and the *justificans* ((E1), (E2), (E3)) must satisfy (a) referential relevance; (b) causal relevance;

(c) that what is causally relevant must be independent of a prior commitment to the *justificandum*; (d) if the *justificans* satisfies (a), (b) and (c) but is true, then the *justificandum* is corroborated or supported; (e) if the *justificans* satisfies (a), (b) and (c) but is false, then the *justificandum* has been falsified; (f) there is neither 'conclusive$_{D/A}$' verification under (d) nor 'conclusive$_{D/A}$' falsification under (e), although there is 'conclusive$_M$' verification under (d) and 'conclusive$_M$' falsification under (e).

VI

FACT AND VALUE WITHIN CONTEMPORARY LIBERALISM

(J. S. Mill and Karl Popper)

Contemporary intellectual orthodoxy accepts the twentieth-century positivist fact/value distinction for two reasons: (a) on explicit logical grounds that normative/value statements cannot be logically derived from factual ones; and (b) on implicit ideological grounds that a free and open (i.e. liberal) society requires a meta-ethics of either subjectivism or relativism to sustain it. The foregoing chapters of this book set out to undermine the logical argument which, although conclusive within its own terms, need not lead to the conclusion that normative/value statements are necessarily non-objective or irrational, as 'ought' may epistemically imply 'is' even if 'is' does not strictly imply 'ought'. This chapter will show that the subjectivist/relativist meta-ethical underpinning is irrelevant to the sustenance of a liberal society. If it can be shown that liberalism is not only perfectly compatible with, but positively requires (contrary to current conventional wisdom) a meta-ethics of objectivity/rationality, a great deal of the innate fear and hostility to an attempt to establish the possibility of objectivity and rationality in moral values would be diminished, making it possible to re-assess the necessity for the fact/value distinction as it is usually understood today.[1]

To show that the anxiety is misplaced it would be helpful to recall Basil Mitchell's distinction between new and old liberalism.[2] It is the former which is underpinned by a meta-ethics of subjectivism and/or relativism. The latter, on the contrary, is both

192

compatible with and requires the possibility of objectivity/rationality in the determination of values. J. S. Mill is an outstanding instance of so-called old liberalism; his arguments (to be investigated below) for the central liberal value of freedom of thought and discussion are essentially different from those proffered by new liberals. In this connection it would be instructive to look at Popper and his philosophy, as he seems to be exceedingly ambivalent about old liberalism, an ambivalence which, under the pressure of his political preferences, turns into a rejection of it, in spite of the fact that increasingly the direction of his own wider metaphysical evolution is towards it. While his epistemology inclines him to old liberalism, he seems mistakenly to believe that his politics requires him to embrace new liberalism. This produces an irresolvable tension and schizophrenia in his thought robbing it in the end of coherence and leading him to self-defeat.

1 NEW LIBERALISM AND ITS PRESUPPOSITIONS

But before examining Mill and Popper, let us first look at new liberalism. It may be set out as follows: (1) a free and open society is one that tolerates diversity of opinions and beliefs; (2) the expression of conflicting opinions and beliefs must be tolerated precisely because it is logically not possible to establish that some beliefs may be true, correct or justified and others may not; (3) given that they are irredeemably subjective (or relativistic), one opinion or belief has as much right as any other to be deemed correct or justified; (4) therefore, to suppress one but not another is unjustified; (5) the final conclusion must be that a free and open society tolerates pluralism because pluralism is alone compatible with a subjective/relativist meta-ethics; (6) the corollary of (5) is that pluralism and the possibility of objectivity are not compatible with each other; (7) if objectivity were to be established, pluralism would be rendered superfluous and meaningless and its abolition would go hand in hand with the demise of the free and open society; (8) hence, it becomes almost a dogmatic article of faith that the possibility of objectivity does not and cannot obtain.

This view, however, rests on several errors, the central one being that tolerance and pluralism make no sense and are not required if objectivity were to be possible. The mistake may itself be traced to a confusion between objectivity on the one hand and dogmatism, absolutism or infallibility on the other. Very briefly, objectivity amounts to the following: (a) what is objective is independent of psychological states of mind or attitudes, whether these be plain intuitions or feelings of certainty, conviction, sincerity or of being self-evidently true.[3] What is objective can be inter-subjectively established (although what is inter-subjective is not necessarily objective). It thus rules out privileged access and an epistemology where the individual (or group) is the sovereign or the final arbiter of what is true, correct or justified; (b) conflicting objective claims may be settled by methods which themselves satisfy (a) just mentioned; (c) *via* (a) and (b), it is possible to establish what is correct (or incorrect), justified (or unjustified).

However, what is objectively established (as thus characterised) makes no claim to being absolutely, infallibly or dogmatically true or correct. Mill has put it well: 'There is the greatest difference between presuming an opinion to be true, because with every opportunity for contesting it, it has not been refuted, and assuming its truth for the purpose of not permitting its refutation.'[4] To assume the latter is to assume infallibility (Mill defines infallibility as an undertaking to decide the question about the truth of an opinion *'for others*, without allowing them to hear what can be said on the contrary side'[5]), and to aspire to dogmatism. To assume the former is to assume that the quest for 'truth' is an open-ended one, that is, to eschew absolutism and to recognise that new arguments could arise to challenge one's conclusion and if these were cogent one would have to modify it or give it up.

The possibility of objectivity implies the possibility of detecting errors; errors can as a matter of fact be detected if people are permitted to scrutinise the claims made critically and express their doubts, their reservations, in short their criticisms of them. Far from the possibility of objectivity annihilating the basis of a free and open society, such a society alone is compatible with it. Dogmatism, absolutism and infallibility have no need for liberalism, it is true; but neither have these values anything to do with objectivity. It is by a most unfortunate technique, association of guilt, that objectivity comes to be regarded as the prerequisite for the pursuit of intolerance and illiberalism. The claim for objectivity is a minimal one, namely, that it is possible to find out whether a belief is warranted or not by subjecting it to criticism.

It does not guarantee an outcome which is certain, holds true for all times and under all circumstances; nor does it require that a conclusion arrived at critically should itself be protected from and be immune to all future criticism.

The new liberals could not have misunderstood the claim of objectivity more seriously than in maintaining that a free and open society rests upon its repudiation. Logically, the link between objectivity and intolerance is unfounded. Psychologically, a person with a coherent good argument has less need, if any, to resort to silencing an opponent than someone who believes that one opinion is as good as another. Politically speaking, from the point of view of *praxis*, either meta-ethics could prove equally impotent in instigating change – both are equally compatible with the preservation of the *status quo*. If one opinion or set of moral ideas is as valid as any other set, then why bother to change; but if you could indeed convince your opponents on objective grounds that their set of ideas is defective, they might agree and yet do nothing. Observation shows that many people can tolerate a high degree of discrepancy between rational conviction and behaviour. Such discrepancy does not always provoke a crisis of identity following the loss of integrity. There is nothing inherently revolutionary in political terms about the claim to the possibility of objectivity; claims objectively established may or may not lead to revolutionary changes in society depending on the conjuncture of events and forces, structural and fortuitous in any particular historical context. It would be simplistic in the extreme to maintain that a causal connection necessarily exists between an objective meta-ethics and revolution (with or without violence). The only necessary link between belief and action lies in the thesis of prescriptivism – *pace* Hare, one may say that any 'ought' proposition entails a prescription to carry out whatever is embodied in it. But this thesis is itself neutral with regard to the rival meta-ethical positions. An 'ought' proposition, whether established as justified in an objective manner, or simply sincerely held, would entail the appropriate prescription.[6]

New liberalism has gone wrong because it is ultimately suspicious of rationalism (with a small 'r') which Popper says is nothing more than the critical method:

The Western rationalist tradition, which derives from the

Greeks, is the tradition of critical discussion – of examining and testing propositions or theories by attempting to refute them. This critical rational method must not be mistaken for a method of proof, that is to say, for a method of finally establishing truth; nor is it a method which always secures agreement. Its value lies, rather, in the fact that participants in a discussion will, to some extent, change their minds, and part as wiser men.[7]

The spiritual fountainhead of new liberalism is not the Greek tradition but the Romantic tradition of self-assertion and of epistemological sovereignty in the self. While the former emphasises the centrality of an 'impersonal, interpersonal objective'[8] epistemological authority, the latter emphasises the will of the individual as the final arbiter of what is correct/incorrect, justified/unjustified. Freedom of expression and discussion, on this view, is merely an aspect of freedom of choice. To choose is all. Since the content of such choices is really irrelevant, being ultimately beyond critical assessment, all that is left is indeed the very context of choice itself. Freedom sanctifies the values of life as each sees fit to commit himself or herself. The 'truth' about values is an existential one which has no reference outside the preferences of the ego (or the collective consciousness.) It implies that there is nothing good or bad but choosing makes it so. A necessary consequence of this view, given the differences in their inclinations amongst human beings, is the existence of diversity of choices. Diversity is then celebrated and cherished for its own sake as an intrinsic good.

2   OLD LIBERALISM AND ITS PRESUPPOSITIONS

However, before looking into the presuppositions of old liberalism as exemplified by Mill, one must remove an important misunderstanding about Mill's moral philosophy. As mentioned in Chapter One, Mill, at least since Moore, is often taken to be a moral philosopher notorious for having committed the Naturalistic Fallacy, thereby undermining his entire system of morality. Upon closer examination, however, this accusation turns out to be groundless.

Attempts to defend any so-called ultimate moral principles (including the utilitarian one) fall into at least five categories: (a) by trying to logically derive, for instance, the utilitarian ultimate principle 'one ought to maximise happiness' from 'people want happiness'; (b) by saying that it is a self-evident truth which requires no further evidence; (c) by regarding it as an irrational/ non-rational commitment; (d) by admitting that although it is not logically derivable from factual propositions, nevertheless, it is capable of being rationally supported by citing factual evidence about human nature; (e) that it is transcendently given.

The first is the argument that the ultimate principle is capable of 'direct proof'; but it is easily demolished by saying that it commits the Naturalistic Fallacy. The second is fraught with those difficulties usually associated with intuitionism as an epistemology. The third runs into problems already rehearsed in Chapters One and Two. The fourth is an instance (or near instance) of applying the thesis of fallibilism as epistemic implication which this book pursues; and moreover, one can make a case for saying that Mill follows this method. The fifth also presents problems which have been briefly looked into in Chapter Four (section 7).

Mill explicitly rejects the first method by saying that the ultimate premise of his system is not capable of direct proof.[9] Direct proof amounts to logical derivation from factual premises. Moore was simply mistaken in claiming that Mill attempted to (logically) derive his ultimate principle from statements about human psychology.

Neither did Mill resort to the second method. It is well known that he spent a good proportion of his intellectual energy combatting intuitionism, regarding it as a most pernicious (that is, having socially harmful effects) epistemology, and therefore, a great evil of his time.[10] Mill had no use for theology; and it would have gone against his general epistemology to base morality upon it. Implicitly, he rejected the third method by actually arguing for and using the fourth.

Mill could be said to have anticipated the twentieth-century view (though not in the case of logical positivism) that 'ought' propositions (moral and non-moral) are prescriptions.[11] That is to say, values/norms are non-cognitive, but conative, as far as their ontological status is concerned. However, as Mill did not make the mistake of inferring their epistemological status, as one of irrationality, from their ontological status as twentieth-century positivism tends to do, he, like Kant, argued that prescriptions can be rationally supported – their epistemological status is one of rationality. (His arguments, of course, differ from those of Kant's, but that is not relevant to the point at issue.)

Very briefly,[12] Mill's arguments may be reconstructed as follows:

(i) people as a matter of fact find certain things or doing certain things pleasurable and other things or activities painful;

(ii) people as a matter of fact avoid painful things/activities and seek pleasurable things/activities;

(iii) that human beings find certain things/activities painful or pleasurable may be explained in terms of their physiology, neurology and psychology as well as the nature of the things/activities themselves;

(iv) in support of the principle 'one ought to maximise pleasure and minimise pain', it would be in order to cite factual evidence of the type mentioned in (i), (ii) and (iii) above;

(v) this support does not amount to logical derivation, but (in the version of fallibilism advanced by this book) epistemic implication may be said to obtain between the principle and these other factual premises;

(vi) to show that epistemic implication obtains, let us first cast the ultimate premise of Mill's system into the form 'people ought to maximise pleasure and minimise pain' – call it p. The factual premises may be cast in the form 'people find being warmed by a fire on a cold day pleasurable, and would strive to get warmth, given the state of their physiology, neurology and psychology and the nature of fire itself' – call such propositions q.

It can be seen that p and q share the same subject term; they, therefore, satisfy referential relevance. There is also causal relevance because the meaning of the term 'maximising pleasure/ minimising pain' is partially explicated by referring to terms like 'being warmed by a fire on a cold day', 'avoiding touching exposed live electric wires' and so on. The partial meaning link exists because we find out that these things/activities referred to by the terms in question are what we as a matter of fact seek to do/avoid doing, other things being equal. We also find out through scientific investigation that the human organism has certain properties (neural, physiological, psychological) so that the stimulus provided by the fire or the electric current would indeed produce the response in people which they come to characterise as pleasurable or painful. Moreover, the causally relevant evidence is itself causally independent of and prior to the adoption of the norm of maximising pleasure and minimising pain.

Mill's account has been shown to satisfy the demands of epistemic implication. If so his moral system does not need to rest on a free-floating commitment; nor can it be accused of committing the Naturalistic Fallacy.

We can now return to the task of examining the presuppositions of old liberalism. Freedom under the critical tradition or fallibilism is conceived very differently from that which obtains under new liberalism. Mill gives two closely related sorts of reasons to justify freedom of expression and discussion: (1) that freedom of expression is a precondition for the discovery of objective truths; and (2) that it is a precondition of the existence of a moral and rational being.

The first argument may be called the Assumption of Infallibility Argument[13] and it rests on the following presuppositions: (a) that there exists such a thing as 'attainable, communicable, objective truth in the field of value judgments';[14] (b) that its discovery is only possible in a society (a necessary condition) which permits an ample degree of freedom of inquiry and discussion; (c) that people are, however, fallible and less than omniscient; so that (d) with discoveries, no matter how well supported by evidence now which indicate that they are correct or justified, there can never be ruled out the possibility of their being false; hence truths can never be final, nor discussion about them terminated once and for all. The search, the discovery and the justification is an open-ended affair.

Presuppositions (b) and (d) given (a) and (c) emphasise the very conditions under which alone we can hope to acquire true/correct beliefs (or discover them to be false/incorrect) in a rational systematic manner through criticism. Presupposition (a) distinguishes Mill in the main from new liberalism. Mill believes without reservation that there are objective truths to be discovered even though one can never be certain once and for all that one has discovered them. New liberals, as we have seen, deny that there are such truths which may be discovered (no matter how tentative). Under old liberalism, freedom of expression is not merely a manifestation of the freely-choosing will; it is a causal requirement (a necessary condition) for the discovery of truth. Pluralism and diversity are, therefore, not cherished for their own sakes but are tolerated as necessary elements in the process of competition for 'truth survival'. One person's opinion is not necessarily as well-founded as another's. Epistemological equality makes nonsense in the end of what we say. Epistemological discrimination both requires and generates a proliferation of competing and conflicting theses. Its aim is to sort out the sheep from the goats. It is what Gellner[15] calls a 'Selector' theory of knowledge.

New liberalism, on the other hand, is in keeping with an epistemology of 'negative endorsement'. Gellner says that

> re-endorsement theories are those which, after profound reflection, reach the conclusion that all is well with existing banks of beliefs, or at least with a substantial part of it, simply in virtue of it *being* the existing bank of beliefs. They act like a commission of inquiry into some suspect establishment, which ends by clearing its name and declaring the suspicions which had caused the inquiry to be in substance unfounded.[16]

Gellner also observes that an epistemology of negative endorsement has very considerable ideological charms, because he who practises it may pose as both modest and liberal, even when he is in fact neither modest nor liberal, which helps to account for its popularity. So while this kind of epistemology goes with the image of universal benevolence, of tolerance, of live and let live, a Selector epistemology is grimly associated with the image of inquisitorial intolerance, of revolutionary ferment, fanaticism and excesses. However, it would be silly to allow oneself to be taken in by the epistemological equivalents of Satchi and Satchi.

Freedom of criticism as the precondition for the acquisition of truths in a rational systematic manner is for Mill one side of the coin; the other side is his argument which says that freedom is the precondition of the existence of a moral and rational being. This may be called the Devil's Advocate Argument.[17] It is not enough simply to hold the right opinions. One must know the grounds for their rightness, their implications for action, how they are to be applied to actual situations, how they are akin to other beliefs and yet differ from them, what courses of action are opened and what closed as a result of applying them, etc. In other words, it is what is implied in the notion of a critical morality, the morality which alone is in keeping with the nature of a rational moral agent.[18] Holding true beliefs which may come from authority or revelation, passively and unreflectively, violates the rational endowment of people which constitutes their peculiar nature. Fitzjames Stephen takes the contrary view, and considers as 'the greatest of all intellectual blessings' the sharing of true beliefs by all men regardless of the manner, provided that the cost in attaining the goal in question is not too high – a typically utilitarian approach.[19]

All people, in spite of their differing intellectual and other abilities, in Mill's opinion, can attain the status and dignity of thinking beings, provided there is freedom of inquiry and criticism. On this question he cannot be accused of elitist leanings. He says:

> Not that it is solely, or chiefly, to form great thinkers, that freedom of thinking is required. On the contrary, it is as much and even more to enable average human beings to attain the mental stature which they are capable of. There have been, and may again be, great individual thinkers in a general atmosphere of mental slavery. But there never has been, nor ever will be, in that atmosphere an intellectually active people.[20]

3 BERLIN'S (A NEW LIBERAL) MISUNDERSTANDING OF MILL

It would be instructive to study Berlin's reaction to Mill on this point. Berlin may be said to be a new liberal (although at first sight, he might not appear to be straightforwardly so), and hence one would expect a certain inability on his part to appreciate this argument of Mill. Berlin says that 'there are many possible courses of action and forms of life worth living, and therefore to choose between them is part of being rational or capable of moral judg-ment'.[21] However, Berlin seems to forget that to be a rational moral being is not independent of the possibility of objective communicable truths being discovered in the field of value judg-ment. To be rational is to be critical. To be critical is to be argumentative, that is, to deploy arguments.

Arguments are regulated by *truth* and *validity*. As Popper correctly says:

> the argumentative use (of language) has led to the evolution of ideal standards of control, or of *'regulative ideas'* (using a Kantian term): the main regulative idea of the descriptive use of language is *truth* (as distinct from *falsity*); and that of the argumentative use of language, in critical discussion, is *validity* (as distinct from *invalidity*).[22]

If truth and validity are satisfied, then one has produced a coherent and correct (or good) argument. Mill believes that such arguments may be found in the field of values (and so does Popper up to a point as we shall see). For Mill, then, his belief that objectivity is possible (a presupposition of his first argument) is very intimately bound up with his second argument. It would not make sense to adhere to the second and jettison the first. Yet this is precisely what Berlin proposes to do, which shows a real incomprehension on his part of the thesis of old liberalism. By so doing, he gives the misleading impression that it is possible to talk meaningfully about being a rational moral being even if rational choices cannot be made and objective claims cannot be arrived at.

He then goes on to say that in any case choice is inevitable because ends collide. According to him, there are several ultimate values (not one), such as freedom, justice, security, etc. He gives no account of why they are ultimate values. But he believes that these are often incapable of simultaneous fulfilment in any one situation, and since he does not believe that they can be arranged in an objective order of priority (that it is not possible to argue critically for such an order), a choice between them is inevitable. This context of choice constitutes a moral dilemma. His quarrel with what he calls the 'classical vision' lies in its belief in just such a possibility of constructing a hierarchy of values, so that in a conflict, one knows which value has to be subordinated to another.

But for Berlin, the priority of values is merely an expression of choice. 'In the end men choose between ultimate values; they choose as they do, because their life and thought are determined by fundamental moral categories and concepts that are, at any rate over large stretches of time and space, a part of their being and thought and sense of their own identity; part of what makes them human.'[23]

Short of interpreting this remark to mean we are deterministic creatures, Berlin may be understood to be saying what amounts to the form of life argument. One chooses in a certain way because one is a member of a community which happens to rate one so-called ultimate value above another. So in Berlin's own society, the value of freedom may be preferred to the value of equality should the two clash, and Berlin would go along with it and choose accordingly. In other words, the pluralism of values that he talks of, and the value of freedom to choose ends, happen to be embedded in a form of life of which he is a participant. If so, he must be committed to ethical relativism. Freedom is chosen above other ends because he is committed to a way of life which endorses this order of priority.

Given that Berlin is a new liberal, it comes as no surprise that he regards Mill's Devil's Advocate Argument as feeble in the extreme and really to be redundant since Mill, after all, does believe that there are objective truths to be discovered. This indicates that he again misunderstands the intricate tie-up between the two arguments – just as the second makes no sense without the first, the first is incomplete without the second. It matters how the truth is obtained and not that one simply happens to hold it. It must be critically arrived at by the individual agent. Berlin says that he (Mill)

> declared that if there were no genuine dissenters, we had an obligation to invent arguments against ourselves, in order to keep ourselves in a state of intellectual fitness. This resembles nothing so much as Hegel's argument for war as keeping human society from stagnation. Yet if the truth about human affairs were in principle demonstrable, as it is, say, in arithmetic, the invention of false propositions in order to be knocked down would scarcely be needed to preserve our understanding of it.[24]

The arithmetical analogy is ill-conceived – the real point of similarity lies in the ability not merely to apply mechanically although successfully a mathematical formula, but to understand fully the operation involved. Getting the answers right through learning by heart an equation is not the point.

Berlin then foists on Mill a view which he never held, namely, that 'what Mill seems really to be asking for is diversity of opinion for its own sake'.[25] Diversity for its own sake, as we saw earlier, is really incompatible with a belief in the possibility of discovering objective truths. If such a possibility is taken seriously, the diversity that appears is only a necessary concomitant of the process of discovering truths in a context of free, rational and critical inquiry. Diversity for its own sake is true of the new liberals. Berlin distorts Mill to make him one of them. Yet he remains uneasy in doing so, since it is so obvious that Mill is not a new liberal. Consequently he vacillates between saying that Mill takes the first argument seriously and that he in fact does not.[26] In so doing, he shows that he has also failed to understand that argument itself – while the belief in objective truths *tout court* is irrelevant to the issue of freedom of inquiry and criticism, however, the belief in the possible discovery of objective truths rationally and critically arrived at, necessarily requires freedom of inquiry; moreover, a critical morality is the only sort compatible with the nature and dignity of a rational thinking being.

So far the two central arguments of Mill have been examined. In fact there is a third, a utilitarian one which may be developed as follows:[27] (a) true beliefs produce good consequences. They promote welfare or progress. It matters vitally that we get hold of and act upon them. Disutility would be generated if we were to act upon false beliefs. So it matters equally that we should be able to discover that we have been mistaken; (b) the presuppositions in the Assumption of Infallibility Argument lead to the conclusion that continuous freedom of criticism and expression is a necessary condition for discovering truth and detecting falsehood; (c) therefore, freedom of expression may also be defended on instrumental grounds as a mean/end relationship. Mill believes that true opinions are more likely to emerge through freedom of inquiry and discussion. However, this instrumental assumption should not be assessed on its own independent of the other two arguments; otherwise, it could lead to the conclusion that Mill would be prepared to jettison or modify that freedom if there is another more efficient alternative to being apprised of the truth, such as through revelation or indoctrination. But for Mill, such alternatives would be neither available nor acceptable.[28]

In the light of the discussion above, one may conclude that new liberalism rests on a subjective/relativist epistemology where reason ultimately plays no part. Tolerance, it appears, is required only because one norm or standard is as 'valid' as another. But if all norms, including the norm of tolerance, are deemed to be valid because the individual/community has merely chosen to adopt and live by them, then the norm of tolerance, the central value of liberalism, stands in danger of being rendered 'invalid' should individuals or sufficient numbers in a community decide to reject it. This leads to the so-called paradox of tolerance – must a tolerant society allow the intolerant to destroy or undermine it? Within new liberalism, there is no way of surmounting it. The epistemology upon which it rests may ultimately thus destroy it. Nor within its epistemological framework is there any need to change an intolerant society to a tolerant or less intolerant one, unless individuals happen to wish to change by adopting or committing themselves to such a norm. In other words, given its epistemological underpinning, new liberalism cannot help but be a smug complacent philosophy – new liberals happen to live and be brought up in a society where the ideals of freedom of expression and tolerance are practised; they in turn practice them themselves and hope that no one in their society would have sufficient initiative to reject the dominant values and upset the social order to which they have become accustomed. The new liberals may happen to have fastened on to a truth. But for Mill, that is not sufficient, for it is not in keeping with the dignity of thinking beings to be simply creatures of custom or habit, and in the long run, uncritical habitual conduct destroys the critical faculty.

4 POPPER'S SCHIZOPHRENIA INDUCED BY POLITICAL FEARS LEADING TO EPISTEMOLOGICAL *HARA-KIRI*

A seemingly forceful proponent of old liberalism today is Karl Popper. The word 'seemingly' is used deliberately and the reasons would be made clear later on. But in brief these are: there is a deep tension between Popper's epistemology and his politics. The central tenet of his epistemology is the possibility of objective knowledge *via* the method of criticism and argument, that is, of fallibilism. He maintains that his epistemology leads him to hold certain views about society and politics[29] – to liberalism, democracy, anti-historicism, piecemeal social engineering.[30] The unity of method, based on fallibilism, is said to exist both in the natural sciences and the studies of society which involve norms and values. If Popper's epistemology is taken seriously and allowed to reach its logical conclusions in the field of values, then Popper may undoubtedly be said to be a straightforward old-fashioned liberal of the Millean ilk. However, things are not straightforward in Popper's thought, for in the end, far from allowing his epistemology to generate his political philosophy, it is his politics which rides rough-shod over his epistemology and undermines it. According to Millean liberalism and the epistemology of this conception of Popper – call it Popper 1 – fallibilism allows us to discover objective truths in morals. But according to the epistemology of Popper 2, when fallibilism is replaced by 'critical rationalism', this new method allows us to discover no such thing. On the contrary, critical rationalism is itself a faith based on irrational choice. Since, for Popper, there is unity of method, this conclusion could not but serve to undermine his entire philosophy. The possibility of objective knowledge both in science and elsewhere goes by the board, and in its place is enthroned irrationalism, the very ogre he seems to have spent his entire philosophical career combatting.

In Popper, we see the struggle between old and new liberalism. For political reasons, he is driven to embrace the new and in embracing it, also embraces the kiss of death for his entire philosophy. It would, therefore, be instructive to study more closely his view of liberalism, its relation to the currently accepted positivist fact/value distinction and its place within his overall philosophy.

Suppose one has never read Popper's explicitly political writings, but has confined oneself only to his work on the philosophy of science, epistemology and metaphysics and to the programmatic remarks he makes in these tomes about the unity of method in science and in morals, then it would strike one how remarkably similar he is to Mill in the essay *On Liberty*. Indeed there are several passages (stylistic considerations apart) which could have come interchangeably from the pens of either philosopher. So striking, indeed, that it is surprising that he nowhere claims to have been influenced by Mill on this matter, or acknowledges the parallels between his own thoughts and those of the Victorian thinker.[31]

If Popper 1's epistemological considerations alone are taken into account, then for both, tolerance and freedom of expression are linked to the possibility of criticism and argument, and hence of objective knowledge in the field of values. For both then, diversity and pluralism are by-products of the competitive process of survival through the elimination of error. For both, because of fallibilism, there is no absolute certainty. But the absence of certainty is not worrying because the human mind, being critical and rational, may discover that it has made mistakes and so learns from them.[32] The only certainty which a critical and less than omniscient being may attain in knowledge is the certainty that so far the claims made have not been successfully challenged and refuted. Mill says:

> The beliefs which we have most warrant for have no safeguard to rest on, but a standing invitation to the whole world to prove them unfounded. If the challenge is not accepted, or is accepted and the attempt fails, we are far enough from certainty still; but we have done the best that the existing state of human reason admits of; we have neglected nothing that could give the truth a chance of reaching us: if the lists are kept open, we may hope that if there be a better truth, it will be found when the human mind is capable of receiving it; and in the meantime we may rely on having attained such approach to truth as is possible in our own day. This is the amount of certainty attainable by a fallible being, and this is the sole way of attaining it.[33]

The starting point of Popper 1's epistemology is the existence of human language (a theme implicit in Mill's *On Liberty* but not worked out by him). Human language is a man-made product, just as bee-language is a bee-made product. Both are artefacts. What, however, distinguishes human from animal language is that the latter possesses only two functions, whereas the former has four. (Popper says he owes this to his teacher, Bühler, who, however, identified only three functions; the fourth, he, Popper has added.[34]) The shared functions are: the symptomatic or expressive (of the state of the organism) and the releasing or signalling (the receiver responds to the symptomatic expression of the sender). Those characteristic of human language are the descriptive[35] (the ability to make statements which are factually true or false) and the argumentative. Without the descriptive function, the argumentative is not possible as one argues not in a vacuum but ultimately for or against descriptive statements. This holds true even in arguments for or against proposals which involve what ought to be done[36] (the 'ought' may be a moral or a non-moral 'ought'). The descriptive-cum-argumentative functions render critical discussion possible. But like Mill, Popper 1 too wishes to say that in criticism and argument lies not only the possibility of discovering truths but also the dignity of human beings. He says: 'It is to this development of the higher functions of language that we owe our humanity, our reason. For our powers of reasoning are nothing but powers of critical argument.'[37]

Rationality plays a dual role in their respective *Weltanschauung* – the cognitive dimension (rationality as a precondition for the discovery and growth of knowledge) and the existential dimension (rationality as a manifestation of the uniqueness and dignity of man). However, in Popper 1 these two dimensions create an almost unbearable tension which he finds difficult to hold in balance, which comes out clearly in his attitude to the scientific enterprise itself. Although it is obvious that to him the first dimension is imperative, nevertheless, he can often be carried away by the second to such an extent that he appears to give the impression that one may lose sight of the former in the pursuit of the latter, which becomes an autonomous activity to be indulged in for its own sake, as a sheer affirmation of that unique characteristic of the human being who alone possesses the two higher functions of language. The idea that, therefore, there must be a permanent revolution in science is an outcome of this, at times, lopsided emphasis. His fear that the critical spirit might be lulled or deadened by success leads him to imply that in principle a comprehensive true theory in science is impossible. There must be an infinite series of revolutions, each improving upon the other in its approximation to the truth.

Kneale[38] challenges Popper on these points and tries to show

(a) that the idea of a comprehensive true theory cannot be ruled out of court if the claim that it can is based on a postulate of thought that nature is infinitely complex and hence cannot be accounted for in any finally satisfactory theory; (b) that the degree of fear should such success ever appear is unfounded. There may be some decline of free critical inquiry, but not to the extent of being superseded by a non-rational, non-empirical attitude and view of the world. The spirit of critical inquiry would be kept alive through the teaching of scientific achievements *via* a philosophical study of the history of science. The history and the philosophy of science will then come into their own and be the central intellectual disciplines.

Popper fails to make use of Mill's Devil Advocate's Argument, for this is precisely the sort of analogous situation Mill has envisaged in the field of values, where he says that even if we were to come to hold the whole truth, and know that we hold it, nevertheless, it matters that it should be 'fully, frequently, and fearlessly discussed, [or] it will be held as a dead dogma, not a living truth.'[39] Knowing the truth is not simply a matter of being able to recite from memory a list of claims which are true but to know the reasons, to be able to defend them critically if challenged. Human dignity would indeed be impaired if we were to mouth truths. It looks as if Mill was able to resolve the internal tension better than Popper 1.

In spite of these striking similarities, there are very important differences between their general philosophical preoccupations. Although both belong to the positivist tradition, Mill's positivism requires a firm foundation (in experience); but Popper is against foundations, arguing for an epistemology which he says rests on piles driven into swamps. Mill, in his philosophy of science, was an arch inductivist, one of Popper's *bêtes noires*. (As already mentioned, perhaps for these reasons, Popper fails to pay adequate attention to Mill's writings, and this would account for the lack of observation on his part about the remarkable similarity between their views on the method of fallibilism.) Yet Mill, in applying refutability to the field of values –

It is the fashion of the present time to disparage negative logic – that which points out weaknesses in theory or errors in practice, without establishing positive truths. Such negative

criticism would indeed be poor enough as an ultimate result;
but as a means to attaining any positive knowledge or
conviction worthy the name, it cannot be valued too highly;
and until people are again systematically trained to it, there
will be few great thinkers, and a low general average of
intellect, in any but the mathematical and physical
departments of speculation.[40]

– was happy to do away with foundations and to lay open to
criticism and possible refutation every moral belief and opinion.

Mill's immediate political preoccupation was with the threat
posed by democracy to liberalism. In particular he was worried
about the mediocrity of the majority and the pressure of majority
opinion towards conformity, limiting the expression of non-
conforming ideas and lifestyles. It is for this reason too that Mill
regarded not only legal prohibitions as an obstacle to the freedom
of the individual, but also the tyranny of opinion. For Mill, these
threats could be averted only by vigilance in a free and critical
society. Popper, on the other hand, is concerned with the threat
posed by the growth of totalitarianism in this century. He regarded
and still regards his books *The Open Society and Its Enemies* and
The Poverty of Historicism as his war effort.[41] He believes that
Nazism is the product of a decline in intellectual honesty and
integrity, of the critical tradition in general which in the end
undermined the liberal movement in Germany.[42] Totalitarianism
of the left as exemplified in Marxism is again the product of an
unscientific (that is, uncritical) attitude, the refusal to give up a
theory even when it has been refuted, thus offending the logic
of falsification which is the *organon of criticism*. His horror of
totalitarianism is perfectly understandable and he is right to be
exercised by its excesses. However, it has led him to panic action,
to endorse in the end an epistemological programme which denies
the very possibility of unmasking the errors of totalitarian beliefs
themselves, which surely is a self-defeating thing to do.

The slippery road to self-defeat is a pretty long and tortuous
one. To begin with, he realises that his initial epistemology might
have implications for a political philosophy which he might not
find congenial. For it is an epistemology which leads him in science
to celebrate radical leaps and revolutionary changes – scientific
progress consists of bold conjectures (the bolder the better)

surviving refutation when subjected to testing. Given the unity of method he adheres to, one would expect him to welcome equally bold conjectures in the sphere of norms and values. But he does not. Instead, he favours ideas which have as little radical implications for the society of which he is a member as possible. It would be unfair to say that he is a conservative with regard to moral/social ideas and a revolutionary *apropos* scientific ones; it would not be unfair to say that he performs a *volte face* to become an evolutionist in moral/social ideas and a gradualist in action. This constitutes the first breakdown in the unity of method. Such a dramatic turnabout is bound to have further severe repercussions on his whole philosophy.

The liberalism, reformism and gradualism in his political philosophy spring essentially from his horror and abhorrence of totalitarianism (both right and left). Totalitarianism which entails radical changes and large-scale social planning, he argues, is intellectually misconceived because it rests on historicism and holism; methodologically misconceived because it fails to appreciate that there are unintended consequences of actions performed by individuals; and humanly speaking also misconceived because it ignores the disturbance and the upset, not to mention the suffering to individuals who are caught up in the maelstrom of change and planning. Popper is, of course, more than eager and anxious to argue for the correctness of these views just mentioned and to defend them against critical challenge, and no doubt he is even of the opinion that his theses so far have survived criticism. However, in his eagerness to defend his political preferences, he has unwittingly cut the ground from under his feet. For his defence now of liberalism against totalitarianism consists of (1) destroying the method of fallibilism and replacing it with 'critical rationalism'; (2) in embracing critical rationalism, he ultimately embraces irrationalism; (3) under the revised epistemology, he is able to maintain unity of method (in science and in morals) but at the price of admitting that argument and criticism make sense only to those who have decided as a matter of faith that they do matter and make sense. But this surely makes nonsense of his entire philosophy.

'Utopia and Violence' is an exceptionally revealing piece. Within its few brief pages is manifest the conflict between his original epistemology and his politics, with the conflict being resolved by politics displacing the epistemology. Although this article was first delivered/published in 1947/8, nevertheless, it remains a faithful reflection in microcosm of the fundamental tension in his philosophy which endures throughout his long and still continuing career.[43]

In it, he argues against Utopianism on the grounds that basically it, too, is a form of rationalism, but unfortunately rationalism of the wrong sort. Now so far, in following his original epistemology, we know that he approves of rationalism as fallibilism which is the thesis he develops in *Logik der Forschung*. Under unity of method, this means, as we know, that he must maintain that it is possible for objective knowledge to obtain in both science and in the value sphere. Rationalism as fallibilism is contrasted with another type of rationalism which is supposed to be disreputable and which may be written with a capital 'R' and with the word 'classical' qualifying it. This objectionable and sterile form is also sometimes called Intellectualism, which is an epistemology based on deduction from a first premise constituted by an intellectual intuition. So when he says that Utopianism is an unacceptable form of rationalism, one might think that he is accusing it of being a variant of Intellectualism. But not so – in fact the offence he accuses it of perpetrating is that of (a) trying to formulate so-called 'ultimate' ends or ideals to guide and determine political action, and (b) of believing that these ideals can be rationally justified.

Now this is very odd indeed, for if fallibilism is correct, under unity of method, would not Popper himself subscribe to the possibility of determining ideals rationally? Is he not then accusing the Utopian thinker of doing something which cannot be done but which he himself also engages in? His opponent as much as himself uses arguments in defence of the ideals that they respectively uphold. Popper might claim that those arguments marshalled by the Utopian thinkers in support of their ideals and ends are bad arguments which do not stand up to critical scrutiny, while his own set of arguments in support of his ideals are superior and survive critical challenge. However, this would only show that Utopian ideals are incorrect or inadequate, and not that they are by their very nature incapable of being rationally justified. Just as one should distinguish between saying that a scientific theory has been falsified and is false and saying that a theory is unfalsifiable and therefore unscientific, so too one should distinguish between saying that certain arguments on behalf of certain ends have been demolished and saying that these ends are incapable of rational justification.

But perhaps Popper wishes to maintain that the ideals he is keen to defend are not 'ultimate' and that only ultimate ends are incapable of rational justification. One does not know what he has in mind when he talks of ultimate ends as opposed to less ultimate ones. But if justice or equality counts as ultimate ends (these are the ones pursued by certain Utopian thinkers of the left), then it is difficult to see why freedom (defended by Popper) should not also count as an ultimate end. He has given no reason why they do not all belong to that same category. So, either no political thinker pursues ultimate ends (including Utopian ones) or every such thinker does and must (including Popper himself). If the latter is true, then Popper as much as the Utopian theorist endeavours to argue rationally for such ends. Under his original epistemological programme, this is precisely what Popper says should and can be done. But is he then backtracking on this? It looks to be so.

He goes on to say that the programme of Utopianism is self-defeating and leads necessarily to violence: 'That it is self-defeating is connected with the fact that it is impossible to determine ends scientifically. There is no scientific way of choosing between two ends.'[44] But what could Popper mean in this context by 'science', or 'scientific means' or 'scientific argument', terms which he uses in this indictment throughout the article? Originally, the method of fallibilism is supposed to be the method of science. But now he seems to be restricting the method of science (whatever it may mean in this context) so that it no longer entirely overlaps with fallibilism. Just to remind ourselves: fallibilism, as understood by Popper, is the method of deploying arguments and criticisms against a thesis and aims at approximating to the truth *via* the elimination of error. Scientific method in this context turns out to refer to something quite different. He now says that it is the method of *proof*. In arguing with those who hold ends different from your own 'you cannot prove to them that they are wrong'.[45] He does not go on to elaborate what a scientific proof is. However, the only sort of proof available is in mathematics and logic which are sometimes called the formal sciences. But in the factual

213

sciences there can be no proof comparable to those in mathematics. No philosopher has been more persistent and more adamant than Popper in arguing against the possibility of obtaining proof and hence certainty in the factual sciences. The whole brunt of his epistemology and philosophy of science is precisely to emphasise the essential tentativeness of even those conjectures which survive refutation, and the open-ended nature of the sequence – $P_1 \rightarrow TT \rightarrow EE \rightarrow P_2$. It is extremely odd then for him in this context to imply that there can be proofs in the factual sciences. But unless proof is available, it hardly makes sense to complain that one cannot determine ends *scientifically*, that is, give *proofs* for their correctness or otherwise.

To make confusion worse, he next goes on to say that although moral/social ends are not susceptible of being proved, all the same, one can argue rationally for or against choosing such ends.

> I do not wish to create the impression that there is a realm –
> such as the realm of ends – which goes altogether beyond
> the power of rational criticism (even though I certainly wish
> to say that the realm of ends goes largely beyond the power
> of *scientific* argument). For I myself try to argue about this
> realm; and by pointing out the difficulty of deciding between
> competing Utopian blueprints, I try to argue rationally against
> choosing ideal ends of this kind.[46]

But to be able to argue rationally about a certain matter is precisely to employ fallibilism which in any case is for Popper the method of science.

And to make matters even worse, he reduces fallibilism to an attitude of reasonableness. A rationalist, he declares, is a man who 'attempts to reach decisions by argument'.[47] But propaganda, it appears, also uses arguments. So what distinguishes rational argument from arguments deployed in propaganda? It is, he says, the attitude of reasonableness.

> It lies rather in an attitude of give and take, in a readiness not
> only to convince the other man but also possibly to be
> convinced by him. What I call the attitude of reasonableness
> may be characterized by a remark like this: 'I think I am
> right, but I may be wrong and you may be right, and in any
> case let us discuss it, for in this way we are likely to get

214

nearer to a true understanding than if we each merely insist that we are right.'[48]

Now it may be that an attitude of reasonableness is a necessary condition for rationalism as fallibilism to operate, but the one should not be confused with the other. Any attitude, reasonable or otherwise, belongs to what Popper, in his later writings, calls World 2. Attitudes are subjective states of mind. Knowledge, its possibility and its end-products belong to World 3. He goes so far as to call his theory of knowledge 'Epistemology Without a Knowing Subject' (lecture delivered in 1967 and published in 1968). But even if the attitude of reasonableness were to be translated into methodological rules of procedure and not understood as mentalistic states of the parties to a dispute, as he suggests ('first, that one should always hear both sides, and secondly, that one does not make a good judge if one is a party to the case'[49]), this would still not be comparable to the thesis of rationalism as fallibilism. Neither does faithful conformity to these two rules of evidence-taking necessarily yield knowledge which is objective.

Having reduced the thesis of rationalism as fallibilism to a thesis about the attitude of reasonableness, he next admits that he cannot produce a rational defence of the attitude of reasonableness itself. The admission is, however, not bald, for he adduces arguments to show why he cannot produce such a defence. These consist of saying (a) that such a defence involves what he calls 'uncritical' or 'comprehensive rationalism' which 'can be described as the attitude of the person who says "I am not prepared to accept anything that cannot be defended by means of argument or experience"';[50] and (b) that comprehensive rationalism is logically untenable, since the thesis itself cannot be supported by argument or by experience without committing circularity, and hence upon its own criterion be discarded; (c) that if no logically coherent defence can be given, irrationalism appears to be logically superior, and therefore ought to be embraced. At this stage, Popper looks set to embrace outright irrationalism. But being unwilling to succumb to it in this naked form, he finds a way out of the impasse by choosing to embrace instead the faith of critical rationalism, a form of rationalism which 'frankly admits its origin in irrational decision (and which to that extent, admits a certain priority of irrationalism)'.[51] However, such a paradoxical compro-

215

mise could hardly be satisfactory to one whose central epistemological tenet is the possibility of objective knowledge.

It appears that he gets into this impasse through a failure to concentrate on the thesis of fallibilism, which leads him mistakenly to address himself to the quite separate and different thesis about the attitude of reasonableness or the rational attitude.[52] But if he had stuck to the task of defending the thesis of rationalism as fallibilism, there would have been no need to commit epistemological *hara-kiri*. The thesis of rationalism as fallibilism[53] rests upon the following propositions: (1) a rational being is one which possesses human language; (2) human language with its descriptive-cum-argumentative functions make criticism and argument possible; (3) which means that one can distinguish truth from falsehood, validity from invalidity; (4) which entails the possibility of eliminating error and in turn the possibility of objective knowledge; (5) such knowledge is not absolutely or logically certain in the way logical and mathematical propositions can be said to be certain, but tentative and in principle open to future refutation; (6) that mistakes can and will be made but the possibility of detecting errors is built into such an epistemology.

The possibility of argument and criticism is crucial to the method of fallibilism. Any thesis which claims to be superior to another for no reason other than that the individual says it is so (what in Chapter Two is called a flippant reason) or because some unquestioned authority asserts it to be so (the command theory of knowledge) is outside the domain of the rational as characterised by fallibilism. The irrationalists, in so far as they use arguments to establish the superiority of their claim over some form of rationalism, are well within the ken of fallibilism. Fallibilism is not a ladder that you can kick away once you have made use of it to get to the dizzy heights of irrationalism. So long as the irrationalists wish to remain critical irrationalists (and not merely rest irrationalism on a declaration of faith), they cannot afford to kick the ladder away. But if they were to abandon the ladder and change into an uncritical irrationalist, the fallibilist needs not take further notice of their claim as a claim to knowledge.[54] Even in arguing for the superiority of irrationalism over comprehensive rationalism, and of critical rationalism over irrationalism, Popper has not as a matter of fact deserted fallibilism.

If the new unity of method is indeed critical rationalism, then this makes nonsense of his claim that his epistemology enables one to surmount both intellectual (or cognitive) and moral relativism. In the Addendum to the second volume (4th edition) of *The Open Society*, he diagnoses 'the main philosophical malady of our time [to be] an intellectual and moral relativism'.⁵⁵ In his intellectual autobiography, he re-affirms that 'one of the main arguments of *The Open Society* is directed *against moral relativism*'.⁵⁶ However, his arguments do not support that claim at all but ironically the very opposite. Little needs be said about the cognitive shakiness of science if the decision to accept the rules of procedure in science including those about argumentation, criticism and refutation were a mere matter of dogmatic faith or sincere commitment – Kuhn and Winch would have a point which the revised Popperian epistemology could not begin to meet. As for moral relativism, far from having dislodged and overcome it, the thesis of critical rationalism serves only to reinforce it.

We have already seen how under pressure of his political preferences, he concedes that ethical ends or values cannot be scientifically established (meaning by this 'proved'). Next, he also has to retract what he implies under his original epistemology, namely, that it is possible to establish objective truths in the field of values. It will also follow that 'arguments cannot *determine*'⁵⁷ fundamental moral decisions. Relativism is thereby vindicated rather than vanquished, Popper's protestations to the contrary notwithstanding. Moreover, moral relativism is used by Popper for the very purpose of undermining cognitive objectivity, for he represents the choice between rationalism and irrationalism itself as a moral choice. He says, 'To be sure, it is impossible to prove the rightness of any ethical principle, or even to argue in its favour in just the manner in which we argue in favour of a scientific statement. Ethics is not a science. But although there is no rational scientific basis of ethics, there is an ethical basis of science and of rationalism.'⁵⁸ In being faithful to his political preferences, Popper gives a new twist to the contemporary positivist dichotomy between fact and value. Facts, as it were, become as problematic as values because they rest on values.

If it is true that arguments cannot determine moral decisions, then the *raison d'être* for liberalism comes close to that of those who wish to celebrate pluralism and diversity for their own sakes, and who regard choice merely as an existential affirmation of our dignity and autonomy. In arguing for critical dualism, that is, the distinction between nature and convention, facts and standards, Popper says:

> Norms are man-made in the sense that we must blame nobody but ourselves for them; neither nature, nor God. It is our business to improve them as much as we can, if we find that they are objectionable. This last remark implies that by describing norms as conventional, I do not mean that they must be arbitrary, or that one set of normative laws will do just as well as another. By saying that some systems of laws can be improved, that some laws may be better than others, I rather imply that we can compare the existing normative laws (or social institutions) with some standard norms which we have decided are worthy of being realised. But even these standards are of our making in the sense that our decision in favour of them is our own decision, and that we alone carry the responsibility for adopting them.[59]

All norms and standards are our decisions and the recognition of this responsibility is the distinguishing mark between an open and a closed one. The latter, resting on naive monism, is characterised by a confusion between laws of nature which describe physical regularities and normative laws which are conventions and man-made. The reduction of norms to facts, he says, is 'based upon our fear of admitting to ourselves that the responsibility for our ethical decisions is entirely ours and cannot be shifted to anybody else; neither to God, nor to nature, nor to society, nor to history'.[60]

Critical dualism is correct – norms cannot be reduced to facts and are man-made. Popper might also be correct in saying that it is our fear of the responsibility for decision-making which motivates the reduction of norms to facts. He is also right in maintaining in the passage cited above that critical dualism is neutral as to meta-ethics – it does not necessarily entail arbitrariness, irrationalism or the lack of objectivity. However, if he also says that arguments cannot determine moral decisions (even though one might cite them), then he cannot be said to have surmounted the thesis of subjectivism/relativism. The responsibility is indeed all that there is left to legitimate moral choices if such decisions are ultimately not amenable to argument and criticism.

In this respect he is no different from Berlin who argues, as we have seen, that the way we choose is determined by the prevalent values in the society of which we are members. For Popper, we are members of the critical and open society, one which recognises that norms cannot logically be reduced to facts. Moreover, it is one which uses arguments to establish that it would be logically improper to effect such a reduction, but we find these arguments cogent and compelling simply because in the end we have already committed ourselves to the faith of reason. We had made an irrational ethical choice to submit to the demands of reason. But if we had not, no argument would have cut any ice. No notice needs be taken of the thesis of critical dualism. An irrationalist, for instance, could simply ignore all of Popper's arguments against his philosophy by the expediency of saying that he is not committed to rationalism.

The arguments he deploys against Utopian blueprints on the grounds that such ideals are bound to lead to violence would only work if the audience already as a matter of fact hate violence, or have adopted an anti-attitude towards it. In other words, arguments only have purchase within means-end rationality. If you already hate violence (as the result of a personal or collective commitment), then it would be rational for you to reject a set of policies whose implementation is very likely or practically certain to produce violence. But if an individual or community is already committed to violence (or whatever other ideal) as an end, there is no rational argument possible to decide between ends. Disagreement of facts is susceptible to rational resolution (and in this respect, one's decision is not arbitrary) but disagreement of values or ends escape rational, critical discussion. This does then commit him to a meta-ethics of subjectivism/relativism. It puts him squarely within the contemporary positivist tradition which views rationality as purely instrumental in scope and nature. Arguments can help us make rational choices by forcing us to consider the consequences which may result from the alternatives before us;[61] but arguments are not available when it is a choice between ends.

In opting for new liberalism, Popper not only embraces its central tenet, namely, that tolerance is required precisely because all moral ideas are equally sound and valid, but also its central prejudice, namely, that the possibility of objectivity leads to intolerance and violence. Without this prejudice, his analysis of Utopianism would not hold water. He says the Utopian method requires one to be as clear as possible about ultimate ends which a state ought to pursue; then to be as clear as possible about the best means to implement these ends. However, since ultimate ends are not determined scientifically, arguments cannot settle differences of opinion, which then take on the character of religious differences. Utopian religions are necessarily intolerant of one another, and the end result is the triumph of one over the other competitors through violence. Moreover, since a Utopian programme requires an extended time scale for its implementation, during its period of construction, Utopian rulers must also resort continuously to violence, intolerance, suppression of its rivals and anyone who criticises their programme.[62]

It is misleading, as we have already mentioned, to identify only Utopianism with the need for a clarification of so-called ultimate ends and the best means for implementing such ends. All political programmes require such intellectual clarification. Popper's own piecemeal social engineering is indeed the product of such an exercise – he argues that it is required by the ends or ideals of liberalism and negative utilitarianism, ends which may be said to be 'ultimate'. The distinction then between Utopian and piecemeal does not coincide with the distinction between ultimate and non-ultimate ends. It lies elsewhere – in Popper's context of discussion, it lies in the discrepancy between the ideal society and social reality as it exists, and in the quantity and quality of the change that would be required to bring reality to approximate to the ideal. A Utopianist may then be characterised as someone who opts for as near an approximation to the ideal as possible, whereas the piecemeal theorist would be satisfied with some gesture towards approximation, no matter how minimal. Those who recognise the need for radical changes may be called Utopians, and those who would like to see only some peripheral changes may be called the piecemeal social engineers. For instance, a critic diagnosing present-day Soviet society to be deficient when measured against the ideal of a free and liberal society, and recognising that very fundamental and large-scale changes would have to be effected in order to transform such a society to approximate to his ideal, is utopian in outlook. Similarly, the Ayatollah Khomeini is a Utopianist in judging his country under the Pahlavi regime to be very deficient when measured against his ideal of Islamic fundamentalism, and in recognising that vast fundamental changes would have to be effected to turn it into an Islamic republic.

The distinction between those committed to radical large-scale changes and those who prefer marginal ones does not necessarily coincide with the distinction between violent and non-violent changes. Revolutionary changes are not necessarily violent upheavals. Whether a radical/revolutionary change involves violence, and in contrast, whether a marginal/piecemeal change involves no violence is not a matter that can be decided in an *a priori* manner. It is conceivable that revolutionary changes in a certain society could be brought about by peaceful non-violent means. Now it could be true that given existing power structures in any society, radical changes are difficult (if not impossible) to effect without resorting to violence. But this would be true whether the existing power structure is that of present-day Soviet totalitarianism (judged deficient by the end of liberalism) or that of American capitalism (judged deficient by the end of socialism). Whether violence is morally and/or tactically justified in achieving radical changes are separate legitimate questions for the philosopher and others to ponder.[63]

Furthermore, one may distinguish between two possible kinds of Utopian thinkers (when 'Utopian' is now defined not as Popper does in terms of those who clarify ultimate ends, but in terms of those who perceive the need for radical changes in order to approximate to an ideal) – the fallibilist who believes that moral arguments are rational and the irrationalist who does not believe this to be possible. The fallibilist has argued that tolerance, diversity and pluralism are required for the elimination of error *via* competition. To such a fallibilist Utopian thinker, it does not follow, as Popper appears to foist on him, that he necessarily has to resort to violence. On the contrary, the violence would only follow if he were an irrationalist Utopian thinker, and this is precisely what Popper says, that violence is required if ultimate ends are not susceptible to rational arguments. According to the logic of fallibilism, large-scale radical proposals for reforms and the reforms themselves, as well as small-scale ones, could be continuously monitored and assessed, and would be open to continuous criticism and discussion in the hope of detecting and eliminating errors.[64] As Mill says, 'Complete liberty of contradicting and disproving our opinion is the very condition which justifies us in assuming its truth for purposes of action; and on no other terms can a being with human faculties have any rational assurance of being right.'[65]

The conclusion that Popper arrives at, that Utopian engineering must lead to violence, may be due to two mistakes in his thinking. One, that under the pressure from his revised epistemology of critical rationalism, he has failed to appreciate that from the standpoint of fallibilism, the critical assessment of large-scale radical proposals for changes and the changes themselves are nevertheless possible; two, under the pressure from new liberalism, he comes to believe that fallibilism itself entails violence for the very possibility of objective knowledge leads to intolerance and violence, and that tolerance alone is compatible with an epistemology which bestows universal validity on moral ideas, no matter what they are.

Under the spell of new liberalism, he seems falsely to think that the level of critical activity can only be sustained if people are to believe that one opinion is really as good as another, and that it would decline, if not totally disappear, if indeed one opinion can be shown to be objectively defective or inadequate. A similar fear about the decline of critical activity in science leads him, we saw, to argue for the necessity of permanent revolutions in science. In politics it leads him to urge for the necessity of permanent conflict (not revolution) in society. He says:

> There can be no human society without conflict: such a society would be a society not of friends but of ants. Even if it were attainable, there are human values of the greatest importance which would be destroyed by its attainment, and which therefore should prevent us from attempting to bring it about. On the other hand, we certainly ought to bring about a reduction of conflict. So already we have an example of a clash of values or principles. This example also shows that clashes of values and principles may be valuable, and indeed essential for an open society.[66]

Implicit in the faith of critical rationalism, he admits, is the view that 'there always exist irresolvable clashes of values: there are many moral problems which are insoluble because moral principles conflict'.[67] One sense of conflict that Popper could be talking about is the conflict that arises out of the disagreement between people in their assessment of what is the right way to act when confronted by a set of circumstances, actual or hypothetical. Conflict in this sense will always exist in any society because it is hard to envisage that people would never disagree in their assessment of what is correct conduct in every possible case under consideration. But to maintain this is simply to maintain a factual thesis about human behaviour. Disagreement and conflict in this sense can exist without prejudice to the thesis that such disagreement is in principle rationally resolvable even when it is about so-called ultimate ends. Therefore, if fallibilism is true, disagreement, even if it exists and is endemic in human society, is not by its very nature irresolvable. To believe that it must be is to subscribe to ethical relativism, and not to surmount it as Popper seems mistakenly to believe. (Incidentally, Popper does not always state the thesis of ethical/cognitive relativism correctly. He gets it right in the Addendum to Volume Two of *The Open Society*:

> By relativism . . . I mean here, briefly, that the choice between competing theories is arbitrary; since either, there is no such thing as objective truth; or, if there is, no such thing as a theory which is true or at any rate (though perhaps not true) nearer to the truth than another theory; or, if there are two or more theories, no ways or means of deciding whether one of them is better than another.[68]

Yet in his intellectual biography, he defines ethical relativism as the doctrine that 'any set of values can be defended'.[69] This doctrine, whatever it may be called, is most certainly not the thesis of philosophical ethical relativism.)

The conflict that is said to be incapable of rational resolution, according to the ethical relativist, occurs typically in two sorts of way: (1) one person or group maintains that principle A is correct (such as that slavery is wrong), and another person or group that principle B is correct (that slavery is right), where B is a straightforward negation of A; (2) moral dilemmas where two principles which are subscribed to are involved in a particular case but only one can be acted on – A, for instance, is 'One ought to fight what is evil, like Nazism', and B is 'One ought to take care of one's aged parent'. The second case is less of an acid test for the thesis of fallibilism than the first, because such dilemmas may be resolvable when set against a wider canvas or a set of so-called higher principles. For instance, the youth and the mother might argue that joining the Free French was the more urgent duty to discharge because if Hitler triumphed, humanism would be destroyed (with the son regretting that he could not discharge his filial obligation and the mother accepting in good spirit the personal sacrifice demanded of her). The further question whether humanism is morally preferable to Nazism becomes an instance of the first sort of conflict, which is why it is the more fundamental of the two sorts of clash between moral principles.

A fallibilist maintains that it is possible to argue rationally about such matters. S/he would attempt to show, in this example, that Nazism based on racial superiority is beset with false premises, that its arguments are incoherent and full of illegitimate steps in reasoning, etc. Pointing out these errors would be a long and tiresome job, but it could be done. One would realise, as a falli-bilist, that one's own assessment of the doctrine must itself be open in turn to critical scrutiny and in this sense one's conclusion is tentative. Only the resolution is tentative, and the conflict is not in principle incapable of rational resolution.

To say as Popper does that it is in principle irresolvable ration-ally, and, moreover, to go so far as to define a human society in terms of such conflicts, is to desert fallibilism for relativism. For him permanent conflict is required to keep up the volume and intensity of critical activity and no longer to eliminate errors as a method of seeking the truth. But in this, Popper 2, like Berlin, could well be mistaken on two counts: (1) a frenzied stirring up of critical activity which is done for its own sake, as a sheer affirmation of human responsibility and dignity becomes a point-less obsession (the fate of philosophers under Gallie's 'agonistic style'), and in the end even makes no sense if the possibility of objectivity/rationality is denied, because, as we have earlier argued, the notion of the dignity of a rational moral being is intimately bound up with the possibility of arriving at objective truths. If the hallmark of rationality is the possession of human language with its two higher functions, then it must be possible through criticism to find out what beliefs or ideas are correct or incorrect, true or false. Critical activity by its very nature serves to maximise the growth of knowledge; (2) if fallibilism is false and relativism is correct, the acceptance of the latter could indeed have the psychological effect of dampening down critical activity or even destroying it altogether. Why bother to argue, for one already knows beforehand that rational argument cannot settle the matter. Either endorse the beliefs or values one finds in one's society with no further ado, or use violence to impose one's own cherished set of beliefs or values regardless of what others think or say. Either possibility, however, would be counter-productive for one as addicted to criticism and as antipathetic to violence as Popper 1 and Popper 2 claim themselves to be.

NOTES

I THE SOURCES OF THE FACT/VALUE DISTINCTION

1 'The Objectivity of Morals', in *Philosophy*, vol. 51, no. 195, January 1976.
2 See R. Bhaskar, *The Possibility of Naturalism*, Harvester Press, Hassocks, Sussex, 1979, p. 54. See also his *A Realist Theory of Science*, Leeds Books, Leeds, 1975, pp. 173–4.
3 W. K. Frankena, 'The Naturalistic Fallacy', *Mind*, vol. 48, 1939.
4 There is another context – his influence outside academic philosophy in British intellectual life in general. The Bloomsbury Circle found in Moore the philosophical backing to their way of life – his vision of good chimed in with that of the adherents of the Bloomsbury Circle, some of whom were, of course, equally prominent figures in Cambridge itself.
5 Remford Banbrough, in *Moral Scepticism and Moral Knowledge*, Routledge & Kegan Paul, London, 1979, is right in pointing out the inconsistency of those who uphold commonsense beliefs and common language but reject the possibility of objectivity and rationality in moral beliefs. However, he seems to have fallen somewhat uncritically for Moore's proof; and his own extended application of it to the moral realm is no more convincing than the originator's application of it to the physical realm. See pp. 15–16.
6 Hare's *Freedom and Reason* may be regarded as an attempt to provide such a rational basis without offending the Naturalistic Fallacy. But as the rational basis is narrowly construed in terms of consistency, all that Hare seems to have succeeded in doing is to sanction every individual agent to apply consistently the principles of universalisability and prescriptivism. This method may yield, as he says, a fortunate consensus of opinion amongst agents, but it at no time leaves the egocentric circle which is its starting point. As a result, it is a

226

sophisticated, refined form of subjectivism, but cannot be used to provide for the possibility of objectivity and criticism (detecting incon-sistencies in the agent's thinking apart) in moral discourse. See section 9 of this chapter for an assessment of Hare's later writing.

7 See L. Kolakowski, *Positivist Philosophy*, Penguin, Harmondsworth, 1972.

8 See G. Kerner, *The Revolution in Ethical Theory*, Clarendon Press, Oxford, 1966, chapter 2 sections 3 and 4.

9 See R. Trigg, *Reason and Commitment*, Cambridge University Press, 1973; W. W. Bartley III, *The Retreat to Commitment*, Chatto & Windus, London, 1964 and *The Critical Approach to Science and Philosophy*, Collier-Macmillan, London, 1964; R. B. Wilson (ed.), *Rationality*, Blackwell, Oxford, 1970; E. Gellner, *Cause and Meaning in the Social Sciences*, ed. I. C. Jarvie, Routledge & Kegan Paul, London, 1973.

10 See Bartley, *op. cit.*

11 Trigg, *op. cit.*, p. 152.

12 *Ibid.*, pp. 167–8.

13 E. Gellner, *Legitimation of Belief*, Cambridge University Press, 1974, p. 52.

14 Gellner, *Cause and Meaning in the Social Sciences*, *op. cit.*

15 Trigg, *op. cit.*, pp. 68–72.

16 *Ibid.*, p. 154.

17 This was later refurbished and published in *Philosophy and the Historical Understanding*, Chatto & Windus, London, 1964. Quotations will be from this volume.

18 *Op. cit.*, p. 183.

19 *Ibid.*, p. 168.

20 See, for instance, A. Giddens, *New Rules of Sociological Method*, Hutchinson, London, 1976, who shows the convergence of the hermeneutical school of today and the relativism of Winch.

21 See C. Hempel, *Aspects of Scientific Explanation*, Free Press, New York, 1965, chapter 10.

22 See R. Harré, *The Philosophies of Science*, Oxford University Press, 1978, p. 55 and *The Principles of Scientific Thinking*, Macmillan, London, 1970, in which he gives a trenchant critique of positivism in the philosophy of science.

23 Harré, *The Principles of Scientific Thinking*, *op. cit.*, p. 4.

24 See Kolakowski, *op. cit.*, p. 53.

25 See M. Bunge, *Semantics II: Interpretation and Truth* (*Treatise on Basic Philosophy*, vol. 2), D. Reidel, Hingham, Mass., 1974, pp. 13–15. Bunge says one should distinguish between various kinds of interpretation: (a) designation – sign S, for instance, designates a generic construct like 'set'; (b) mathematical – 'set' is interpreted as 'the set of pairs', for instance; (c) factual – 'the set of pairs' as the collection of married couples; (d) pragmatic – 'the set of pairs' as the collection of married couples counted by the census bureau. Any conceptual system must satisfy (a). Logic satisfies it and is, therefore,

the most abstract since it is least interpreted. Next comes mathematics. Factual science goes beyond (b) to (c) but does not at all times go beyond (b) to (d). Those who maintain that it must tend to equate empirical testability with factual meaning. On this point, see *op. cit.*, p. 38.

26 See Bunge, *op. cit.*, and Harré, *The Philosophies of Science*, *op. cit.*, pp. 76–8.

27 This, however, is not to say that the various philosophers involved are agreed on an agenda as to what the issues are and how to deal with them; on the contrary, they each have their own preoccupations and their own philosophical axes to grind. Their work, read in conjunction with one another, gives rise to the impression that each is working away from the old constraints and working towards a reformulation of realism. In the philosophy of science in particular, see Harré and Bhaskar, whose works have already been cited, and also I. Hacking, *Representing and Intervening*, Cambridge University Press, 1983; in the philosophy of the social sciences, see Bhaskar, *The Possibility of Naturalism*, 1979; in philosophy and the philosophy of science, see Bunge's works already cited; in epistemology, see D. M. Armstrong, *Universals and Scientific Realism*, two volumes, Cambridge University Press, 1978.

28 Some of these theses have been isolated by Peter Halfpenny in *Positivism and Sociology: Explaining Social Life*, Allen & Unwin, London, 1982.

29 On its history and complexity, see Halfpenny, *op. cit.*; Kolakowski, *op. cit.*; and K. Lee, *Positivism and Law* (in preparation), in which it will be argued that Hobbes is the first systematic positivist, although his unique brand of positivism based on geometry as the paradigmatic science did not enter mainstream positivism.

30 See Halfpenny, *op. cit.*; Lee, *op. cit.*, chapter 2.

31 See Halfpenny, *op. cit.*; Lee, *op. cit.*, chapter 3.

32 See Lee, *op. cit.*, chapters 2, 3 and 5.

33 *Ibid.*, chapter 4.

34 See 'Moral Arguments' (1958), reprinted in *Virtues and Vices*, Blackwell, Oxford, 1978.

35 *Proceedings of the British Academy*, 1976, p. 331.

36 See D. Donaldson, 'Theories of Meaning and Learnable Languages', in *Proceedings of the 1964 Congress for Logic, Methodology, and Philosophy of Science*, Amsterdam, 1964; 'Truth and Meaning', *Synthese*, 17, 1967; 'Semantics for Natural Languages', in *Linguaggi, Nella Societe e Nella Technica*, Milan, 1970. For a succinct account of Davidson's theory of meaning and the controversy generated, see A. C. Grayling, *An Introduction to Philosophical Logic*, Harvester Press, Hassocks, Sussex, 1982, chapters 8 and 9.

37 See, for instance, M. Dummett, 'What is a Theory of Meaning? (II)' in *Truth and Meaning*, ed. J. McDowell and G. Evans, Clarendon Press, Oxford, 1976. (Dummett is actually a critic of realism.)

38 Grayling, *op. cit.*, p. 233.

39 Mark Platts, *Ways of Meaning*, Routledge & Kegan Paul, London, 1979, p. 243.
40 See *ibid.*, pp. 243–7.
41 A term introduced by Dummett in his critique of the realist position – see McDowell and Evans, *op. cit.*
42 Sabina Lovibond, *Realism and Imagination in Ethics*, Blackwell, Oxford, 1983, pp. 10–11.
43 Platts, *op. cit.*, p. 247.
44 A precursor is J. McDowell's 'Non-Cognitivism and Rule-following', in *Wittgenstein: To Follow a Rule*, ed. S. Holtzman and C. Leich, Routledge & Kegan Paul, London, 1981.

   The connection between Davidsonian semantics and the later Wittgenstein appears to be this (the Wittgenstein of the *Tractatus* clearly holds the truth-conditional view of language) – the concept of truth, fundamental to such a theory of meaning, requires a more general theory to explicate the links between truth and meaning on the one hand and behaviour on the other. This task, McDowell sets out to do by falling back on a theory of behaviour, both linguistic and non-linguistic. (See Grayling, *op. cit.*, pp. 231–3.) It is obvious that Wittgenstein's later writings provide one such inclusive theory of behaviour. Hence the renewed interest in the later Wittgenstein prompted by the controversy thrown up by Davidsonian semantics. This constitutes yet another phase in Wittgensteinian interpretation which tends to see his view of language as yielding a non-relativist realist account of concepts. (On McDowell's contribution, see also especially 'Truth-Conditions, Bivalence, Verificationism', in McDowell and Evans, *op. cit.*)
45 See Simon Blackburn's reply, 'Rule-Following and Moral Realism', to McDowell's paper in Holtzman and Leich, *op. cit.*, sections 2 and 4. Also compare D. Wiggins's following comment:

   It is also to be remarked that for someone who wanted to combine objectivity with non-cognitivism, or cognitive underdetermination, there could be no better model than Wittgenstein's extended normative conception of the objectivity of mathematics; and no better exemplar than Wittgenstein's extended description of how an ongoing cumulative making can reflect the creation of a shared form of life which is constitutive of rationality itself, can yield proofs which are not compulsions but procedures that guide our conceptions, and can still explain our sense that sometimes we have no alternative but to infer this from that. (*Proceedings of the British Academy*, 1976, p. 369.)

46 See, for instance, Lovibond, *op. cit.*, pp. 29–30.
47 See S. Lukes, *Individualism*, Blackwell, Oxford, 1973.
48 See Lovibond, *op. cit.*, especially sections 14 and 15.
49 *Ibid.*, pp. 55–6.
50 *Ibid.*, pp. 55–7.
51 *Ibid.*, p. 63.

52 *Ibid.*, p. 133.
53 *Ibid.*, p. 65.
54 Hilary Putnam also points out that philosophers are prone to confuse the two senses:

> Nor should commitment to ethical objectivity be confused with what is a very different matter, commitment to ethical or moral authoritarianism. It is perhaps this confusion that has led one outstanding philosopher (David Wiggins) to espouse what he himself regards as a limited version of 'non-cognitivism', and to say 'Concerning what "living most fully" is for each man, the final authority must be the man himself'. (Notice the ambiguity in 'the final authority': does he mean the final *political* authority? The final *epistemological* authority? Or does he mean that *there is no fact of the matter*, as his use of the term 'non-cognitivism' suggests?). (*Reason, Truth and History*, Cambridge University Press, 1981, p. 149)

55 Lovibond, *op. cit.*, p. 57.
56 *Ibid.*, pp. 57–8.
57 For a recent criticism of expressivism, see Putnam, *op. cit.*, especially pp. 110–13. See also Lovibond, *op. cit.*, p. 145.
58 Putnam, *op. cit.*, p. 113.
59 Lovibond, *op. cit.*, pp. 127–8.
60 *Ibid.*, p. 138.
61 This point will be elaborated upon in chapter 3, section 12.
62 R. M. Hare, *Moral Thinking*, Clarendon Press, Oxford, 1981. In the bibliography, Hare has conveniently listed all his publications. Between 1963 and 1981 he wrote several books and numerous articles. But from the point of view of economy and of assessing his method of generating rationality in moral discourse, it is sufficient to concentrate on his latest major effort. A book dedicated solely to an examination of Hare's total contribution to moral philosophy would, no doubt, have to be comprehensive. But this one is not.
63 Hare, *op. cit.*, pp. 42–3.
64 See *The Observer*, 17 August 1980. The name of the employee is Stanley Adams who has since written a book, *Roche versus Adams*, Jonathan Cape, London, 1984. For another case, see H. Kohn, *Who Killed Karen Silkwood?*, New English Library, 1983. On 'whistle-blowing' in general, see *New Scientist*, editorial, 23 June 1983.
65 See Robert Whymant's reports in *The Guardian* on 14 August 1982 and 17 September 1982. See also the report in *The Observer* on 10 April 1983.
66 Hare might argue that if critical thinking were brought to bear on the subject of communism, one might come to the conclusion that communism is not such an evil as portrayed by cold war ideologues. But that is another matter. Granted that they already hold the view that communism is evil, it is plausible using utilitarian/critical thinking to arrive at the conclusion that such an exchange of expertise behind

closed doors is justifiable. To get out of having to admit this possibility, Hare would have to argue that utilitarian/critical thinking must be an all-or-nothing affair – before one applies it to one issue, one must also have applied it to all other issues presupposed by or related to that issue. This might render his method impotent in practice.

67 See, for instance, Jonathan Steele, *World Power*, Michael Joseph, London, 1983, and Brian May, *Russia, America, The Bomb and the Fall of Western Europe*, Routledge & Kegan Paul, London, 1984.

68 Hare, *op. cit.*, pp. 134–45.

69 *Ibid.*, pp. 141–2.

70 *Ibid.*, p. 171.

71 *Ibid.*, p. 181.

72 *Ibid.*, p. 182.

73 Bentham argued that the principle of maximising utility in conjunction with the principle of marginal utility entails the principle of equality in the distribution of resources (of income, anyway). See *The Theory of Legislation*, ed. C. K. Ogden, Kegan Paul, London, 1931, p. 105 and pp. 103–4, and *The Works of Jeremy Bentham*, ed. J. Bowring, Edinburgh, 1843, vol. 2, p. 578. In the social pleasure calculus, Bentham treated rich and poor, high-born and low-born alike whereas historically, slaves, serfs, lower castes, the working classes, etc. had not always been considered to be fit subjects for the receipt of welfare. This assumption was therefore revolutionary. (See *The Theory of Legislation*, p. 103.) However, Bentham could not in the end accept the radical implications of his own arguments as they entail the modification of the institution of private property, if not its outright abolition. Bentham in the end decided that an egalitarian income distribution had to be sacrificed for the greater advantage of security and stability of private property. See *The Theory of Legislation*, pp. 96–120.

In later utilitarian thought, the principle of marginal or diminishing utility was rendered altogether harmless by adopting the device of denying the possibility of intertemporal comparison of utility – see C. B. Macpherson, 'Politics: Post-Liberal-Democracy?', in *Ideology in Social Sciences*, ed. R. Blackburn, Collins, London, 1972, p. 25. The jettisoning of the principle of marginal utility and the principle of equality means that the injunction 'maximise utility' could entail a less equal rather than a more equal distribution of resources, welfare or utility. See A. K. Sen, *On Economic Inequality*, Clarendon Press, Oxford, 1973, pp. 16–17.

74 Hare, *op. cit.*, p. 172.

II THE CONSEQUENCES OF STRICT IMPLICATION

1 See Richard B. Brandt, 'The Status of Empirical Assertion Theories in Ethics', *Mind*, new series, vol. 61, 1952. He points out that the

crude emotive view did not last long and modifications were introduced.

2 See H. Kelsen, *General Theory of Law and State* (tr. A. Wedburg), Russell & Russell, New York, 1961, and *The Pure Theory of Law* (tr. M. Knight), University of California Press, Berkeley and Los Angeles, 1967.

3 See H. L. A. Hart, *The Concept of Law*, Clarendon Press, Oxford, 1961. See also J. Austin, *The Province of Jurisprudence Determined*, ed. Hart, London, 1964 or J. Austin, *Lectures on Jurisprudence*, 5th edn, R. Campbell, John Murray, London, 1885; also Hobbes, *The Leviathan* – any respectable edition would be acceptable.

4 A legal system, to be workable and efficient, does have to satisfy norms like generality, certainty, accessibility, etc., but these should not be identified with moral norms like 'Thou shalt not kill'. See, for instance, the controversy centered on L. Fuller's *The Morality of Law*, Yale University Press, New Haven and London, revised edn, 1969.

5 See Hart's distinction between internal and external aspects or points of view in Hart, *op. cit.*

6 There are also problems relating to the reduction of laws to commands on the Austinian view. Even the criminal law, never mind the civil law, or the law of evidence, cannot be easily analysed as commands to citizens without distortion. To get over these difficulties, some positivists like Kelsen say that laws do not command citizens to do X or forbid them to do X but are ultimately addressed to officials who will apply sanctions should certain behaviour be indulged in by the citizens. Other positivists, like Hart, distinguish between primary and secondary rules. The former are more like those belonging to the criminal law which may appear to the individual citizen like commands. The latter (akin to Kelsen's thesis) are really rules of adjudication, etc. addressed to officials laying down how they conduct their business. The rules of civil law are neither primary nor secondary since they are not commands nor are they addressed to officials. They merely enable citizens who may wish to, say, make a will or enter into marriage, to do so in a way the law would recognise as valid.

In general legal positivism is not short of critics. The aftermath of the Third Reich produced an anguished soul-searching and a revival of its rival, the natural law tradition. (For a recent formulation of natural law, see John Finnis, *Natural Law and Natural Rights*, Clarendon Press, Oxford, 1980.) For a recent critique of legal positivism, see R. Dworkin, *Taking Rights Seriously*, Duckworth, London, 1977. For a recent version of positivism in law, see N. MacCormick, *Legal Reasoning and Legal Theory*, Clarendon Press, Oxford, 1978.

7 See N. Rescher, *The Logic of Commands*, Routledge & Kegan Paul, London, 1966, p. 16, note 12.

III THE NOTION OF EPISTEMIC IMPLICATION

1 See J. L. Mackie, *The Cement of the Universe: A Study of Causation*, Oxford University Press, 1974; M. Brand (ed.), *The Nature of Causation*, University of Illinois Press, 1976; Ted Honderich, 'Causes and If p, even if x, still q', in *Philosophy*, 57, 1982.
2 If the positivist conception were rejected as inadequate, then it might not be so easy to dislodge the notion of cause, or to understand it as no more than constant conjunction.
3 See H. L. A. Hart and A. M. Honoré, *Causation in the Law*, Clarendon Press, Oxford, 1959.
4 *Op. cit.*
5 See R. Harré, *The Principles of Scientific Thinking*, Macmillan, London, 1970. Also see R. Bhaskar, *A Realist Theory of Science*, Leeds Books, Leeds, 1975.
6 See B. Williams, 'The Idea of Equality', in *Philosophy, Politics and Society*, ed. P. Laslett and W. G. Runciman, Blackwell, Oxford, second series, 1962.
7 See A. R. Anderson and N. D. Belnap, *Entailment: The Logic of Relevance and Necessity*, vol. 1, Princeton University Press, Princeton and London, 1975. See also A. Flew, *A Dictionary of Philosophy*, Macmillan, London, 1979, pp. 153–4.
8 However, to argue that epistemic implication is stronger than material implication is not to say that such a form of implication entails a weaker form like material implication. This is because while the two forms of implication vary in strength, they also differently construe what we mean by 'if . . . then'. (I owe this point to Peter Halfpenny.)
9 See Belnap and Anderson, *op. cit.*
10 S. Haack, 'Theories of Knowledge: An Analytic Framework', in *Proceedings of the Aristotelian Society*, vol. 83, 1982/83, p. 145.
11 See S. Haack, *op. cit.*, for one such attempt. She favours what she calls foundherentism which consists of three theses – fallibilism, epistemic inegalitarianism and up-and-backism. (She kindly drew my attention to the relevance to my concern of this and other articles of hers.)
12 See Harré, *op. cit.*, pp. 196–200.
13 A view which is commonly attributed to Hobbes. This, however, is a misunderstanding of Hobbes's epistemology – see K. Lee, *Positivism and Law* (in preparation), chapter 7.
14 See J. Hintikka, *Knowledge and Belief*, Cornell University Press, New York, 1962.
15 This point will be discussed at greater length in chapter 5.
16 See M. Bunge, *Treatise on Basic Philosophy*, D. Reidel, Hingham, Mass., 1974, vol. 1, p. 123. See also vol. 2, pp. 127–9.
17 *Op. cit.*, vol. 1, p. 122.
18 R. M. Chisholm, (I), *Theory of Knowledge*, Prentice-Hall, Englewood Cliffs, New Jersey, 1966, chapter 4. See also (II), *The Foundations*

of Knowledge, Harvester Press, Hassocks, Sussex, 1982, part 2, chapter 5. (S. Haack drew my attention to Chisholm's attempt.)

19 Chisholm extends the thesis to cover assertions about other minds and even theological discourse – see *op. cit.*, (I), pp. 67–8. (See chapter 4, section 7 of this book on the relevance of theological discourse to moral discourse.)

20 See Chisholm, *op. cit.*, (I), pp. 38–40 and pp. 61–2.

21 For the sake of simplicity, I use the terms (A) and (E) in my account of Chisholm's view.

22 So does this book. See section 12 of this chapter.

23 Chisholm, *op. cit.*, (I), p. 62.

24 *Op. cit.*, p. 61.

25 Using this model, one may represent Mark Platts's type of intuitionism (see chapter 1) as follows (with some additional premises): Not-R, Not-Q, L (experiential knowledge is obtained by looking and seeing, that is to say, it is non-inferential), NI (moral knowledge is non-inferential knowledge obtained by looking and seeing), ∴ P.

26 Chisholm, *op. cit.* (I), pp. 59–60.

27 Chisholm's reference to inductive inference is left out because sceptics regard inductive logic to be unsound anyway.

28 W. Sellars, 'Are There Non-Deductive Logics?' in *Essays in Honor of Carl Hempel*, D. Reidel, Hingham, Mass., 1969, pp. 83–4.

29 For a more complete account, see K. Lee, *Positivism and Law* (in preparation) especially chapters 4 and 9, where the influences of Weber and the Neo-Kantians are also taken into account.

30 In Lee, *op. cit.*, chapter 4, it is argued that Hare's positivist science of morals is an analogue of the conventionalist wing in the philosophy of the natural sciences.

31 For the differences between Popper and the Vienna Circle, see P. Halfpenny, *Positivism and Sociology: Explaining Social Life*, Allen & Unwin, London, 1982, chapters 3 and 5, and Lee, *op. cit.*, chapters 4 and 6.

32 See Lee, *op. cit.*, chapter 4.

33 See chapter 6 of this book.

34 See Lee, *op. cit.*, chapter 4.

35 See H. Putnam, *Reason, Truth and History*, Cambridge University Press, 1981, pp. 135–7.

36 J. L. Mackie, *Ethics, Inventing Right and Wrong*, Penguin, Harmondsworth, 1977, p. 38.

37 *Ibid.*

38 *Op. cit.*, p. 39.

39 See K. Popper, *The Open Society and Its Enemies*, vol. 1, Routledge & Kegan Paul, London, 1962, chapter 5.

IV APPLICATION AND TESTING OF EPISTEMIC IMPLICATION

1 W. W. Bartley III, *Morality and Religion*, Macmillan, London, 1971, p. 14.
2 See G. Myrdal, *Value in Social Theory*, Routledge & Kegan Paul, London, 1958.
3 J. L. Mackie, *Ethics, Inventing Right and Wrong*, Penguin, Harmondsworth, 1977.
4 W. W. Bartley III, *The Retreat to Commitment*, Chatto & Windus, London, 1964.
5 Chapter 6 will investigate why Popper would consider it anathema to regard moral claims as knowledge-claims in spite of his avowed belief in the possibility of rationalism.
6 Bartley, *The Retreat to Commitment*, *op. cit.*, pp. 158–9.
7 See J. Von Neumann and C. Morgenstein, *Theory of Games and Economic Behaviour*, Princeton University Press, 3rd edn, 1953.
8 R. Nozick, *Anarchy, State and Utopia*, Blackwell, Oxford, 1974, pp. 150–1.
9 Nozick deals with this problem when he considers Locke's proviso in relation to his theory of acquisition. Underpinning Locke's theory is the labour theory of value which Nozick is not much concerned with; instead he considers at some length Locke's proviso about the limits of acquisition, namely, that there be 'enough and as good left in common with others' for acts of appropriation to be justified. Nozick gives what he calls a weak interpretation of it – the proviso would be satisfied so long as some of the objects are left for the rest to use, even if most of them have already been appropriated by others. For instance, if 2 per cent of the population has already appropriated, say, 95 per cent of the land, the rest of the population, so long as it can *use* it, the proviso, in his opinion, is satisfied. One thing his interpretation would rule out is monopoly of an item which is necessary for survival – the only waterhole in a desert may not be appropriated by the person who comes across it ahead of the others. This interpretation naturally suits and reflects Nozick's own intuitive sense of justice, but it is open to question whether it satisfies the Lockean proviso as such, for there is an obvious qualitative difference between a case where an individual may appropriate as much of something as s/he fancies (so long as s/he does not take all) and the case of an individual who can only use whatever is left, which may not be much, in the company of numerous others like oneself. This does not appear to be a case of there being 'enough and as good left in common with others'.
10 Nozick, *op. cit.*, p. 7.
11 *Ibid.*, p. 8.
12 Mackie, *op. cit.*, p. 35.

13 See R. Swinburne, 'The Objectivity of Morals', *Philosophy*, vol. 51, 1976.
14 See K. Lee, 'Kuhn – A Re-appraisal', *Explorations in Knowledge*, vol. 1, no. 1, 1984.
15 L. Kolakowski, *Positivist Philosophy*, Penguin, Harmondsworth, 1972, p. 173.
16 See (one such study) K. Lee, 'The Legalist School and Legal Positivism', *Journal of Chinese Philosophy*, 3, 1975.

V THE PHILOSOPHICAL DOMAIN OF ORDINARY KNOWLEDGE

1 Even positivism claims that it does, although it also maintains that the logic of explanation and the logic of prediction are symmetrical.
2 See R. Harré, *The Principles of Scientific Thinking*, Macmillan, London, 1970, pp. 18–19.
3 See R. B. Braithwaite, *Scientific Explanation*, Cambridge University Press, 1968. (For the detailed complexities of positivism, see P. Halfpenny, *Positivism and Sociology*, Allen & Unwin, London, 1982; see also K. Lee, *Positivism and Law* (in preparation)).
4 It is fair to say that this is true of only one form of positivism, namely, conventionalism-cum-instrumentalism. However, conventionalism-cum-instrumentalism is the outcome of trying to overcome certain difficulties inherent in other forms of positivism – see Lee, *op. cit.*, especially chapter 3.
5 See Chapter 1, section 7 for a brief account (a) of the difficulties facing the extension of the logic of prediction to explanation, and (b) of the problems facing its extension to the normative domain. On (b), see also chapter 2, section 4. For a more detailed account of (i) why positivism regards prediction as central for both epistemological and ideological considerations, and (ii) of the transmutation of the logic of prediction-cum-explanation to become the logic of validation in the normative sphere, see Lee, *op. cit.*, chapters 3, 5 and 6.
6 The subscribers to the Naturalistic Fallacy complain about utilitarianism as an attempt to reduce moral norms to empirical propositions by saying 'good' or 'right' means 'pleasure' or 'productive of pleasure'. They are right in maintaining that 'right' does not mean 'productive of pleasure' or 'good' does not mean 'pleasure', but they are wrong in concluding from it that 'right' statements cannot be supported or backed up by statements about pleasure and pain, or that the meaning of 'right' statements cannot be partially explicated in terms of statements about pleasure and pain or other 'is' statements in general. The utilitarian theory may be re-interpreted not as an attempt to meet the requirement that to count as knowledge, a statement must be about empirically observable matters or be reduced

without residue to one which is, but as an attempt to provide a *justificans* for moral statements, the *justificandum*.

7 See, amongst others, Musgrove and Lakatos (eds), *Criticism and Growth of Knowledge*, Cambridge University Press, 1970; Harré, *op. cit.*; R. Bhaskar, *A Realist Theory of Science*, Leeds Books, Leeds, 1975; A. O'Hear, *Karl Popper*, Routledge & Kegan Paul, London, 1980.

Criticisms include: that scientific theories are not dealt an instant death blow by the logical weapon of falsification; instead they are capable of re-suscitation through re-deployment and modification; that when they are finally written off, it is through a cumulation of dead-ends and *culs-de-sac*; it leads to the absurdity that all evidence in science is falsificatory and never confirmatory; it implies that universal existential statements are unscientific because they are unfalsifiable, although they are intrinsic to most (if not all) scientific theories; that falsifiability is not so much about the logic of scientific discovery as a methodological rule for maximising criticism of a scientific theory; that he has not solved the problem of induction as he claims to have done; that he confines rationality merely to the testing of theories and excludes it from the domain of the formation of the theories themselves; the more general type of criticism which centres on the view that Popper's thesis is but a variant of positivism.

See also Popper, *Realism and the Aim of Science*, ed. W. W. Bartley III, Hutchinson, London, 1983.

8 K. Popper, *The Logic of Scientific Discovery*, Science Editions, New York, 1961, p. 102.

9 *Ibid.*, p. 76, note 1.

10 See Popper, *Realism and the Aim of Science*, *op. cit.*, p. 184.

11 *Ibid.*, p. 186.

12 See Harré, *The Principles of Scientific Thinking*, pp. 191–6 where he attempts to grapple with this problem by making use of certain arguments developed by R. A. Putnam and F. I. Dretske.

13 *Ibid.*, p. 191.

14 For a critique of his foundationless epistemology, see O'Hear, *op. cit.*

15 See S. Haack, *Philosophy of Logics*, Cambridge University Press, 1979, p. 16. This distinction, she says, is made by the medieval logicians from whom Peirce borrowed the term.

16 See A. R. Anderson and N. D. Belnap, *Entailment*, vol. 1, Princeton University Press, 1975, for the development of one system of such logic.

17 A. R. Anderson and N. D. Belnap, *op. cit.*, pp. 17–18. In their attempt to explicate the relevance of A to B, they place certain restrictions on deducibility (dubbed by Fogelin 'The Rule of No Funny Business'). This leads to constructing R, the system of 'relevant implication', which is then combined with the modal system S4 to give a system of 'entailment'. This system, as Haack shows, challenges classical logic in the following ways: (i) by introducing a new entail-

ment connective, thus extending the apparatus of classical logic; (ii) it also leads them to reject *modus ponens* as a principle of inference; (iii) and to consider relevance to be itself relevant to validity – see Haack, *op. cit.*, pp. 199–200.

18 Haack, *op. cit.*, pp. 16–17.

19 *Ibid.*, p. 202.

20 *Ibid.*, pp. 202–3.

21 I owe this point to Susan Haack who says that their system of 'relevant implication' is even stronger than strict implication. Moreover, it challenges the two-value system of classical logic which epistemic implication does not intend to do.

VI FACT AND VALUE WITHIN CONTEMPORARY LIBERALISM

1 Put crudely, it amounts to saying that while facts are by and large unproblematic, being objective as well as inter-subjectively checkable, values are subjective, being the expressions of the individual's (or the community's) feelings, choices or commitments. Science deals with facts but must eschew values to remain objective and therefore scientific. Social scientists are hence careful to observe the Weberian rule of being value-free and not to commit the Naturalistic Fallacy. In this way they hope to throw up a *cordon sanitaire* around their domain of investigation. Some of them set out scrupulously to eradicate any bias, prejudice or value which might subvert their claim about the objective nature of their studies; others admit that even a conscious policy of eradication may not be successful as it seems to be endemic in the subject matter of their inquiry – the only honest and viable course of action is simply to declare them publicly, to put one's cards on the table as it were, so that the reader would be made aware of the value standpoint according to which problems have been selected and formulated and solutions propounded. (Myrdal seems to favour this approach.) However, this policy of honest avowal has at least one drawback – what about those values which elude the immediate consciousness of the social scientist? (In *The American Dilemma*, Myrdal tacitly assumed the value of integration, that WASP values are the central American values to which black people ought to aspire and which they ought to assimilate.) It is not obvious then that accepting the fundamental contemporary positivist dichotomy is an easy way out for the social scientist.

2 B. Mitchell, *Law, Morality and Religion in a Secular Society*, Oxford University Press, 1967.

3 See K. Popper, *Objective Knowledge*, Clarendon Press, Oxford, 1974, especially essay 3.

4 Mill, *On Liberty*, in *Utilitarianism, Liberty and Representative Government*, Everyman's edition, London, J. M. Dent, 1954, p. 81.

5 *Ibid.*, p. 85.
6 For Hare, the test of sincerity lies in the execution of the prescription. Failure of execution is evidence of *akrasia* or lack of sincerity.
7 K. Popper, *Conjectures and Refutations*, Routledge & Kegan Paul, London, 1969, p. 352.
8 *Ibid.*, p. 375.
9 Mill says: 'Questions of ultimate ends are not amenable to direct proof. Whatever can be proved to be good must be so by being shown to be a means to something admitted to be good without proof' (*Utilitarianism, Liberty and Representative Government*, Everyman's edition, London, J. M. Dent, 1954, p. 4).
10 See J. S. Mill, *Autobiography*, Columbia University Press, New York, 1924, p. 158.
11 Prescriptivism is not exclusive to twentieth-century positivism, nor even to positivism itself. Hobbes could be said to hold it as a seventeenth-century positivist, and Kant, a non-positivist, may also be said to hold it. On the point that Mill is a prescriptivist, see A. Ryan, *The Philosophy of John Stuart Mill*, Macmillan, London, 1970, pp. 189–90.
12 On the general themes that Mill did not commit the Naturalistic Fallacy, that he distinguished the ontological status of norms/values as products of the will from their epistemological status that they are rational products of the will, for greater details, see Lee, *Positivism and Law* (in preparation), chapter 4, section 5.
13 See C. L. Ten's helpful article 'The Liberal Theory of the Open Society' in *The Open Society in Theory and Practice*, Martinus Nijhoff, The Hague, 1974, in which he uses this name for the argument.
14 I. Berlin, *Four Essays on Liberty*, Oxford University Press, 1969, p. li.
15 E. Gellner, *Legitimation of Belief*, Cambridge University Press, 1974, pp. 37–9 and pp. 56–62.
16 *Ibid.*, pp. 46–7.
17 Ten calls it the Necessity of Error Argument – see *op. cit.*
18 See Mill, *On Liberty*, pp. 94–6.
19 See Fitzjames Stephen, *Liberty, Equality and Fraternity*, Cambridge University Press, 1967, p. 86. (cited by Ten, *op. cit.*, p. 147).
20 Mill, *On Liberty*, p. 94.
21 Berlin, *op. cit.*, p. 144.
22 Popper, *Objective Knowledge*, p. 237.
23 Berlin, *op. cit.*, pp. 171–2 and pp. lii–liii.
24 *Ibid.*, p. 189.
25 *Ibid.*, pp. 189–90.
26 *Ibid.*
27 Ten calls it The Avoidance of Mistake Argument – see *op. cit.*, pp. 143–4.
28 Ten puts the point well:

> [Mill] believes that these arguments are connected. Rational and thinking men who seek to know the truth are more likely to

arrive at true opinions than those who wish to suppress false opinions. So, though in a particular case, false opinions may prevail over true ones if freedom of discussion is permitted, in the long run many more true doctrines will be discovered in a free atmosphere which breeds thinking than in an atmosphere where there are restrictions in freedom of expression. (Ten, *op. cit.*, p. 148)

29 K. Popper, *Unended Quest*, Collins, London, 1978, p. 115.
30 Piecemeal social engineering is the result of modifying the hypothetico-deductive method of testing when applied to society; the modification is required because of the Oedipal effect which exists when social policies are enunciated and carried out because there are no laws in society analogous to laws of physics; and because there are unintended consequences of actions.
31 Popper admitted a similarity (which he discovered later but not at the time when he first propounded his thesis) between his model of explanation-cum-prediction and Mill's formulation of it. See *Unended Quest*, p. 117. (Mill himself acknowledged his debt to Whewell on this point.)
32 Mill says:

Why is it, then that there is on the whole a preponderance among mankind of rational opinions and rational conduct? If there really is this preponderance – which there must be unless human affairs are, and have always been, in an almost desperate state – it is owing to a quality of the human mind, the source of everything respectable in man either as an intellectual or as a moral being, namely, that his errors are corrigible. He is capable of rectifying his mistakes by discussion and experience. Not by experience alone. There must be discussion, to show how experience is to be interpreted. Wrong opinions and practices gradually yield to fact and argument; but facts and arguments, to produce any effect on the mind, must be brought before it. (*On Liberty*, p. 82)

Compare the gist with Popper's view:

For these standards of rational criticism and of objective truth make his knowledge structurally different from its evolutionary antecedents. . . . It is the acceptance of these standards which creates the dignity of the individual man; which makes him responsible, morally as well as intellectually; which enables him not only to act rationally, but also to contemplate and adjudicate, and to discriminate between, competing theories. These standards of objective truth and criticism may teach him to try again, and to think again; to challenge his own conclusions, and to use his imagination in trying to find whether and where his own conclusions are at fault. They may teach him to apply the method of trial and error in every field, and especially in science; and thus they may teach him how to learn from his mistakes, and how to search for them. (*Conjectures and Refutations*, p. 384)

33 Mill, *On Liberty*, p. 83.
34 An extensive version of this recurrent theme may be found in 'Of Clouds and Clocks' in Popper, *Objective Knowledge*.
35 He concedes that bee-language could satisfy this requirement. One does not know, however, what he thinks about Washoe and Koko and other apes and their linguistic achievements. He could say that they are in any case being taught a human language.
36 Popper, *Objective Knowledge*, pp. 237–8.
37 *Ibid.*, pp. 120–1.
38 Kneale writes:

> If my argument is sound, the programme of perpetual revolution in science cannot be justified by appeal to the principle of the infinite complexity of nature. So far as I can see, a scientist may someday formulate a comprehensive theory which is wholly true and therefore incapable of refutation. I do not wish to say that this will happen. The human race may be too stupid for the task, or it may be overtaken by some natural disaster while it is still far from its scientific goal. Still less do I wish to say that, if we produce the theory we want, we can also be sure that we have done so. For in order to attain such certainty we should have to know everything about nature, including the fact that we knew everything about nature; and I believe that to be impossible in principle. But the ideal of comprehensive true theory remains unaffected by these reservations, and I think it is essential to the scientific enterprise. (W. Kneale, 'Scientific Revolution for Ever?', *British Journal for the Philosophy of Science*, vol. 19, 1968–9)

There may be, of course, other reasons apart from this one attributed to Popper by Kneale for maintaining that there must be permanent revolutions in science. See, for example, R. Bhaskar, *A Realist Theory of Science*, Leeds Books, Leeds, 1975. The point of citing Kneale is to show that for Popper, the thesis about permanent revolutions in science cannot be sustained on scientific grounds. As we suggest in the text, the motive is a 'political' one, the fear of a decline in critical activity and the ushering in of the closed society.

39 Mill, *On Liberty*, p. 95.
40 *Ibid.*, pp. 104–5.
41 Popper, *Unended Quest*, p. 115.
42 See especially Addendum, *The Open Society and its Enemies*, vol. 2, (4th edn), Routledge & Kegan Paul, London, 1962, pp. 393–5.
43 See also the chapter entitled 'Revolt Against Reason' in *The Open Society and its Enemies*, vol. 2, and *Unended Quest*, pp. 113–16.
44 Popper, *Conjectives and Refutations*, pp. 358–9.

45 *Ibid.*
46 *Ibid.*
47 *Ibid.*, p. 356.
48 *Ibid.*
49 *Ibid.*
50 Popper, *The Open Society and its Enemies*, 1962, vol. 2, p. 230.
51 *Ibid.*, p. 231.
52 See Popper, *ibid.*, pp. 230–1.
53 See Popper's own account in *ibid.*, pp. 375–6. This account suits Popper's view of fallibilism more directly than the one given earlier in Chapter 3, although the two accounts are compatible.
54 See A. O'Hear, *Karl Popper*, Routledge & Kegan Paul, London, 1980, pp. 147–53, for a related way out of the impasse. Also see R. Trigg, *Reason and Commitment*, Cambridge University Press, 1973.
55 Popper, *The Open Society and its Enemies*, vol. 2, p. 369.
56 Popper, *Unended Quest*, p. 116.
57 Popper, *The Open Society and its Enemies*, vol. 2, p. 232.
58 *Ibid.*, p. 238.
59 *The Open Society and its Enemies*, vol. 1, p. 61.
60 *Ibid.*, p. 73.
61 See *The Open Society and its Enemies*, vol. 2, p. 232.
62 Popper, *Conjectures and Refutations*, pp. 358–60.
63 See, for instance, Ted Honderich, *Violence for Equality*, Penguin, Harmondsworth, 1980.
64 O'Hear makes a similar point – see *op. cit.*, p. 158.
65 Mill, *On Liberty*, p. 81.
66 Popper, *Unended Quest*, p. 116.
67 *Ibid.*
68 Popper, *The Open Society and its Enemies*, vol. 2, p. 369.
69 Popper, *Unended Quest*, p. 116.

BIBLIOGRAPHY

Adams, S., *Roche versus Adams*, Jonathan Cape, London, 1984.

Anderson, A. R. and Belnap, N. D., *Entailment: The Logic of Relevance and Necessity*, vol. 1, Princeton University Press, 1975.

Armstrong, D. M., *Universals and Scientific Realism*, 2 vols, Cambridge University Press, 1978.

Austin, J., *The Province of Jurisprudence Determined*, ed. H. L. A. Hart, London, 1964.

Banbrough, R., *Moral Scepticism and Moral Knowledge*, Routledge & Kegan Paul, London, 1979.

Bartley, W. W. III, *The Retreat to Commitment*, Chatto & Windus, London, 1964.

Bartley, W. W. III, *The Critical Approach to Science and Philosophy*, Collier-Macmillan, London, 1964.

Bartley, W. W. III, *Morality and Religion*, Macmillan, London, 1971.

Beardsmore, R. W., *Moral Reasoning*, Routledge & Kegan Paul, London, 1969.

Bentham, J., *The Works of Jeremy Bentham*, ed. J. Bowring, Edinburgh, vol. 2, 1843.

Bentham, J., *The Theory of Legislation*, ed. C. K. Ogden, Kegan Paul, London, 1931.

Berlin, I., *Four Essays on Liberty*, Oxford University Press, 1969.

Bhaskar, R., *A Realist Theory of Science*, Leeds Books, Leeds, 1975.

Bhaskar, R., *The Possibility of Naturalism*, Harvester Press, Hassocks, Sussex, 1979.

Blackburn, S., 'Rule-Following and Moral Realism', in *Wittgenstein: To Follow a Rule*, ed. S. Holtzman and C. Leich, Routledge & Kegan Paul, London, 1981.

Braithwaite, R. B., *Scientific Explanation*, Cambridge University Press, 1968.

Brand, M. (ed.), *The Nature of Causation*, University of Illinois Press, 1974.

243

Bibliography

Brandt, R. B., 'The Status of Empirical Assertion Theories in Ethics', *Mind*, new series, vol. 61, 1952.

Bunge, M., *Treatise on Basic Philosophy*, vols. 1 and 2, D. Reidel, Hingham, Mass., 1974.

Chisholm, R. M., *Theory of Knowledge*, Prentice-Hall, Englewood Cliffs, New Jersey, 1966.

Chisholm, R. M., *The Foundations of Knowledge*, Harvester Press, Hassocks, Sussex, 1982.

Donaldson, D., 'Theories of Meaning and Learnable Languages', in *Proceedings of 1964 Congress for Logic, Methodology, and Philosophy of Science*, Amsterdam, 1964.

Donaldson, D., 'Truth and Meaning', in *Synthese*, 17, 1967.

Donaldson, D., 'Semantics for Natural Languages', in *Linguaggi, Nella Societe e Nella Technica*, Milan, 1970.

Dummett, M., 'What is a Theory of Meaning? II', in *Truth and Meaning*, ed. J. McDowell and G. Evans, Clarendon Press, Oxford, 1976.

Dworkin, R., *Taking Rights Seriously*, Duckworth, London, 1977.

Finnis, J., *Natural Law and Natural Rights*, Clarendon Press, Oxford, 1980.

Flew, A., *A Dictionary of Philosophy*, Macmillan, London, 1979.

Foot, P., *Virtues and Vices*, Blackwell, Oxford, 1978.

Frankena, W. K., 'The Naturalistic Fallacy', *Mind*, vol. 48, 1939.

Fuller, L., *The Morality of Law*, Yale University Press, New Haven and London, revised edn, 1969.

Gallie, W. B., *Philosophy and the Historical Understanding*, Chatto & Windus, London, 1964.

Gellner, E., 'Cause and Meaning in the Social Sciences', in *Cause and Meaning in the Social Sciences*, ed. I. C. Jarvie, Routledge & Kegan Paul, London, 1973.

Gellner, E., *Legitimation of Belief*, Cambridge University Press, 1974.

Giddens, A., *New Rules of Sociological Method*, Hutchinson, London, 1976.

Grayling, A. C., *An Introduction to Philosophical Logic*, Harvester Press, Hassocks, Sussex, 1982.

Haack, S., *Philosophy of Logics*, Cambridge University Press, 1979.

Haack, S., 'Theories of Knowledge: An Analytic Framework', in *Proceedings of the Aristotelian Society*, vol. 83, 1982/3.

Hacking, I., *Representing and Intervening: Introductory Topics in the Philosophy of Science*, Cambridge University Press, 1983.

Halfpenny, P., *Positivism and Sociology: Explaining Social Life*, Allen & Unwin, London, 1982.

Hare, R. M., *The Language of Morals*, Clarendon Press, Oxford, 1952.

Hare, R. M., *Freedom and Reason*, Clarendon Press, Oxford, 1963.

Hare, R. M., *Moral Thinking*, Clarendon Press, Oxford, 1981.

Harré, R., *The Principles of Scientific Thinking*, Macmillan, London, 1970.

Harré, R., *The Philosophies of Science*, Oxford University Press, 1978.

Bibliography

Hempel, G., *Aspects of Scientific Explanation*, Free Press, New York, 1965.

Hintikka, J., *Knowledge and Belief*, Cornell University Press, New York, 1962.

Hobbes, T., *Leviathan*, 1651. Collier Books edition, Introduction by R. S. Peters, New York, 1962.

Honderich, T., *Violence for Equality*, Penguin, Harmondsworth, 1980.

Honderich, T., 'Causes and if p, even if x, still q', in *Philosophy*, 57, 1982.

Kelsen, H., *General Theory of Law and State*, tr. A. Wedburg, Russell & Russell, New York, 1961.

Kelsen, H., *The Pure Theory of Law*, tr. M. Knight, University of California Press, Berkeley and Los Angeles, 1967.

Kerner, G., *The Revolution in Ethical Theory*, Clarendon Press, Oxford, 1966.

Kneale, W., 'Scientific Revolution for Ever?', *British Journal for the Philosophy of Science*, vol. 19, 1968–9.

Kohn, H., *Who Killed Karen Silkwood?* New English Library, London, 1983.

Kolakowski, L., *Positivist Philosophy*, Penguin, Harmondsworth, 1972.

Kuhn, T. S., 'The Structure of Scientific Revolutions', in *International Encyclopaedia of Unified Science*, vol. 2, no. 2, Chicago, 1962.

Lee, K., 'The Legalist School and Legal Positivism', *Journal of Chinese Philosophy*, 3, 1975.

Lee, K., 'Kuhn – A Re-appraisal', *Explorations in Knowledge*, vol. 1, no. 1, 1984.

Lee, K., *Positivism and Law* (in preparation).

Lovibond, S., *Realism and Imagination in Ethics*, Blackwell, Oxford, 1983.

Lukes, S., *Individualism*, Blackwell, Oxford, 1973.

MacCormick, N., *Legal Reasoning and Legal Theory*, Clarendon Press, Oxford, 1978.

McDowell, J., 'Non-Cognitivism and Rule-Following', in *Wittgenstein: To Follow a Rule*, ed. S. Holtzman and C. Leich, Routledge & Kegan Paul, London, 1981.

Mackie, J. L., *The Cement of the Universe: A Study of Causation*, Oxford University Press, 1974.

Mackie, J. L., *Ethics, Inventing Right and Wrong*, Penguin, Harmondsworth, 1977.

Macpherson, C. B., 'Politics: Post-Liberal-Democracy?', in *Ideology in Social Sciences*, ed. R. Blackburn, Collins, London, 1972.

May, B., *Russia, America, The Bomb and the Fall of Western Europe*, Routledge & Kegan Paul, London, 1984.

Mill, J. S., *Autobiography*, Columbia University Press, New York, 1924.

Mill, J. S., *Utilitarianism, Liberty and Representative Government*, J. M. Dent, London, 1954.

Mitchell, B., *Law, Morality and Religion in a Secular Society*, Oxford University Press, 1967.

Bibliography

Moore, G. E., *Principia Ethica*, Cambridge University Press, 1903.

Murdoch, I., *The Sovereignty of the Good*, Routledge & Kegan Paul, London, 1970.

Musgrove, A. and Lakatos, I. (eds), *Criticism and Growth of Knowledge*, Cambridge University Press, 1970.

Myrdal, G., 'An American Dilemma: The Negro Problem and Modern Democracy', in *Carnegie Corporation of New York Study on the American Negro*, vol. 5, 1944.

Myrdal, G., *Value in Social Theory*, Routledge & Kegan Paul, London, 1958.

New Scientist, editorial, 23 June 1983.

Nowell-Smith, P. H., *Ethics*, Penguin, London, 1954.

Nozick, R., *Anarchy, State and Utopia*, Blackwell, Oxford, 1974.

Observer, 17 August 1980 and 10 April 1983.

O'Hear, A., *Karl Popper*, Routledge & Kegan Paul, London, 1980.

Phillips, D. Z. and Mounce, H. O., *Moral Practices*, Routledge & Kegan Paul, London, 1969.

Platts, M., *Ways of Meaning*, Routledge & Kegan Paul, London, 1979.

Popper, K., *The Logic of Scientific Discovery*, Science Editions, New York, 1961.

Popper, K., *The Open Society and its Enemies*, 2 vols, Routledge & Kegan Paul, London, 1962.

Popper, K., *Conjectures and Refutations*, Routledge & Kegan Paul, London, 1969.

Popper, K., *Objective Knowledge*, Clarendon Press, Oxford, 1974.

Popper, K., *Unended Quest*, Collins, London, 1978.

Popper, K., *Realism and the Aim of Science*, ed. W. W. Bartley, Hutchinson, London, 1983.

Putnam, H., *Reason, Truth and History*, Cambridge University Press, 1981.

Rescher, N., *The Logic of Commands*, Routledge & Kegan Paul, London, 1966.

Ryan, A., *The Philosophy of John Stuart Mill*, Macmillan, London, 1970.

Sellars, W., 'Are there non-Deductive Logics?', in *Essays in Honour of Carl Hempel*, D. Reidel, Hingham, Mass., 1969.

Sen, A. K., *On Economic Inequality*, Clarendon Press, Oxford, 1973.

Steele, J., *World Power*, Michael Joseph, London, 1983.

Stephens, F., *Liberty, Equality and Fraternity*, Cambridge University Press, 1967.

Stevenson, C. L., *Ethics and Language*, Yale University Press, New Haven, 1944.

Swinburne, R., 'The Objectivity of Morals', in *Philosophy*, vol. 51, 1976.

Ten, C. L., 'The Liberal Theory of the Open Society', in *The Open Society in Theory and Practice*, Martinus Nijhoff, The Hague, 1974.

Trigg, R., *Reason and Commitment*, Cambridge University Press, 1973.

Von Neumann, J. and Morgenstein, C., *Theory of Games and Economic Behaviour*, Princeton University Press, 3rd edn, 1953.

Bibliography

Whymant, R., reports in the *Guardian*, 14 August 1982 and 17 September 1982.

Wiggins, D., 'Truth, Invention and the Meaning of Life', in *Proceedings of the British Academy*, 1976.

Williams, B., 'The Idea of Equality', in *Philosophy, Politics and Society*, ed. P. Laslett and W. G. Runciman, Blackwell, Oxford, second series, 1962.

Wilson, R. B., *Rationality*, Blackwell, Oxford, 1970.

Winch, P., *The Idea of a Social Science*, Routledge & Kegan Paul, London, 1958.

Wittgenstein, L., *Philosophical Investigations*, ed. G. E. M. Anscombe and R. Rhees, tr. Anscombe, Blackwell, Oxford, 1953.

INDEX

abortion, 16, 47, 128, 140–7
agonistic style (*Sturm und Drang*),
  see Gallie; Popper
analytic/synthetic, 8–10, 27–8
Anderson, A. R., 188–90
a priori/a posteriori, 8–10, 27–8
assertions (A1, A2, A3)/evidence
  (E1, E2, E3), 37, 67–75, 83,
  86–109, 112–13, 116, 119,
  121–4, 132–6, 139, 148, 151,
  166–7, 169, 175–7, 181–3,
  189–91
Austin, J., 77, 79
authority, two senses of, 39–42,
  45, 83–5
Ayer, A. J., 8, 11

Bartley, W. W. III, 133, 152
Beardsmore, R. W., 11
Belnap, N. D., 188–90
Benthamite utilitarianism, 60–1,
  63
Berlin, I., 201–5, 219, 224

causal independence, 96–100, 119,
  132, 135–6, 139, 163–5, 191,
  199
cause, 88–9, 170, 172, 174
checks of adequacy, 111, 152–8,
  163–5
Chisholm's critical cognitivism,
  116–19

class, 110–12
classification, 107–14
command theory of knowledge,
  40–1, 78–82, 85, 216
conative, 36, 46, 124–7, 129, 197
critical assessment of moral
  theory, *see* checks of adequacy,
  epistemic implication,
  fallibilism
critical dualism, 124–6, 130, 216,
  218–19
critical rationalism, 206, 211,
  215–17, 222; *see also* Popper

Davidson, D., 34–5, 37
Deducibility-Commitment model,
  10–11, 46, 71, 78, 115, 124
deductive logic, 2, 27, 116–17,
  120–1, 136–8, 142, 177–81
Deductive-Nomological model,
  see Hempel; logic of
  explanation-cum-prediction
definition, 4, 7
descriptivism, 47–8, 131; *see also*
  Hare
doxastic logic, 114–16
Duhem, P., 160–1

emotivism, 10, 12, 36, 68, 124; *see
  also* Stevenson
Empiricism, 184–5
epistemic implication, 33, 46–7,

249

International Library of Philosophy

Editor: Ted Honderich

(Demy 8vo)

Allen, R.E. and Furley, David J. (eds.), **Studies in Presocratic Philosophy**
   Vol. 1: The Beginnings of Philosophy *326 pp. 1970.*
   Vol. 2: Eleatics and Pluralists *448 pp. 1975.*
Armstrong, D.M., **Perception and the Physical World** *208 pp. 1961.* **A Materialist Theory of the Mind** *376 pp. 1967.*
Bambrough, Renford (Ed.), **New Essays on Plato and Aristotle** *184 pp. 1965.*
Barry, Brian, **Political Argument** *382 pp. 1965.*
Becker, Lawrence C. **On Justifying Moral Judgments 212 pp. 1973.**
† Benenson, F.C., **Probability, Objectivity and Evidence** *224 pp. 1984.*
†* Blum, Lawrence, **Friendship, Altruism and Morality** *256 pp. 1980.*
Brentano, Franz, **The Foundation and Construction of Ethics** *398 pp. 1973.*
   The Origin of our Knowledge of Right and Wrong *184 pp. 1969.*
   Psychology from an Empirical Standpoint *436 pp. 1973.*
   Sensory and Noetic Consciousness *168 pp. 1981.*
† Budd, M., **Music and the Emotions** *208 pp. 1985.*
† Clarke, D.S., **Practical Inferences** *160 pp. 1985.*
Crombie, I.M., **An Examination of Plato's Doctrine**
   Vol. 1: Plato on Man and Society *408 pp. 1962.*
   Vol. 2: Plato on Knowledge and Reality *584 pp. 1963.*
† Davies, Martin, **Meaning, Quantification, Necessity** *294 pp. 1981.*
Dennett, D.C., **Content and Conciousness** *202 pp. 1969.*
Detmold, M.J., **The Unity of Law and Morality** *288 pp. 1984.*
Ducasse, C.J., **Truth, Knowledge and Causation** *264 pp. 1969.*
Fann, K.T. (Ed.), **Symposium on J.L. Austin** *512 pp. 1969.*
Findlay, J.N., **Plato: The Written and Unwritten Doctrines** *498 pp. 1974.*
† Findlay, J.N., **Wittgenstein: A Critique** *240 pp. 1984.*
Flew, Anthony, **Hume's Philosophy of Belief** *296 pp. 1961.*
† Fogelin, Robert J., **Hume's skepticism in the Treatise of Human Nature** *192 pp. 1985.*
† Foster, John, **The Case for Idealism** *280 pp. 1982.*
Goldman, Lucien, **The Hidden God** *424 pp. 1964.*
† Gray, John, **Mill on Liberty: A Defence** *160 pp. 1983.*
Holzman, Steven M. and Leich, Christopher H., **Wittgenstein: to Follow a Rule** *264 pp. 1981.*
† Honderich, Ted (Ed.), **Morality and Objectivity** *256 pp. 1985.*
†* Hornsby, Jennifer, **Actions** *152 pp. 1980.*
Husserl, Edmund, **Logical Investigations** *Vol. 1: 456 pp.*
   Vol. 2: 464 pp. 1970.
* Linsky, Leonard, **Referring** *152 pp. 1967.*
Mackenzie, Brian D., **Behaviourism and the Limits of Scientific Method** *208 pp. 1977.*
†* Mackie, J.L., **Hume's Moral Theory** *176 pp. 1980.*